A HISTORY OF
BRITISH RAIL
ENGINEERING
LIMITED

A HISTORY OF
BRITISH RAIL
ENGINEERING
LIMITED

RICHARD MARKS

PEN & SWORD
TRANSPORT
AN IMPRINT OF PEN & SWORD BOOKS LTD.
YORKSHIRE – PHILADELPHIA

First published in Great Britain in 2024 by
Pen and Sword Transport
An imprint of
Pen & Sword Books Ltd.
Yorkshire - Philadelphia

ISBN 978 1 39906 635 8

Typeset in 11/14 Palatino by SJmagic DESIGN SERVICES, India.

Printed and bound in the UK on paper from a sustainable source by CPI Group (UK) Ltd., Croydon. CR0 4YY.

Pen & Sword Books Ltd incorporates the Imprints of Pen & Sword Books After the Battle, Archaeology, Atlas, Aviation, Battleground, Discovery, Family History, History, Maritime, Military, Naval, Politics, Railways, Select, Transport, True Crime, Fiction, Frontline Books, Leo Cooper, Praetorian Press, Seaforth Publishing, Wharncliffe and White Owl.

For a complete list of Pen & Sword titles please contact

PEN & SWORD BOOKS LIMITED
George House, Units 12 & 13, Beevor Street, Off Pontefract Road,
Barnsley, South Yorkshire, S71 1HN, England
E-mail: enquiries@pen-and-sword.co.uk
Website: www.pen-and-sword.co.uk

or

PEN AND SWORD BOOKS
1950 Lawrence Rd, Havertown, PA 19083, USA
E-mail: uspen-and-sword@casematepublishers.com
Website: www.penandswordbooks.com

CONTENTS

ACKNOWLEDGEMENTS

I would like to thank the staff at The National Archives at Kew for all their professional help so readily given. The mass of British Rail Engineering Limited (BREL) files released during the last few years at Kew have been consulted in great depth for this work, allowing a huge amount of primary evidence, never used before, to be included in the creation of this new history of the company.

I would specifically like to thank Neil Barker for sharing his contacts in the rail industry and for his encouragement and assistance. I would also particularly like to thank Colin Marsden for his help and advice during the project from which this book has resulted.

I would also like to thank John Scott-Morgan not only for commissioning this book, but also for his advice and assistance during the research and production of this volume.

Finally, I would link to thank Ros for her patience and support during the research and creation of the book, as well as being able to find railway documents which have been so valuable in the creation of this new history of BREL in various antique and ephemera shops which would otherwise have been missed.

All cover images are copyright Colin J. Marsden

INTRODUCTION

Britain's railway companies had to a large extent been self-sufficient with regard to the provision of locomotives, rolling stock and other materials they needed until the advent of British Railways in 1948. In the earliest days of the railways in the nineteenth century, many of the locomotives used on the embryonic network were sourced from outside contractors. Companies such as Robert Stephenson in Newcastle, Peckett in Bristol and Vulcan Foundry in Newton-le-WIllows, among others, supported the embryonic railways until such time as the companies had established their own works.

The trend toward reliance upon outside providers would continue throughout the history of Britain's railways to a lesser extent, although the smaller companies without their own workshops would have to continue to rely on outside industry. Despite the presence of large and capable workshops within the larger railway companies, they sought to temporarily expand their manufacturing capacity through outsourcing work to independent locomotive manufacturers, something that would continue under British Rail.

When British Railways was formed in 1948, the company inherited all of the works from the Big Four which it had absorbed and in many cases this resulted in duplication of capability. The works continued to provide British Railways with a disparate selection of pre-nationalisation designs, which when constrained within the regions relating to the old companies was not a great issue. Experience in maintaining those designs could be found at works such as Doncaster, Swindon, Eastleigh or Crewe alongside stocks of spare parts. When travelling further afield however, difficulty was experienced due to unfamiliarity with operational requirements and maintenance needs among crews and staff at depots. The visit of an unfamiliar locomotive or item of rolling stock at a depot could cause difficulties where no correct or interchangeable spare parts on site caused delay in returning a locomotive to traffic after a minor failure. The railway also inherited a large number of older designs which were coming towards the end of their operational life and were becoming due for replacement.

The high levels of traffic being carried on the railways after the Second World War, coupled with the lack of finance available for the massive investment in new technologies required to help the railways recover from the ravages of the war provided no reason to change the status quo. The availability of a range of proven and reliable designs inherited by British Railways in 1948, gave no reason for immediate change within the railway's production facilities. The continued construction of pre-nationalisation designs and the heavy maintenance workload to support a broad inventory of older locomotives and rolling stock, provided plenty of work for the workshops. No thoughts towards any form of rationalisation were necessary at British Railways Board (the BRB) level in its earliest days.

As time progressed and older designs became less suitable for the modern railway with their high maintenance overheads, a programme of standardisation was embarked upon. Robert Riddles had been appointed as the member of the Railway Executive for Mechanical and Electrical Engineering, assisted by Roland Bond (Chief Officer, Locomotive Construction and Maintenance) and Ernest Cox (Executive Officer – Design) in 1947. The need to adopt common manufacturing and maintenance procedures grew and it was decided that some degree of change was required. As a result, a small amount of rationalisation occurred during the 1950s.

The condition of the railways by the mid-1950s and the perilous state of British Railways' finances, mainly due to increased road competition from the newly re-privatised road haulage industry and the growth of private car ownership, resulted in the production of the *Modernisation and Re-equipment of the British Railways* report in 1954. The government white paper which followed in 1956 stated that modernisation would resolve the decline in the railway's fortunes. The report unfortunately failed to address the need to modernise the way in which the railways were operating, how passengers were carried and freight was being transported. Instead, the modernisation report adopted a position of modernising the railways as they were rather than evolving them to be more relevant to the needs of their customers which may have attracted passengers and freight back to the rail network and reduced the need for later route closures.

The plan also called for the elimination of steam traction and its replacement with diesel locomotives and multiple units with a longer-term desire for the electrification of all major trunk routes. The Railways' own response was to adopt a wide-ranging pilot programme for 174 diesel locomotives from 6 independent British manufacturers, some of whom had little experience of diesel locomotive design and construction, as well as its own internal design offices and workshops. British Rail's own workshops at least had some experience in new types of traction through the experiments undertaken by the railway companies prior to nationalisation. The railway also had some experience of other forms of traction through the electrification of routes such as the Woodhead route between Sheffield and Manchester and the suburban routes on Southern Railway lines around London.

The designs, spread across three power categories that British Railways believed would cover its needs, were a mixed selection of successful, unsuccessful and, by the time they entered service, irrelevant designs for which the traffic they were supposed to be used was disappearing from the network.

Construction of the new designs and the need to maintain the existing steam fleet provided a higher level of work than was needed to keep the railway's works fully occupied and manned. The increased maintenance loads in the early days of the new locomotives saw the manpower allocated to the maintenance departments of all the works provided with more work than could be met by existing staffing levels. In Swindon, the adoption of diesel-hydraulic power plants for the locomotives to be produced for Western Region (whilst other regions favoured diesel-electric power plants) saw the development of a unique skill set which, for a time, would continue to make the works a centre of excellence for a part of British Railways' locomotive inventory. In the long term, however, that decision may have contributed partly to its eventual demise. Once the railway had settled on the more common diesel-electric powered locomotives for its fleet, and for the withdrawal and scrapping of the now non-standard diesel-hydraulic fleet, the workload available for the workshops in Swindon steadily declined.

The run-down of steam would see the first of the works closures and concentration of construction and maintenance facilities at the larger regional works. For a time, these sites were busy and successful as continued developments in new technology resulted in new classes of locomotives and multiple units being designed and built to meet changing needs on the network. The continued construction of British Railways standard Mark

I coaching stock followed by the introduction of the Mark II programme provided ample work for the various coach works. The increasing amount of coal, parcels and container traffic, and an optimistic view of future traffic patterns, coupled with the need to eradicate old vacuum braked freight wagons from the network in order to increase the speed of freight trains, provided constant requirements for the construction of new freight stock at all of the wagon works.

Despite the healthy amount of work available for the workshops, the smaller works were viewed as being uneconomic to keep open, and a programme of rationalisation was undertaken which resulted in the closure of a large number of the railway's workshops. The remaining workshops at Ashford, Crewe, Derby (both the Locomotive Works and the Carriage Works at Litchurch Lane), Eastleigh, Glasgow (St Rollox), Horwich, Shildon, Swindon, Temple Mills (Stratford), Wolverton and York specialised to some extent in certain types of work. (Ashford, Shildon and Temple Mills upon wagon construction for example.) In addition, the steel foundry at Worcester remained open to provide the railway with in-house steel making capability.

The remaining workshops were seen as not only being sufficient for the needs of the by then rebranded British Rail for the short term, but with investment to modernise them, for the future. A continual investment programme was thus embarked upon from the mid-1960s to replace worn out machine tools, create modern apprentice schools onsite at many works, and provide new facilities to meet the needs of the modern railway.

The government legislation passed in 1962 which famously allowed for the closure of railway routes, also contained clauses which created the BRB and which would also impact the future of the railway's workshops. The Transport Act 1962 stated in Section 13 of the provision of the Act that the BRB would have the power to 'construct, manufacture, produce or purchase, maintain or repair anything required for the purpose of the business'. The Transport Act 1968 which followed created the environment within which it was possible for the BRB to create a wholly owned subsidiary to undertake the construction of new rolling stock for its fleet, the maintenance of the entire fleet, but importantly also to be able to manufacture and supply or to repair 'anything which the authority consider can advantageously be so manufactured or … repaired' where the skills and facilities were available in its workshops.

The clause of the 1968 Act was important in the creation of an independent but viable subsidiary company which was able to tender for business outside of the needs of its parent, increasing its ability to become profitable and self-sustaining. The promise of a new 'independent' manufacturing and engineering company affiliated to British Rail offered much.

The abolition of the British Transport Commission in 1962 and the drive throughout the 1960s towards separating the functions not directly linked to running trains from the BRB into wholly owned subsidiaries saw the creation of a number of wholly owned companies created to manage the various diverse elements of British Rail's Business.

British Transport Hotels was created in 1963 to run the portfolio of hotels which had been inherited by British Rail from the four railway companies under nationalisation. British Rail Shipping and International Services, formed in 1969, operated the railway shipping services including the car ferry services between Britain and Europe under the Sealink Consortium, a joint venture with SNCF, the Belgian Maritime Transport Authority (Regie voor Maritiem Transport) and the Dutch Zeeland Steamship Company (Stoomvaart Maatschappij Zeeland).

The engineering provision within British Rail was also to be split off into a wholly owned subsidiary of the BRB. All the remaining workshops were transferred into the ownership of a new company from 1 January 1970, British Rail Engineering Limited. The new independent company began trading but the restrictions placed upon it by the BRB and the constant interference in its running would cause great difficulty and unnecessary trouble throughout the existence of the company. The lack of autonomy that a truly independent engineering company would have had contributed to BREL not reaching its full potential.

Chapter 1

BRITISH RAILWAYS ENGINEERING BEFORE BREL

As the clocks chimed midnight on 31 January 1947 and people across Britain raised their glasses to toast the new year, the Big Four railway companies ceased to exist and British Railways was born under the control of the BRB within the British Transport Commission. At the same moment, all of the company's railway works became part of the new nationalised railway.

The new British Railways inherited a large number of workshops, which under the auspices of a single nationalised company, caused a degree of duplication. The new board would seek to rationalise their engineering arm over time to concentrate different types of work on fewer sites in order to achieve greater economy of scale than could be achieved through a disparate group of workshops undertaking the same work on smaller scales. The large number of works across the network was viewed as being inefficient and uneconomic by the mid-1950s, with financial pressures beginning to be felt by the BRB after the re-privatisation of the road haulage elements of the British Transport Commission in 1953. The resulting competition from road hauliers offering cheap transport services and the resulting decrease in freight revenues as customers moved from rail to road eroded British Railways' financial health. As a result, the board began a programme of rationalisation across its workshops to add to the economies that it had already looked to achieve through the reallocation of workload from some of its smaller works, and closure of those sites.

The Great Western Railway's works at Swindon continued to produce Great Western locomotive, carriage and wagon designs, as well as other railway equipment. The works was later heavily involved in the production of a large number of Riddles' standard classes as well as a large proportion of the diesel-hydraulic locomotives constructed for Western Region to ultimately replace its steam fleet. The works produced thirty of the seventy-four Class 52 (Western) locomotives, the remainder being constructed at Crewe between 1961 and 1964. The thirty-eight members of Class 42 (Warship) were constructed solely at Swindon between 1958 and 1961, with all members of the Class 41 and 43 Warships being built at North British in Glasgow. The works also constructed all fifty-six of the Class 14 locomotives between 1964 and 1965, but the work for which they had been designed – short trip workings between goods yards and short distance freight trains – had begun to disappear from the railway by the time they started to arrive in service. Swindon would be the centre for maintenance of the majority of the diesel-hydraulics, including the 101 Class 35 (Hymek) locomotives built for British Railways by Beyer Peacock in Manchester.

The other two Great Western workshops which were located in Wales remained open at the time of nationalisation. The works at Caerphilly had ceased to build new stock under the Great Western Railway and was

Western Region's mainline diesel-hydraulic locomotives D821, D1015, D818 and D7029 at Swindon Works, 4 April 1977. *Laurence Waters*

Collett 4,000 gallon tender at Swindon Works, 11 April 1984. *Laurence Waters*

concentrating purely on locomotive and carriage maintenance. Wagons had ceased to be built or maintained at Caerphilly after a new wagon works was built at the old Taff Vale Railways' works site in the Cathays suburbs of Cardiff. Coaching stock ceased to be built at Caerphilly under the Great Western Railways although a new maintenance facility was built and opened in 1939.

The London, Midland and Scottish Railway's (LMS) remaining thirteen works in England and Scotland were also all absorbed into British Rail, although only the works at Derby (Locomotive and Litchurch Lane), Crewe, Horwich and St Rollox in Glasgow were producing new locomotives and rolling stock at that point.

The works at Wolverton had ceased producing locomotives and was concentrating solely on the production of coaches by 1948, remaining open until the final years of British Rail Engineering Limited, and being used for the maintenance and storage of the Royal Train.

Other works had also ceased some aspects of locomotive and rolling stock production before nationalisation. Bromsgrove had become focused upon manufacturing wagons under the LMS, but nevertheless had a reputation for high quality work. Bromsgrove Works continued constructing wagons under the auspices of British Railways. The site gained a reputation for an extremely high level of productivity as well as high quality work. The changing traffic demands as mixed freight trains with single wagon load freight began to disappear from the railway onto the roads, and the resulting need to rationalise the network's workshops, resulted in the transfer of all work from Bromsgrove to Derby Litchurch Lane. The resulting complete closure of the works in 1964 ended 123 years of railway rolling stock construction in Bromsgrove.

The works at Bow in East London had ceased to manufacture new rolling stock under the LMS, undertaking repairs to locomotives only. In 1956 the works began to undertake repairs to the diesel-electric fleet allocated to the nearby Devon's Road Depot, one of the first depots to be allocated only diesel locomotives. In 1960, under a rationalisation programme designed to reduce maintenance overheads, British Rail transferred the work undertaken at Bow Works to Derby Locomotive Works and the site in East London was closed.

In Scotland, the LMS had inherited the works of its Scottish constituents. The Scottish engineering facilities were scattered over the country. The Caledonian Railway had workshops at St Rollox (Glasgow), the Glasgow and South Western Railway at Barassie (South Ayrshire) and Kilmarnock and finally, the Highland Railway's main workshops had been located at Lochgorm (Inverness).

The works at Barassie were opened in 1901 by the Glasgow and South Western Railway. The wagon and carriage repair work previously undertaken at Kilmarnock Works was reallocated to the new works to release capacity at Kilmarnock for locomotive construction and maintenance. The works remained focused solely on the maintenance of wagons, the LMS continuing to use the works in the same way. Despite occasional threats to Barassie when the LMS Board considered closing the works, the company continued to invest in the site. In 1929, wagon construction work was reallocated from St Rollox Works, which became the centre of locomotive and carriage repairs in Scotland. Wagon repair and maintenance work was relocated to Barassie at the same time to release further capacity at St Rollox for locomotive related work.

Barassie's workshops were extended and modernised in the early 1960s by British Railways in order to take over all of the wagon repair work for Scottish Region. However, the reduction in wagon load traffic and the reduction in wagon stock requirements which followed on the railway reduced the need for maintenance and repair of the now less intensively used fleet. The loss of work impacted upon Barassie which was closed in 1972, although part of the works remained open as Barassie Permanent Way Depot.

The Glasgow and South Western Railway's works at Kilmarnock opened in 1856, producing the first locomotive for the company the following year. The workshops continued to be busy until locomotive construction ceased in 1921 although the site continued to serve as a maintenance and repair centre for the LMS. Kilmarnock remained open, performing the same function for British Railways until rationalisation of the railway's workshops saw locomotive maintenance cease there, the site being retained for the maintenance of cranes for Scottish Region. The workshops closed in 1959, although part of the mothballed site was reopened in 1971 under the civil engineering department of Scottish Region for heavy repairs of civil engineering rail vehicles such as Tampers and Ballast Cleaners.

Lochgorm Works was opened by the Inverness and Nairn Railway in 1855, becoming part of the Highland Railway in 1865. The workshops were located directly adjacent to the north of the approach lines to Inverness station. The workshop site originally included the locomotive sheds until 1863 when the company built the half roundhouse opposite the works, which opened in 1863. The works constructed a number of locomotives for the Highland Railway, the northern part of the site being dedicated to that function. The southern part of the workshops undertook the construction and maintenance of coaches. Locomotive construction ceased in 1906, after which the Highland Railway contracted locomotive building out to the North British Locomotive Company and Hawthorne Leslie in Newcastle-upon-Tyne. The workshops continued to construct coaches and wagons for the Highland Railway with the works also being responsible for the maintenance of the company's fleet.

The site continued to operate in this guise under the LMS and into the early days of British Railways, but was one of the early casualties of nationalisation, closing completely in 1959. The site became Inverness Depot after the closure of Inverness Locomotive Shed with the facilities for locomotive maintenance moving across the railway tracks into some of the old works buildings, the site remaining open in 2024. The works site was partly cleared in 1984, for the construction of Inverness Signalling Centre which also remains open in 2024.

The LMS inherited the works of the Warrington and Newton Railway through the acquisition of the London and North Western Railway at the grouping in 1923. The works had been built on the original company's line a mile west of Newton-le-Willows at a junction with the Liverpool and Manchester Railway. A new town for the workers employed in the works was created and named Earlestown. Earlestown Works built a small number of locomotives, but the main locomotive construction in the area was concentrated at the Vulcan Foundry Works at Newton-le-Willows. The site continued to manufacture locomotives as part of Vulcan until it was sold to English Electric in 1957. Locomotive manufacturing continued under the new owner until it finished at the site in 1970, although the works remained open producing Ruston Paxman diesel engines. Under Ruston Paxman, the workshops became the manufacturer of choice for diesel power plants for locomotives built at Crewe and Doncaster by British Rail Engineering Limited.

Earlestown continued to repair wagons for the LMS and was still doing so at nationalisation and British Railways continued to use the workshops for the same work. The works was important in the early days of British Railways, being involved in the conversion of steel mineral wagons which were built as the Second World War was coming to an end with the intention of sending them to France. The wagons were to have been used to replace stock damaged during military action against the French railways during the Allied advance following D-Day, but not all were sent to the continent. The converted wagons were purchased by the Railway Executive to replace worn out old stock in use on Britain's railways after the war. The replacement wagons were bought to resolve shortages of reliable freight stock on Britain's railways caused by continual failures of mineral wagons, caused by delayed maintenance, after the war. The wagons required modification to suit Britain's railways and the work was undertaken at Earlestown. The works was also used as a centre for the repair of Scammell trailers used with the railway's fleet of Scammell mechanical horse lorries. British Railways reintroduced coaching stock construction to Earlestown in the 1950s, allocating the construction of non-passenger coaches to the works. The first series of vehicles produced at the works were thirty motor-car vans, followed in 1952 by twenty-five cattle vans. A further two orders were placed in 1953 and 1954 for a total of 100 horse-boxes to an older pre-nationalisation design that originated with the London and North Eastern Railway (LNER), with two vehicles a week being completed.

A new apprentice training school for the site was authorised by the BRB in 1952. The works continued to undertake the repair of wagons and road vehicles and the construction of non-passenger carrying coaching stock for British Railways until 1964, when demand for wagons across the network was reducing. The board was seeking to rationalise the engineering elements of the business into the larger works, at which point the works at Earlestown was closed and the site sold, becoming a Trading Estate which in turn was closed and redeveloped for housing more recently.

The LMS main works at Crewe, Derby (both Locomotive and Litchurch Lane), Horwich, St Rollox and Wolverton all remained fully open and were invested in heavily by British Railways during the 1950s and 1960s. Wolverton remained dedicated purely to coach construction and maintenance, with Derby Litchurch Lane continuing to operate as it had under the LMS, also as a dedicated coach works. The other works site in Derby concentrated on construction and maintenance of locomotives. Crewe and St Rollox continued to operate as locomotive construction and maintenance centres. Horwich Works, located just to the south-east of Manchester, continued to construct locomotives and rolling stock for British Railways, with the foundry located within the works continuing to be the major supplier of castings, including brake blocks, for the newly nationalised railways.

The nationalised railways also inherited all of the works which had been part of the LNER that remained open in 1948, both in England and Scotland.

The Great Central Railway's workshops at Gorton, just east of Manchester, opened as the works for the Manchester, Sheffield and Lincolnshire Railway in 1848, for construction and maintenance of its locomotives, coaches and wagons. The company's locomotive superintendent, Richard Peacock, left the company in 1854 to form a partnership with Charles Beyer which created the Beyer Peacock Locomotive Company at Gorton Foundry directly opposite the Manchester, Sheffield and Lincolnshire Railway's works. The two works should not be confused, Gorton Foundry remaining a private concern throughout the life of both the companies. The company would be an important contractor to the Great Central Railway, the LNER, the LMS (in the construction of the Beyer Garrett articulated locomotives among others) and as a subcontractor to British Railways for the manufacture of locomotives and parts.

Gorton (Great Central Railway) mostly ceased to manufacture locomotives after the grouping in 1923. The LNER concentrated new locomotive construction at the larger workshops at Doncaster and Darlington shortly after the grouping. The workshops continued to undertake maintenance of locomotives and the manufacture of parts for Doncaster and Darlington until nationalisation. Gorton Works continued to perform locomotive maintenance tasks under British Railways but also undertook the scrapping of many steam locomotives under the railway's modernisation plan as steam gave way to diesel traction. The works closed in 1963 when its workload was transferred to Doncaster as part of British Railways' reorganisation of its workshops.

The Great Northern Railway's (GNR) Works at Doncaster was one of the larger works inherited by British Railways and remained an important site after nationalisation. The works opened in 1853 to replace workshops at Peterborough, although the site initially only undertook maintenance and repair functions. The works gradually expanded, becoming the main locomotive, carriage and wagon works for the GNR, constructing Patrick Stirling's 'Stirling Single' class express locomotives, Henry Ivatt's Atlantics and Sir Nigel Gresley's Pacifics, including the *Flying Scotsman* and *Mallard*. The works produced the first corridor coaching stock and the first dining cars in Britain.

Doncaster Locomotive Works

AI CLASS "PACIFIC" LOCOMOTIVE No. 60154 LEAVING THE DONCASTER LOCOMOTIVE WORKS ON A TRIAL TRIP

BRITISH RAILWAYS

PRINTED IN GREAT BRITAIN

British Railways Doncaster Works open days leaflet. *Author's collection*

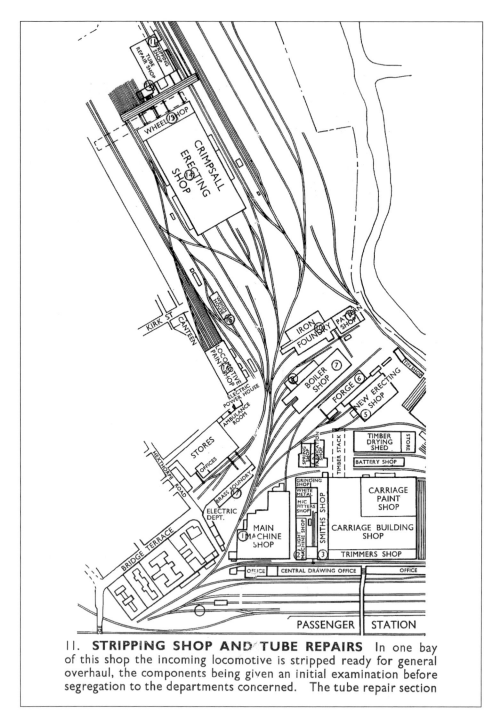

II. **STRIPPING SHOP AND TUBE REPAIRS** In one bay of this shop the incoming locomotive is stripped ready for general overhaul, the components being given an initial examination before segregation to the departments concerned.   The tube repair section

Map of Doncaster Works from a British Railways open day leaflet. *Author's collection*

WHEELING AN A2 CLASS LOCOMOTIVE IN THE NEW ERECTING SHOP

DONCASTER LOCOMOTIVE WORKS

Built in 1853 for the former Great Northern Railway Company these works, together with the adjacent Carriage Works, are known familiarly as "The Plant" and cover a total area of 84 acres. The Locomotive Works have so developed that they now employ 3,000 men and have over 600 machines installed.

Responsible for the maintenance in good repair of 1,250 locomotives allocated to districts principally in the Eastern and North Eastern regions, some 700 classified repairs are undertaken annually as well as the construction of new locomotives for British Railways. Another important aspect of the work is the provision of items for stock, the repair of material sent from Motive Power depots, and work for other departments which have no such facilities.

Doncaster Locomotive Works have been responsible for the construction of many locomotives of historical interest, such as Stirling's 8-foot "Single-Wheel" Locomotive, the famous Ivatt "Atlantics" and more recently the Gresley, Thompson and Peppercorn "Pacifics" most famous of which—the Gresley streamlined "Mallard"—achieved a world speed record for steam traction of 126 m.p.h.

ABOVE "CRIMPSALL" REPAIR SHOPS

LEFT   MAIN BOILER SHOP

Published by The Railway Executive (Eastern Region) PP/152/29. Printed by S. H. Peters & Sons Ltd., Sydenham & Selhurst.

British Railways Doncaster Works open day leaflet showing the inside of the works. *Author's collection*

Doncaster became the main centre of rolling stock engineering alongside Darlington Works under the LNER after the grouping.

The works was still important to British Railways after the nationalisation of the railways, remaining open and intact throughout the existence of British Rail and BREL, receiving continual investment until the last days of BREL when the works was split up and partially sold. A small part of the works remains open in 2024, but the majority has closed with the main locomotive repair shop demolished to make way for housing.

The LNER's other main works was that at Darlington. The works was established by the Stockton and Darlington Railway in 1863 to supplement the company's works at Shildon. The company was absorbed by the North Eastern Railway (NER), with Darlington becoming the main locomotive works for the company in 1910, taking over from the facility at Gateshead which had until then been the company's locomotive building centre. The NER allocated construction of its coaching stock to York, with Shildon becoming the company's wagon works. Gateshead continued to undertake locomotive maintenance and repair work until 1932 when the site was closed by the LNER.

When the company was absorbed into the LNER at the grouping, a strong sense of rivalry remained between the two works, even manifesting in the colour used to paint passenger locomotives. The company standard 'apple green' was different between Doncaster and Darlington, one being the GNR colour and one the NER colour. Darlington was still involved in locomotive construction when the railways were nationalised in 1948, constructing both steam and diesel locomotives for British Railways. The site was enlarged in 1954 but in 1964 the rationalisation of the company's workshops resulted in the closure of Darlington Works long before the new machinery and buildings had reached the end of their useful working life.

The NER's Gateshead Works reopened during the Second World War to ease the pressure on Darlington and to take some of the maintenance and repair work back. The works was refurbished by the LNER and remained open until 1959 when the site was closed by British Railways for the last time.

The works at Shildon and York both continued to serve the NER, the LNER and British Railways, and finally BREL. The Holgate Road Works at York first opened in 1884, replacing the original NER workshops in Queen Street which the company had outgrown. Wagon construction had already been transferred away from York, the workload being transferred to Shildon in 1867, with the new Holgate Road site designed from the outset as a purpose-built carriage works. York became one of the main centres of coach building for the LNER, many of the company's trademark teak coaches being produced there. The works was inherited by British Railways when the railways were nationalised. York continued to be an important coach construction and maintenance facility for the railway. The site started to take responsibility for the maintenance of the new Diesel Multiple Unit (DMU) fleet allocated locally from the early 1950s, and later for the construction of Diesel and Electric Multiple Units. The works remained open performing the same tasks after the reorganisation of the British Rail workshops in the early 1960s, going on to become an important element of BREL's workshop estate.

The first works at Shildon, the Soho Works, originally opened as the main works for the Stockton and Darlington Railway in 1825, although under the private ownership of Timothy Hackworth. The works were purchased by the Stockton and Darlington in 1855 due to the company's expansion, the need for more locomotives and for its own repair facilities. The works grew in size under the Stockton and Darlington, including the addition of an expanded foundry to the site. When the Stockton company was absorbed into the NER, Shildon ceased construction of locomotives, focusing mainly upon the construction of wagons, but also forgings for the other NER Works. Shildon remained important to the LNER after the grouping, remaining a key production centre for freight vehicles for the company as well as iron forgings. At the creation of British Railways in 1948, the works remained open, undertaking the same types of work, producing many freight vehicles for the new company to replace life expired vehicles. The works was modernised in 1962 as part of the reorganisation of the railway's works. The modernisation programme gave the works the capability to construct, maintain and repair the new generation of air-braked goods vehicles that the railway required to meet the changing needs of its freight division and customers. Shildon was one of the works, alongside Doncaster, that was transferred to the ownership of BREL at the creation of the company in 1970.

The Great Eastern Railway's (GER) Works in London were also inherited by British Railways. The GER's main works was built at Stratford in East London. The site originally opened in 1850 under the Eastern Counties Railway which then closed its original works at Romford, producing its first locomotive the same year. The GER took over in 1862 and Stratford became its main works, constructing and maintaining the company's passenger and freight stock. The work connected with the construction and maintenance of wagons transferred to Temple Mills Wagon Works in 1896.

Stratford Works continued to manufacture and service locomotives up until the amalgamation of the railway companies in the 1923 grouping. The LNER ceased construction at Stratford soon after inheriting the works, the works purely undertaking maintenance and repair activities from that point. At nationalisation, the works became part of the engineering estate of British Railways, who closed part of the works early in 1949. The workshops fell victim, as did many others, to the reorganisation of the railway's workshops in the early 1960s, closing completely in 1963. Repair of diesel locomotives was transferred to the old 1915 locomotive shed, which from then on became a maintenance site purely for modern traction. British Railways had begun to learn of the difficulties inherent in attempting to maintain diesel and electric traction alongside steam locomotives. The site was never again involved in construction and so did not pass into the ownership of BREL at its formation in 1970. The story was very different for the wagon works at Temple Mills.

The GER Works at Temple Mills was opened on a site in Leyton just off the Stratford to Lea Bridge Line (referred to on the 1921 Ordnance Survey Map as the 'Cambridge Old Main Line'), close to Temple Mills freight yards. The works was well equipped from the start, built specifically for the construction and maintenance of the GER's wagon fleet. Its location was well chosen, being just the other side of the Buckholt Road from the Temple Mills freight yards where wagons would finish their journeys and once unloaded could be shunted across to the works for attention. When taken over by the LNER, the works at Temple Mills continued to construct new wagons for the LNER's fleet, as well as maintenance and repair as before. The advent of nationalisation changed little other than the name over the door, as the works continued as before under the nationalised railway.

The site at Temple Mills saw almost immediate investment from British Railways who built a new repair workshop on the site to enhance the capabilities of the works. Investment continued to be made in their East London Works by British Railways. New machinery replaced worn out and life expired equipment and a continual programme of improvements was implemented on the site. Temple Mills design office was responsible for the creation of the Freightliner and car carrying wagons, with many being constructed at the same site. The works continued to be an important part of the engineering capability of the railway, passing to BREL at its creation in 1970.

The workshops which had been part of the Midland and Great Northern Joint Railway (M&GN), like all the other works in operation in 1948, passed to British Railways upon nationalisation. The M&GN Works at Melton Constable was originally opened in 1883 by the Eastern and Midlands Railway to provide a construction and maintenance capability to the company. The site at Melton Constable was chosen as it sat on a major junction located near a small village, which grew dramatically to serve the workforce of the town in a similar but perhaps more modest manner than at Crewe or Swindon. The works constructed wagons and a small number of locomotives, although the majority of the workload was related to the maintenance and repair of the company's existing locomotive and rolling stock fleets. The works foundry produced castings and other iron and steel components, with the concrete works providing cast concrete products for use across the railway.

The workshops were inherited by the LMS and LNER upon the grouping when the M&GN was absorbed. The LNER took over operation of the entire M&GN network and infrastructure in 1936, and closed part of the works at Melton Constable, transferring repair and maintenance work, along with the employees impacted, to the larger and more modern workshops at Doncaster and Stratford. Simple repairs and other work, such as the manufacture of wagon sheets for open freight wagons, was still carried out at the site which continued into the period of nationalisation.

British Railways inherited the site at Melton Constable and for a short time continued to invest to a modest level in the works, however with the closure of most the of the M&GN network in the 1950s, the works became redundant and was closed in its entirety.

The LNER's workshops in Scotland all survived to some extent to be nationalised. The Great North of Scotland Railway moved their works from Kittybrewster in Aberdeen to Inverurie, the new works opening alongside Inverurie station in 1902. The works was mainly involved in maintenance and repair, constructing only a small number of locomotives until 1921. The works was absorbed by the LNER at the grouping, continuing to undertake maintenance of locomotives until nationalisation. The works carried on performing the same functions for British Railways and then British Rail until 1969. The second rationalisation of the railway works across British Railways that occurred at the end of the 1960s, in preparation for the creation of BREL, resulted in the closure of Inverurie Works and the transfer of the maintenance activities undertaken there to St Rollox in Glasgow.

The railway works at Cowlairs in Springburn, opened in the north-eastern suburbs of Glasgow adjacent to Cowlairs station to serve the needs of the Edinburgh and Glasgow Railway in 1841. The works was acquired by the North British Railway in 1865 when the Edinburgh and Glasgow Railway purchased the company. The better facilities available at the Glasgow Works resulted in the decision by the North British Railway to close its works at St Margaret's in Edinburgh, transferring all work to the Glasgow site from 1865. The Cowlairs Works constructed locomotives, coaches and wagons on the same site, although it shared locomotive construction with Neilson and Company, and Dübs and Company, both also in Glasgow. Neilson and Company (later Neilson Reid) were extremely successful, experiencing continued business growth, and in order to meet the orders they had on hand, built a new works in Springburn which opened in 1861 on Ayr Street, very close to the North British Railway's works. Like the Cowlairs Works, Neilson's new site was served by direct connections to the Sighthill Branch. Henry Dübs left the company in 1864 to set up his own locomotive building business, selecting a site for his works at Polmadie in Glasgow.

A new works was established opposite Neilson's works and also served by direct rail links from the Sighthill branch, which was opened as the Clyde Locomotive Works in 1884. The company was taken over in 1888 by Sharp Stewart and Company when they moved to Glasgow from Manchester. The works was renamed the Atlas Works, inheriting the name of Sharp Stewart's old Manchester Works. Sharp Stewart merged with Neilson Reid and Company, and Dübs and Company in 1903, confusingly for the railway historian, naming the combined company North British Locomotive Company. The company had no connection with the North British Railway other than as a contractor involved in the construction of locomotives for the company in the twentieth century and then for British Railways until the company's liquidation in 1963.

The North British Railway's Cowlairs Works was expanded in 1904 with the construction of the Eastfield Running Sheds just north of the works site at Cowlairs East Junction on the opposite side of the Sighthill Branch. Maintenance work was transferred to the new depot to free up space in the main workshop to allow the site to meet the new construction needs of railway. Cowlairs continued to construct new locomotives and rolling stock for the North British Railway until the grouping, at which point the LNER took the decision, as it had done elsewhere, to cease production in Glasgow. Its requirements for new locomotives, coaches and wagons were to be met by its main works at Doncaster, Darlington, York and Shildon. The works continued to produce new boilers and castings for the company but ceased building new stock, although it continued to undertake heavy locomotive repairs. The works remained open, still undertaking these tasks at the time of the nationalisation of Britain's railways.

The rationalisation of the railway works undertaken by British Railways in the early days saw much of the work being undertaken in the foundry at Cowlairs transferred to the large foundry at Horwich. The works remained open for major locomotive repairs and some construction of new components for use in the railway's main works elsewhere. The newly created British Railways organised the country's railway network into regions, with all of Scotland's railways controlled by Scottish Region.

The amalgamation of control and management resulted in the duplication of works which were undertaking similar tasks. In order to achieve economies, Scottish Region nominated the large works at St Rollox as the primary centre for repair and maintenance of locomotives, coaches and wagons for Scotland. St Rollox continued to construct new locomotives and rolling stock, mainly for Scottish Region.

Despite the decision to centralise the construction workload and the majority of the repair and maintenance tasks to St Rollox, the works on the other side of Sighthill at Cowlairs remained open, undertaking work for St Rollox as well as locomotive repairs in its own right. As the railway modernised and moved toward the replacement of steam with diesel traction, the works at Cowlairs remained responsible for the maintenance and repair of steam locomotives, whilst St Rollox was re-equipped to build, repair and maintain diesel locomotives.

The works fell victim to the rationalisation of British Railways' engineering provision in preparation for the creation of the new subsidiary, BREL, during the late 1960s. The workshops finally closed in 1968 when the last steam locomotives had their fires dropped for the last time and all the remaining locomotives in Scotland were retired and sent for scrapping. The remaining workload at Cowlairs was transferred to St Rollox and the site at Cowlairs was abandoned and sold by British Rail Property Board, becoming an industrial estate. Railway engineering in that area of Glasgow now solely consisted of British Rail's St Rollox Works as North British Locomotive Company had also closed six years before.

One legacy of the North British Works at Cowlairs remained. The maintenance centre in Eastfield remained open to service locomotives, and remains open in 2024, undertaking maintenance and repair for ScotRail's Class 170 DMUs.

The last of the big four railway companies inherited three main locomotive and rolling stock workshops; the London, Brighton and South Coast Railway's (LB&SCR) works on the south coast at Brighton, the South Eastern Railway's (SER) works at Ashford in Kent and the London and South Western Railway's works at Eastleigh near Southampton.

The LB&SCR's works at Brighton was one of Britain's earliest railway owned repair facilities, opening in 1480. In 1841, the company opened a second works at Horley with a view to possibly relocating the workshops at Brighton which were in a very constrained site. Brighton Works was restricted by the railway terminus, a large hill which the railway had made during the construction of the line into Brighton and later by Boston Street as the town expanded. The LB&SCR's locomotive superintendent, John Craven, decided to reverse the plan to move to Horley, the works remaining at Brighton instead. The company established erecting shops to build its own locomotives at Brighton, having until that point used the services of independent locomotive builders, Sharp Stewart (at the time based in Manchester), Jones and Potts (Newton-le-Willows), Bury, Curtiss and Kennedy (Liverpool) and Timothy Hackworth's own company at Shildon. The expanded and re-equipped workshops began to construct new locomotives to Craven's designs from 1852. The company continued to outsource locomotive construction to third parties, as remained common on Britain's railways when additional capacity for construction was needed. The LBSCR subcontracted the construction of some of its Standard Passenger Class 2-4-0 locomotives to Beyer Peacock, and Dübs and Company with all of its 6ft 6in Single Class 2-2-2 locomotives being built by Robert Stephenson and Company (1864) and Nasmyth Wilson (1867) with a final two built by Dodds and Son (1871). Carriage construction moved to Brighton's expanded workshops in 1848, relocating from the workshops of the subcontractor at New Cross who had been building carriages for the company until that point.

Craven found more space to expand by removing the railway's artificial hill in 1861 when a new locomotive depot was built. The existing running sheds were closed and used to expand the works, but, even so, the constrained location would continue to be a problem at the works. The choice of the original site in Brighton would result in consideration of plans to close the site on a number of occasions with relocation to a more open site elsewhere putting the future of the site at risk throughout the life of the works. The LB&SCR and Southern Railways both considered options to move the works. In 1910, Brighton was struggling to cope with demand for new locomotives and the repair and maintenance needs of the existing fleet. In order to alleviate the difficulty caused by the restricted nature of the site, the company purchased land at Lancing where a new carriage and wagon works was established, opening in 1909. The Brighton workshops then concentrated solely upon activities associated with locomotive building and maintenance.

The company was absorbed by the Southern Railway in 1923 with the works at Brighton coming under the control of the new company. The new company relocated the majority of locomotive construction to its larger and more modern works at Eastleigh, with Brighton focusing mostly upon maintenance and repair activities. The electrification programme embarked upon by the Southern Railway reduced the need for locomotives and the maintenance of them, threatening Brighton with closure. The works were run down, with the remaining work and many of the staff being transferred to Ashford and Eastleigh. The works was converted partly to become a maintenance facility for the new Electric Multiple Units (EMUs). The works was reopened in 1941 amid fears of the impact of potential air raids upon Eastleigh and Ashford as well as the need to construct more locomotives and armaments for the war effort.

The revived Brighton Works passed into the ownership of British Railways in 1948 after nationalisation. The works continued to build new locomotives for the railway, being responsible for the design of a number of the new standard classes of locomotives. Despite the contribution that Brighton was making to British Railways, the modernisation plan of 1954 ignored the works. Locomotive construction ended in 1957 when Standard 4MT tank engine 80154 was completed, with maintenance ceasing the following year. The workshops were closed in 1962, with much of the land remaining in railway use. Those buildings not being used by the railway became derelict, although some of the site was used by local manufacturing companies until 1967. The buildings were demolished in 1969.

The workshops at Lancing initially focused purely upon the construction of new wagons for the Brighton company, with the construction of carriages beginning in 1912. The works also became responsible for the maintenance of the company's wagon and carriage stock from 1912. The location of the works, in what was at the time a remote rural location, resulted in the need for the company to run a train between Brighton and Lancing at the beginning and end of the working day due to the staff at Lancing having been transferred from Brighton. After the grouping, the Southern Railway concentrated all the carriage construction for the company upon Lancing with the carriage works at Ashford closing and some of the workforce transferring to Lancing. The carriage workshops at Eastleigh remained open.

Lancing Works continued to construct and maintain coaching stock for British Railways after nationalisation, gaining a reputation for efficiency and experiencing very few industrial disputes. The rationalisation programme undertaken by British Rail in the 1960s resulted in the decision to close Lancing and relocate all the carriage construction and maintenance workload to Eastleigh. The rundown of the works began in 1962, the site finally closing in 1965.

The workshops at Eastleigh and Ashford both passed into the ownership of BREL. The Ashford workshops were opened by the SER in 1847 to replace the original works at New Cross. The new works undertook construction, maintenance and repair activities for all of the company's needs, with locomotives, carriages and wagons being built and maintained there. The company entered into an operating agreement with the London, Chatham and Dover Railway in 1899. The agreement was made in order to remove the aggressive competition between the two companies which had caused both the South Eastern and London, Chatham and Dover Railways to experience financial difficulties. The operating company that resulted, the South East and Chatham Railway, took control of the two companies' works as part of its operational remit. Both the London, Chatham and Dover Railway and the South Eastern Railway continued to exist as an independent company, the South East and Chatham Railway effectively becoming an early version of the post privatisation train operating companies in Britain.

The new company sought to achieve economies in order to reduce the losses being made by both the owning companies. The railway works at Ashford and the London, Chatham and Dover's Works at Longhedge in Battersea which had opened in 1860 both undertook similar activities. In order to achieve the savings that the new company required, locomotive construction became centred upon Ashford, which also undertook repair and maintenance. Longhedge then only undertook maintenance and repair activities, although a small number of locomotives were built there in the early years of the twentieth century. After 1904, locomotive construction at Longhedge finally ceased, the works only undertaking heavy repair and maintenance work from then on. The works ceased heavy maintenance work in 1911 when the South East and Chatham transferred all heavy repair work to Ashford with Longhedge reduced to a light maintenance facility to support the adjacent Stewart's Lane depot.

Ashford Works had been founded in 1846 by the SER in the village in Kent located between Tonbridge and Dover. The company began locomotive construction at the works in 1848, with the works site gradually increasing in size as the SER's network grew. The workshops then became responsible for the construction of locomotives, carriages and wagons, as well as the maintenance of all the SER locomotive and rolling stock fleets. Ashford was key in the electrification programme begun by the South East and Chatham, the frames for the new EMUs being constructed there.

The workshops remained important after the grouping in 1923 which created the Southern Railway, becoming one of the main works for the construction, maintenance and repair activities associated with the railway company's locomotives and rolling stock alongside Brighton and Eastleigh Works, although the Southern Railway decided that Lancing would become the company's main carriage works with wagon construction and maintenance work remaining at Ashford. Ashford continued to build the frames and fabrications used by the Southern Railway for the construction of new EMUs for use on the gradually increasing route mileage which was being electrified.

In 1941, the Southern Railway won a tender to construct a large number of 12-ton mineral wagons for what was then Persia. The wagons were manufactured at Ashford beginning the workshop's role in Britain's railway exports which continued until the closure of the works under BREL.

At the nationalisation of the railways, the works became part of the engineering function of British Railways. The BRB took the decision to split the works into two separate functional areas, one specialising in the construction and maintenance of locomotives and the other that of wagons. The locomotive department at Ashford was closed in 1952 following the British Transport Commission's decision to concentrate all functions associated with locomotives within Southern Region at Eastleigh, ending 114 years of locomotive building in Kent.

The works continued as a wagon building and maintenance facility, which was incorporated, alongside all other surviving British Railways workshops, into the British Railway Workshop Division in 1963. British Railways shortly afterwards won a contract to build a large number of Continental Ferry Vans, which was allocated to Ashford. The order was followed by a large number of orders from the BRB for various types of wagons, including freightliners with their containers and the first batches of Merry-Go-Round hopper wagons for the modernised power station coal trains. The works remained busy and was passed over to the control of BREL with the creation of the new subsidiary in 1970.

The workshops at Eastleigh first opened as the London and South Western Railway's carriage and wagon works in 1891, complementing the company's existing works at Nine Elms in London. In 1903 the company built a new workshop in Eastleigh to replace the facility at Southampton, and in 1910 locomotive building was transferred to the works from Nine

Elms. Eastleigh thus became the main works for the South Western, building locomotives, carriages and wagons as well as taking on the maintenance and repair operations associated with the locomotive and rolling stock fleets.

The works was incorporated into the Southern Railway in 1923, when the London and South Western became absorbed by the new company under the remit of the Railways Act of 1921. The two workshops (Locomotive and Carriage & Wagon) became the central works for the new company, with the sites being modernised under the company's Chief Mechanical Engineer, Richard Maunsell, soon after the grouping. The works pioneered the use of plastics and fibreglass in the construction of carriages for locomotive hauled as well as EMU stock. In 1945 the works created another railway technology milestone, completing the first all-steel passenger coach.

In 1948, the works was absorbed by the British Transport Commission alongside all of the other sites already mentioned. Eastleigh remained responsible for the same work across both parts of the plant. The workshops at Eastleigh were responsible for all the rebuilds of Bulleid's Pacific locomotives between 1956 and 1961. Eastleigh continued to maintain and repair steam locomotives, but from the early 1960s the works took on operations relating to modern locomotives and multiple units. The reorganisation of British Rail's workshops during the early 1960s allocated responsibility for the maintenance of all Southern Region's motive power to Eastleigh, the work at Ashford and Brighton being transferred to the site. The works was involved in the construction of the Class 73 electro-diesel locomotives, but only built the first six prototypes, the remainder of the class being built by Vulcan Foundry in Manchester. The locomotives were built in the carriage works which resulted in hostility from within the locomotive works.

A second reorganisation of the works occurred between 1964 and 1968 when a programme of efficiency improvements and rationalisation was undertaken. The programme saw a desperately needed modernisation of many of the workshops occur within the locomotive works. As a result of the rationalisation of the works, which was also part of British Rail's overall policy towards rationalisation of its workshops during the late 1960s, the carriage works closed. All work was then transferred into the existing locomotive works. The remaining site was transferred to the ownership of BREL at the creation of that company on 1 January 1970.

Chapter 2

THE CREATION OF AN 'INDEPENDENT' RAILWAY WORKS

The railway locomotive, carriage and wagon workshops owned by British Railways had all been transferred into the British Railways Workshop Division from 1963, and rationalised. Work had been concentrated upon a small number of large works, which had been modernised. Some works concentrated on one specific area of rolling stock construction and maintenance, achieving economy of scale and reduction in spares and component holding across the network, although components relating to light repairs to be undertaken at local depots still needed to be held locally.

The workshops which had become redundant due to the changing needs of the railway had closed with their workload transferred to the remaining works. The costs associated with the relocation or redundancy of staff had been absorbed by British Rail during the 1960s. British Railways had also absorbed other costs accrued during the modernisation of the workshops which were to remain open to support the needs of the nationalised railway going into the 1970s. The absorption of these costs prior to the creation of the new commercial company, allowed the new organisation to begin trading free of debt and in such condition that it was able to effectively meet the needs of its main customer, the BRB. Ongoing investment would, of course, be crucial to ensure the long-term viability of the new engineering company. Starting its existence with a relatively modern estate of workshops would allow the company to seamlessly take on the existing workload and requirements of the railway, as well as being able to effectively (it was hoped) bid for outside work.

The railway was reorganised under the powers of the Transport Act of 1968. Sections 48(2) and 48(4) allowed the railway to create subsidiaries for various operational aspects of its business which were used to support the formation of British Rail Engineering as a fully owned subsidiary of the railway. The BRB was to distance itself directly from the manufacture and maintenance of locomotives and rolling stock, as well as other business operations, which were viewed as being ancillary to the railway's main business of running trains. In the case of the railway works, the new subsidiary was to operate as a nominally independent commercial company with its own board of directors. The board of the new company had the remit to run the operation on a commercial basis, allowing it to undertake bids for tenders from outside the main railway business for what the new company would term third parties.

The powers granted to the BRB and its subsidiaries by the 1968 Act increased the breadth of manufacturing options available from those granted in the 1962 Act which restricted manufacturing to only those items directly required for the purposes of the individual boards under the remit of the British Transport Commission. The later Act gave powers for the BRB to undertake manufacturing, through a subsidiary if such a subsidiary existed, not only items related to its own business (locomotives, carriages and wagons), but also to manufacture for sale to other companies any product which the workshops had the capability to construct as a result of the skills and capacity available within any of their workshops. The Act also provided powers to undertake repair work for any outside company of any item which, by having the skills, materials, and capacity in house, the works were able to undertake.

The 1968 Act gave new powers to the railway enabling it to repair motor vehicles, and to manufacture and sell 'spare parts and accessories for motor vehicles' which would enable the board and its intended new subsidiary not only to bid for work in the motor industry but also to tender for work from the Ministry of Defence.

The new company, as a subsidiary of the BRB, would theoretically be able to trade as any other commercial entity was able to, bidding for work as it saw fit to fill its order books and to keep its workforce gainfully and profitably employed.

Despite its 'arm's length' approach to the new company, the BRB would have quite close control over the new company. The BREL directors were to be appointed or reassigned from other parts of the railway or its subsidiaries by the railway board, with the chairman of the BREL board and a number of other directors sitting on the BRB. The BREL board would be unable to appoint its own directors at any point, although it was able to make recommendations which the BRB would consider.

The close relationship between the two boards would be both a blessing and a curse, and, as the company went into the 1980s, would cause complaints of favouritism and inside knowledge from BRELs competitors in the rail industry. Initially, as the sole supplier of the majority of the railway's rolling stock and locomotives, the close interaction would be of benefit to BREL in planning workload and capacity requirements for the future, however the demands of the BRB would continually be a cause for concern within the company, both as the sole supplier to the railway and also in the competitive environment of the 1980s.

The main trouble that BREL experienced throughout its entire existence was its close commercial relationship with the BRB. The arrangements through which the BRB and BREL would trade with each other was defined in 1969 as the plans for the new engineering company were being drawn up. As a nationalised company British Rail was expected to cover its costs, even though it struggled to not make a loss between the late 1960s and its eventual privatisation in 1997. It was further limited by the budget for new investment set by the Department for Transport and the Treasury, which would impact upon orders that could be placed with BREL for new construction. The investment plans drawn up by British Rail for new stock were often for a number of years as part of various 'future rail plans', which BREL was expected to have capacity to meet as and when the BRB approved the orders to be placed.

In order to meet British Rail's expectations, the company would need to have reserved the capacity that British Rail thought it might need against a moving forecast that may never be realised. The lack of certainty that underpinned the earliest days of the company would never be resolved and would cause issues with utilisation of staff when these orders were not forthcoming at the time scale originally planned. Lack of authorisations for promised work left BREL having to find work for the shopfloor at the last moment, or to bring other work forward to fill the gaps in production in order to avoid job losses which would then impact upon future capacity. The decisions made in 1969 to operate in this manner would plague BREL throughout its existence and prevent the company from being able to effectively plan its workload and to meet the potential that being one of Britain's largest engineering companies promised.

The commercial relationship between the BRB and BREL was also defined to not allow the company to make a profit. It was expected that the company would quote for work from British Rail on the basis of covering only costs and interest, no profit being allowed. The only work which BREL would be allowed to tender for based upon a profitable proposal would be for outside work to third parties or for potential export orders. The decisions made in 1969 seem in retrospect to be short sighted and somewhat strange. The company, as a nominally independent business, was expected to become commercially viable and profitable in its own right, yet its major customer would not allow it to make a profit on the work it placed with them.

BREL was also intended to fulfil the railway's need for maintenance on its locomotive, carriage and wagon fleet for which contracts would be awarded as needed. The same restrictions were built into the definition of the maintenance contracts which the BRB issued to BREL as could be found within the orders it placed for new locomotives and rolling stock. No profit was to be included in the quotation provided to the railway for which a maintenance contract would be automatically given subject to the BRB being satisfied that the pricing was acceptable. The major difference between new build and maintenance from the outset was that the maintenance activity work was reliable. Locomotives and rolling stock required regular planned light overhauls and heavy repairs for which BREL was able to plan from the outset, allowing capacity to be defined and the workforce to be kept employed.

The expectation at the formation of the company was that it would become profitable through its ability to win outside business, both rail related and general engineering or fabrication. The lack of clarity in the relationship between the company and its parent around new build work was destined to cause the company a great deal of difficulty in bidding for outside work to maintain both continuous production in the works and foundries and profitability. The company was being constrained by the need to have capacity planned against forecast orders from British Rail that may arrive later than forecast or potentially not at all, whilst looking for outside work to fill capacity that may or may not actually be available.

The BRB agreed to put other restrictions on their new subsidiary before it was created. The new company was not to be as independent operationally as it might have appeared to the outside observer and the historian. The board of directors was only to be allowed to authorise small amounts of expenditure up to a value agreed by the BRB. The amounts authorised would be sufficient for operational expenditure but not for investment in new machine tools and other heavy plant equipment.

In the event that major expenditure was required, the board of the new company would be required to authorise the proposal at their own board meeting, but this was not an authority for the purchase to go ahead, but for the proposal to pass to the Investment Committee of British Railways for deliberation at their next committee meeting. If the committee were to approve the proposal, the purchase was still unable to go ahead, the second approval only allowing the proposal to go forward to the next meeting of the BRB for their deliberation. If the proposal were to be authorised at the meeting, then the permission for the purchase to be undertaken would be cascaded back down to the BREL board so that they could inform the purchasing team to source the required items.

The restrictions on the BREL board's purchasing power would be loosened over time, through authorities given at the BRB meetings, but the lack of autonomy would cause delays in purchasing new machines tools and other equipment. The resulting delays to the constant modernisation of BREL's works over time caused quality issues when obsolete machine tools were unable to meet design tolerances. It consequently resulted in the over manning of machine shops, which became necessary to perform existing work. The delays to investment resulted in BREL being unable to make better use of their highly skilled craftsmen to increase the capacity of the existing works. In turn, that resulted in delays in delivering contracts for the railway and an inability to create extra capacity that could have been used to bid for profitable third party work.

The company was to inherit the existing works estate but was not to have control over its buildings. The BREL board was not to have direct authority over decisions needed for building maintenance nor for the improvement of works sites. The fabric of the works buildings, rail connections, power and water supplies and drainage would remain vested with the British Railways civil engineering department. The buildings would therefore be included in the civil engineers' maintenance plan, with work frequently being scheduled at times inconvenient to the needs of BREL's business.

Despite the lack of control, the company was responsible for the budget expenditure in their own right and from their own funds. The company would later gain control of its sites in their entirety but, even then, would still be at the mercy of the civil engineering department for the actual completion of required work. Budget constraints may also see work required delayed by the civil engineers and the BRB until the expenditure was absolutely necessary. These delays were often a false economy, such as in the case of the roof of one of the buildings at Swindon which was leaking, with the work delayed so as postpone the expenditure, the short termism resulting in the need to replace the entire roof later at far greater cost.

This was the remit that the new board of directors was given and that the management of the company would have to work within throughout the life of the company, a situation that was never ideal.

The company, despite efforts to rationalise and modernise the works that were to be passed on to it, inherited backlogs of work and delays in completion that were not of its making. Over time, the need arose to invest heavily in new plant and machinery as it became obsolete or unable to meet the demands of new standards in engineering tolerances that came into force later in the 1970s and into the 1980s. The commercial contracts that had been agreed with suppliers of raw materials and components

Class 46, 46050 on fire inside Swindon Works, 11 April 1984. *Laurence Waters*

were expected to be honoured until such time as they came up for renewal, at which point BREL could renegotiate contracts with its suppliers and source new ones. The situation that the company inherited, whilst probably ideal in many respects for British Rail as one entity, would be less effective for BREL. The company had little option upon its formation other than to take what its parent company passed to it and then to make the best attempts it could to resolve the problems that were created. Once the difficulties related to British Railways' legacy had been dealt with within the workshops and viable solutions had been implemented, the company would be able to move forward until such a time as it was able to implement its own strategy.

Unlike other new businesses, the company began life with a relatively full order book, work on hand and a large estate of fully equipped and modernised workshops staffed by an experienced workforce. This was, however, offset by problems caused in production by design changes that needed to be made on existing stock. The amendments to the designs would cause disruption on the shopfloor resulting in delay to completion of work on hand, impacting on the delivery of future orders already planned.

The company was to take over the design functions which had been undertaken in-house by British Rail. The design teams located at each of the works and centrally at British Rail headquarters would, like the workforce on the shopfloor, become employees of BREL from 1 January 1970. A central headquarters would be required to which the design staff that were not to remain on site at the various works would be relocated. The decision was taken that the location would be Derby.

The new company received its certificate of incorporation on 31 October 1969, creating British Rail Engineering Limited. The first board of directors was appointed by the BRB shortly afterwards and the company officially came into being. At the same time, a new administrative headquarters, at which the new company was to be registered, was agreed upon. The first board meeting took place at the new offices at Melbury House in Melbury Terrace, London NW1 on 18 December 1969. Present at the meeting were the company's first chairman J.M.W. Bosworth, the engineering director Dr Sydney James, as well as three other directors, P.G. James, L.F. Neal and T.C.B. Miller. The company's appointed managing director A.E. Robson was minuted as being unable to attend the first board meeting, as was L.W. Ibbotson, the company's personnel and industrial relations director. The company solicitor, A.E. Boothroyd, was also in attendance, as were D.C. Allan and L.E. Stanton as acting company secretary and acting assistant company secretary respectively.

The meeting ratified the incorporation of the company and the appointment of the directors as well as the receipt of ownership of the workshops which were to be passed to the company from British Rail as of 1 January 1970. At this point, the Ashford, Crewe, Derby Litchurch Lane, Derby Locomotive, Doncaster, Eastleigh, Glasgow (St Rollox), Horwich, Shildon, Swindon, Temple Mills, Wolverton and York works as well as the steel works at Worcester would become the property of the company with all members of staff, including all management, shopfloor, and clerical grades employed in these works becoming employees of BREL under the same terms and conditions under which they had been employed by British Rail.

The meeting agreed the capitalisation of the company, which was to be by 999,900 shares with the value of £1 per share. The entire shareholding was to be purchased by the BRB making it the single shareholder in the company, thus retaining total control over the business. The company was to be funded by an unsecured loan of £61 million at 6 per cent annual interest, the loan to be provided entirely by the BRB from its own funds. The 6 per cent interest was to be allowed as the interest cost to be included in the prices quoted to British Rail on new build and maintenance

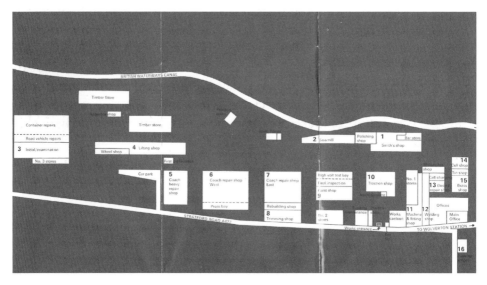

Map of Wolverton Works from an open day leaflet, *Author's collection*

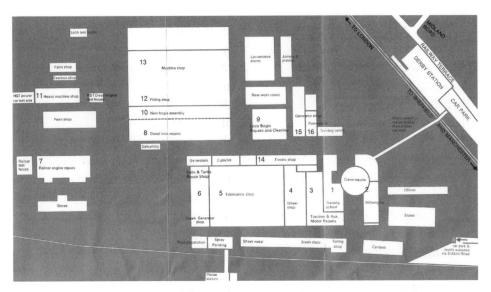

Map of Derby Locomotive Works from an open day leaflet. *Author's collection*

proposals. The unsecured loans provided by British Railways Board were effectively from the Department of Transport and thus government funding. The question of the divestment of a company which owed money against tax payer funded loans would later impact the privatisation of the company and needed to be resolved during the process of the sale of the company to its new owners. The issue of government finance was not relevant at the time for the company though, as it was not intended to be sold off. The expectation was that the business was to become self-sufficient and able to trade as an independent concern at some future point. Decisions made during the formation of the company seem, with the benefit of hindsight, to restrict the potential of the company, leaving a legacy which the company would consistently have to work against in order to succeed.

In 1969, all of these challenges were yet to manifest and the directors and employees of the company looked forward to a future with great potential.

Chapter 3

THE FIRST YEAR OF BREL: 1970

As the clocks struck midnight on 31 December 1969, one of Britain's largest engineering companies came into existence, appearing with little fanfare or celebration. British Rail Engineering Limited was now a live business with orders to be met from its parent company.

The first board meeting of the company was held at Eastleigh Works on 18 January 1970. The meeting was the first of the meetings to be held onsite at one of the company's works at various times over the next twenty years. The schedule was to be agreed in advance and would always involve a tour of the works to allow the directors to see the jobs being undertaken, and the working conditions within the workshops. The meeting also created the tradition of the works manager being invited to at least part of the board meeting to give a report and also to raise any concerns related to the plant and equipment at the works, vehicle designs that were causing trouble in construction, lack of delivery of locomotives and vehicles to the works which were scheduled for planned maintenance, industrial relations difficulties and so on. The board remained keen to continue the visits under the chairmanship of a variety of directors until the company was privatised.

The company had a pressing issue that needed to be resolved in the early stages of its existence, not just at Eastleigh, but across all of its works. Decisions had been taken in the past to cease production of some components and assemblies required for the construction of new vehicles and for maintenance of the existing fleets. The supply of some raw materials had also been outsourced, although many had traditionally been purchased in from large suppliers of glass and steel.

The resulting loss of control over the supply of these important items was causing delay to many projects. Supply of raw materials such as steel sheet and glass was becoming unreliable, and orders were often delivered late. Manufacturers of parts required for new builds were becoming less able to supply on time. Similarly, it was becoming necessary to hold large amounts of spare parts to guarantee the availability of replacements to meet maintenance schedules, and thus to keep the railway's locomotives and rolling stock availability at the level required to meet service demands. The raw materials suppliers and parts manufacturers were also unable to increase the volumes to match the needs of BREL.

The project being impacted the most in January 1970 was the production of Mark II passenger coaches. The suppliers of various parts were supplying in small quantities and often later than the order had been required by when it was placed. The unreliability of supply was causing delay in completion of new coaches at Derby Litchurch Lane, which in turn was delaying the introduction of the new sets into traffic. The yards at Derby were filling with part completed coaches awaiting parts which was in turn causing bottlenecks in the works.

The BREL board discussed the possibility of introducing penalty clauses for late or non-delivery of purchased materials and parts on new orders from the trade going forward. In order to attempt to find a resolution to the delays senior directors of BREL agreed to discuss the situation with

Maybach engines at Swindon Works, 4 April 1977. *Laurence Waters*

the directors of the companies concerned in order to agree a programme to resolve the problem. The company was also to refer the problems that were being experienced within the supply chain with the BRB, something which the company was to continue doing on many occasions over the succeeding years.

The problem had partly been caused by the late authorisation of new construction orders for the Mark II fleet by the BRB and the Ministry of Transport. The late placing of the production orders with the railway workshops had resulted in unnecessary pressure being put onto the supply chain, particularly on long lead time materials such as steel and brake equipment. The erosion of lead time was partly causing suppliers to struggle to meet BREL's timescales due to their own manufacturing lead times. The result was poor quality and non-compliance with scheduled delivery dates by the trade supporting BREL. If the delays to the confirmation of orders could be addressed at British Rail and the Ministry of Transport, the company would have more leverage on the suppliers to guarantee the required quantities and delivery dates.

The workshops at Swindon were facing a new dilemma caused by changes in British Rail's need and policy. The National Traction Plan implemented by British Rail in 1967 and 1968 had impacted upon the Western Region's diesel-hydraulic fleet. The plan had decreed that any locomotive which was unreliable or expensive to maintain should be eliminated from the fleet with more reliable traction replacing it as soon as was viable. The locomotive fleet on the Western Region had been particularly affected by one clause in the plan which stated that any non-standard locomotive was also to be eliminated. The diesel-hydraulic fleet were viewed as not standard due to the majority of the railway's diesel fleet using diesel-electric powerplants, and the lack of electric train supply equipment on the diesel-hydraulic fleet which was needed to be compatible with the newer Mark II fleet's air conditioning and heating systems. The locomotives impacted were the Class 35 Hymek, Class 42 and Class 43 Warship, and Class 52 Western fleets which remained mostly intact in 1970.

The uncertain future of the diesel-hydraulic fleet was not helped by shortages of replacement components that was impacting upon the maintenance schedule at Swindon. The critical state of component stocks was raised at the meeting in Eastleigh by the Chief Engineer (Traction and Rolling Stock) who advised that the shortages in materials and delays in resupply were at that point becoming likely to cause even lower traction

D1015, Western Champion outside Swindon Works, 21 February 1977. *Laurence Waters*

availability than was currently being experienced. In response to the report by the Chief Engineer, the board decided to intervene; A.E. Robson was to discuss the lack of support directly with his counterparts at the suppliers of the materials in question. The intention was to attempt to expedite deliveries in order to keep the fleet at acceptable services levels until such time as the withdrawals had commenced and other traction had been made available from elsewhere to fill the schedule.

Issues with supply remained unresolved by March, at which point serious consideration was being given to sourcing components in different ways to resolve the situation and remove delays that were not the fault of BREL. Plans to purchase materials from Europe were considered, the company opening discussions with German steel mills to complement British mill capacity. This did not come to fruition due to the difficulty in obtaining imperial gauge steel used in British designs at the time from the continent where most steel was manufactured to metric standards. Some materials were sourced from overseas where British manufacturers were unable to meet requirement dates, although this was minimal.

The company looked at their own capability and whether it may be possible to manufacture spares and other parts in-house. Some work was brought back into the company's works where viable to do so, which partly resolved some of the delays being experienced from within the external supply chain. The company was unable to address all of its supply shortages in this way, though.

The delivery of the prototypes for the new high density EMU vehicles was being delayed by late deliveries of traction equipment from the manufacturer. The suppliers were indicating that further deliveries of equipment for the production vehicles planned for the future would not only be subject to delay, but also to considerable price increases. The news impacted the delivery schedule, disrupting work planning on the shop floor and resulting in an increased cost which needed to be passed on to the BRB, for which an authority would need to be sought from the railway. Issues such as these would trouble BREL on many occasions, causing delivery delays and project cost overruns which would be reported negatively in the media but over which BREL had little control.

The variation in stock on the Southern Region was to cause BREL considerable difficulty in its first days. Stock being maintained at Eastleigh was, at the time of the director's visit, experiencing delays in completion of work. The slow return of units to traffic was being caused by the difficulties inherent in having to maintain sixteen different types of non-standard bogies on the vehicle fleet and the complex requirements of coach painting required by the vehicle liveries in use at the time. The works manager proposed that if the painting requirement could be changed to a simple two-tone scheme, that this would considerably reduce the time that stock was kept out of service in the works and assist in a greater throughput of vehicles.

An unwanted question which BREL had to address from the start had been caused by the reorganisation of the various works across Britain during the 1960s. The decisions made by the BRB during the last years of its ownership of the railway works had left a legacy of industrial unrest. The new company needed to find mutually acceptable ways to resolve the problems it had been left with, even though the inherent bad feeling was not of their making. At Eastleigh, the construction of the first Class 73 locomotives in the carriage works had caused discontent within the locomotive works. The unrest spread to the carriage works during the rationalisation at Eastleigh which resulted in the closure of the carriage works with all the facilities moving into the site of the locomotive works to create a single consolidated site.

The works manager at Eastleigh reported that there had been difficulty with finding consensus across the works and that having to negotiate with many different trade unions was causing delays in reconciling the dispute. In order to resolve the situation, a works council was setup, with the agreement of all the trade unions. The council would represent the interests of all unions and act as a single point of negotiation between unions and

BREL Eastleigh, in addition to EMU and DMU classes and hauled stock also provided classified maintenance for locos of Classes 07, 08, 09, 33, 71, 73 and 74, 25 April 1984. ED No.73131 undergoes an intermediate overhaul. *Colin J. Marsden*

management, simplifying the situation for both sides. The success of the introduction of the council at Eastleigh saw the idea rolled out across all of the works that were now owned by BREL.

The works at Eastleigh had experienced a number of stoppages due to industrial action related to staff demands. The members of the Amalgamated Union of Engineering and Foundry Workers (AEF), for example, had called a strike in response to a number of issues with which they had grievances. On 14 April, the works manager at Eastleigh was asked by the board of BREL to report on why the strike had occurred. David Bowick responded with a report that stated that, whilst the strike was unofficial, 300 men had walked out, with the strike now reaching a month in duration. The dispute was believed to be soluble quite simply, as the problem had mainly been caused by lack of training undertaken by British Railways in personnel work for its managers. Messrs Wurr and Barker-Wyatt were sent to Eastleigh and to consult with the AEF Union representatives. The dispute was resolved and all of the men returned to work shortly afterwards.

Despite the improvement in industrial relations brought about by the works councils, conflict between management and staff still remained and could potentially create a flashpoint for further industrial action. The company had begun to undertake various studies to ascertain how to improve efficiency and to reduce delays which were caused by outdated working practices. The main study being undertaken in early 1970 was a work measurement study which resulted in a proposal to change the way in which the works were measured. It had been decided that the works would be paid through an incentive scheme in addition to their base wages, rather than continuing with bonus by piece work. The existing arrangement paid employees by the completion of numbers of parts, completion of a 'job' (such as installing a powerplant in a new locomotive) or completion of entire vehicles. Increasing resistance to the work studies was seen at York and Eastleigh works, with non-cooperation being common elsewhere. The reluctance of the works staff to change to a new system would be resolved over time with all works eventually agreeing to adopt the incentive bonus scheme. The dispute at Eastleigh was resolved locally to the mutual satisfaction of both staff and management with a settlement that was unique to the site and not suitable for roll out across the company.

From the outset, the company was keen to build good industrial relations and began discussions on a new 'Machinery of Negotiation' framework with the union representatives at all their workshops. The intention was to eventually create a jointly agreed system which would replace the shopmen's councils under a single works council, whilst considering the requirements of different trades and skills of the clerical and workshop staff, and hours of work. The negotiations remained ongoing in 1970, but would ultimately prove fruitful and beneficial to both sides. The creation of the new framework was timely as the railway and BREL would be impacted by the new legislation being proposed under consultative documents relating to what would become the Industrial Relations Act 1971. Allowance for the planned legislative requirements could thus be written into the new framework as part of the continuing negotiations.

The Industrial Relations Bill would have an almost immediate impact upon BREL, with industrial action taken in response to the planned legislation common across British industry. Strikes and work to rule protests against the new law impacted upon the company in December 1970. The industrial action in response to the new labour Act which occurred across BREL's workshops added to the loss of working time caused by unrelated industrial action in the electricity supply industry, as well as across British industry at the time.

In order to widen the opportunity for growth, and to provide work for its workshops, create profit and protect the jobs of the workforce, the company from the outset started to look for opportunities to undertake more profitable export and private sector work. An export agency agreement with Arne Glucksman AB of Gothenburg in Sweden which allowed the Swedish company to sell any products manufactured by BREL in Scandinavia, was quickly agreed, with the company seeking other third party and export opportunities.

The company was well aware that it had the capacity to undertake outside work in addition to the work it was guaranteed to receive from British Rail. The company was, however, lacking the commercial experience to undertake a successful sales effort to find and win orders. Despite the lack of a sales group to work with outside customers, the relationship with Glucksman resulted in orders from overseas very quickly.

The first export order won by the company was taken during February 1970 when the Johnson Line of Stockholm in Sweden ordered 2,500 lumber flat trucks worth £1.22million. The work was allocated to Ashford Works, the first of many wagon export orders completed there for BREL. The production of the wagons was delayed by lack of stock within the equipment and materials supply chain, but BREL was able to respond to the situation by using its own resources to make up lost time and to meet the delivery dates requested by the customer. In order to achieve the date promised to the customer, a portion of the order was reallocated to Swindon, providing work for the staff who had been involved in the production of British Rail Universal Trolley Equipment (BRUTE) caged platform trolleys which had by then been completed.

The export drive through BREL's own efforts were proving successful in 1970. In the first three months of the company's existence, it had closed another two major orders, in addition to the order from Sweden.

M.A.F.I. Fahrzeugwerk of Stuttgart had signed a contract worth £6.25million to supply a minimum of 3,250 shipping containers to M.A.F.I.'s designs over the next five years. The containers for the order were to be built at the container works at both Derby Litchurch Lane and Horwich. Malayan Railways had agreed a £650,000 contract with BREL for the construction and supply of 150 covered freight vans to be built to metre gauge and which were to be delivered at the rate of 10 per week. The order was allocated to Shildon with shipments to be undertaken through the docks at Middlesbrough from November 1970. The company had also completed its part of an order for Northern Ireland Railways for three locomotives and eight coaches won jointly with the Hunslet Locomotive Company and English Electric.

BREL completed contract negotiations in late March 1970 with Córas Iompair Éireann (CIE, the Republic of Ireland's national transport company), for the construction and supply of ninety-five coaches and vans at a cost of £2.6million. The year ended with a successful bid for a further order of 62 carriages, 22 boiler vans and 11 generator vans for CIE, worth £2.58million and an order for 2,500 container platforms for Rederiakttiebolaget Norsdtjernan of Sweden.

The company began to consider other options to diversify the work undertaken in its works in order to open up more commercial opportunities. Seeing the growing demand for shipping containers, as maritime freight became progressively more containerised, the company began to explore the possibility of either designing their own standard container or possibly purchasing a proven design for an aluminum/steel container from elsewhere. The design could then be added to the company's portfolio.

From the earliest days, the company began to adopt a programme of investment in its works aimed at improving the machine tools, some of which were past the end of life despite the investments in the 1960s. The machine shop at Crewe was equipped with a new wheel and axle machining lathe and two new automatic chucking lathes, the authority being given by the board at the April meeting. The £41,000 cost for the wheel lathe and £45,000 for the two automatic lathes were within the BREL board's authority level and was also associated with the 1970/71 Machine Tool Replacement Programme. The machine shop at Derby Litchurch Lane was also to receive a new 8-ton capacity crane at a cost of £37,822.

The company began to ask the civil engineers' department to undertake repairs on its buildings which had been deferred to delay expenditure. In March 1970, the company agreed and authorised work to be undertaken to repair the roofs at various works which could no longer be deferred. The DMU workshop at Swindon required major roof repairs costing £42,000.

The roof of the machine shop at Crewe also required complete replacement, during which the company investigated the possibility of replacing glass panels in the roof with corrugated plastics to improve

Western Champion inside Swindon Works, 19 May 1979. The age of the buildings in use at the workshops can be clearly seen and was typical of much of BREL's site. *Laurence Waters*

safety for those working underneath. The new plastic panels were found to be suitable but required additional roof supports which would increase costs dramatically, so a new asbestos roof with safer wired glass windows costing £39,125 was installed. At Horwich, the roof of the mechanised foundry had been found to be dangerous and was replaced at a cost of £51,000. Other work was undertaken across the works estate during 1970, including replacement of the roofs of the erecting shop at Crewe (£86,000) and the crane shop at Glasgow (£34,500).

The company began to embark on a general ongoing machine tool replacement programme which would run annually from 1971 until the sale of the company, although some years would see a reduction in available funds. The 1971 Tool Replacement Programme was agreed at the June BREL board meeting with investments totalling £1.04million being identified and planned for the year. The programme was approved for submission to the British Rail Investment Committee, eventually receiving full approval from the BRB.

The major individual investment planned in 1970 was for Horwich. The foundry in Horwich Works was becoming life expired. Equipment was becoming unreliable and frequent breakdowns caused delay to production. The company was looking to gain better utilisation of the foundry by taking on work for castings from outside the railway, which was also likely to be more profitable. The condition of the equipment at the foundry would not have allowed the works to take on more work from within the railway, let alone from customers elsewhere, so it was recognised that modernisation of the plant was urgently needed. The modernisation was estimated to cost £1.11million, although it was decided to phase the work across the three production units to avoid complete closure of the plant during modernisation. The programme was above the limits set for approvals by the BRB and so had to be submitted to the British Rail Investment Committee for approval and then on to the railway board.

The company was able to attract a small degree of outside funding for improvements. The provision of new Record and Playback Welding Machines at Derby Litchurch Lane in 1970 was to be part funded by Hawker Siddeley, for whom the company was to be undertaking subcontract work at Derby, with the balance of cost being covered by the BRB under their Research Expansion Programme. BREL had its own research group which focused on the creation of new designs and technology for the company, whereas the BRB had their own research department, British Rail Research

Division, which had been formed in 1964 and remained separate from BREL throughout. The research division was located at the Railway Technical Centre in Derby, located on the opposite side of the London Road from BREL's Litchurch Lane Works. BREL's works at Derby and elsewhere would undertake a large amount of fabrication and construction work for the research division over time. As a result, it would have access to some degree of modernisation funding for its machine shops until 1989, when the research division became an independent self-contained business in preparation for the privatisation of the railway.

The work to improve matters in BREL included research being undertaken by the engineering teams. The company was seeking to offer new designs to the railway to meet the BRB's requirement for higher availability of locomotives and multiple units. BREL began work on new designs that would take advantage of new technology to reduce the frequency of maintenance visits, keeping the units in traffic for longer. The Chief Mechanical and Chief Electrical Engineers at BREL reported in March 1970 that more time would be required to perfect new proposals. The work being undertaken in 1970 would ultimately have a huge impact on the employees of BREL and upon the company itself, but for now those challenges were still in the distant future.

The BREL board was keen to look at the wages and salaries being paid across all of its staff from the start. A meeting was held at the London headquarters on 25 June 1970 with the personnel director, at which a programme of job pay evaluations was agreed. Some grades, it was agreed, had fared less well than some of those involved in more specialist roles under previous job evaluation programmes. In order to undertake the re-evaluation of pay, a new evaluation panel was created consisting of the managing and personnel directors of the company, with a Mr Low seconded to the panel from outside BREL to act as 'expert witness' when job grades were being evaluated. To begin with, eight senior posts were to be evaluated, resulting in pay rises for all concerned.

A number of urgent engineering requirements were being addressed in the early days of the company. One of the pressing issues was whether all-steel vehicles should have all the surfaces galvanised prior to painting to extend the life of the panels on the vehicles being constructed in works. The question had been raised by the works manager at Derby as a suggestion to the board meeting in May 1970. The open invitation to suggestions from within the company regarding potential improvements remained a feature of the board's relationship with the company's employees throughout the existence of the company, normally being channelled through the works managers. On this occasion, it was agreed that the panels used in all-steel vehicles should be fully galvanised to extend the life of the vehicles following investigation into the condition of non-galvanised Merry-Go-Round hopper wagons which revealed that the vehicles were deteriorating more quickly than had been expected.

Another factor causing the delays and inefficiency that was plaguing the company related to shopfloor control. Lack of control was proving troublesome, particularly when changes to designs had been made which required the withdrawal of job cards and other paperwork, and the creation of replacement instructions and drawings. The potential use of 'computer-time' was being investigated as it was seen to have potential to reduce the disruption caused on the shopfloor by change to designs or the movement of work to accommodate other more urgent jobs.

Merry-Go-Round hopper wagon at Shildon Works, 11 November 1980. The method of construction involved complex welding of the hopper body in galvanised steel to extend the life of the wagon. *Colin J. Marsden*

At the time, computing was in its early stages in business, with large mainframe computers occupying entire rooms, linked to 'dumb terminals' for users to access the systems being the only available options. Departments needed to book computer time, so that the disc clusters that their work was located on could be loaded in a disc drive machine in the computer centre for them to use. Even in its primitive form, computing had much to offer BREL and the company had agreed to lease a main frame machine from International Computers Limited (ICL), a British computer company established in 1968 which provided both machines and bespoke software for businesses.

The vast business management software industry that exists in the twenty-first century providing standard but configurable business and manufacturing management software systems had not yet begun to appear. Most software was produced by programmers employed by companies such as ICL or by businesses. BREL would later have their own computer programmers but at the beginning were reliant on ICL for the production of the systems upon which they would come to rely. BREL received approval in May 1970 for the replacement of an old machine with a state-of-the-art ICL 1901A series mainframe computer with fifty storage discs on a two-year lease from ICL for the sum of £34,440, with an additional £3,750 for the discs. The computer room was to be located at Derby Loco Works with networked telephone lines giving access to the machine from other works.

The influence of the BRB on the company was exemplified in June 1970 when three new directors were appointed to the BREL board by the parent company. I.D. Gardiner, R.C.S. Low and D.C. Allan were appointed to the board, with D.C. Allan appointed as the company's permanent company secretary.

BREL was constantly to be subject to another influence from the BRB. The predicted need for locomotive and rolling stock, including the plans associated with the Advanced Passenger Train on which much optimism was placed in the early 1970s, would have a constantly varying impact upon the workshops operated by BREL and the futures of the people employed there. The 'Future Rail Plan' usually only covered a period of around four to five years making the long-term planning of investment in BRELs workshops related to the work from British Rail difficult. The Future Rail Plan 1971/75 published by British Rail indicated that a reduction in workshop capacity with the resultant job losses that would cause as the most probable outcome for BREL. Work planned in relation to the introduction into service of the Advanced Passenger Train fleet (then deemed to be likely towards the end of the plan period) was seen to require an increase in both headcount and capability within the workshops. This would need planning for the longer term reinvestment in works capacity and also the need to potentially attempt to rehire staff previously made redundant. A threat which was identified by the board at the time related to the future availability of staff previously employed by BREL, who may have taken new employment elsewhere by that time and would be unlikely to be tempted to return.

BREL's board was keen to avoid job losses wherever possible and wished to explore the manufacture of more components in-house as opposed to the purchase of them from the trade associated with the rail industry. Whilst BREL may have been capable of taking back more work that had been outsourced during the 1960s, the company was restricted by its relationship with the BRB once again. It was against the BRB's policy to reverse the outsourcing that had been undertaken and to revert to higher levels of in-house production of components and equipment. The supposedly independent company was to be hampered in its need to be responsive to market trends by its masters at Euston.

One action that the company could undertake on its own, without interference from the railway board, was the reorganisation of its workshops to resolve working practices that it had inherited which no longer made commercial sense. One such project was undertaken at Temple Mills workshops.

Temple Mills employed 422 staff, and in 1970 was undertaking repair and overhaul work on freight vehicles, containers and road vans. One of the main tasks that were undertaken at the works was the maintenance of Freightliner wagons in a dedicated workshop, which was also where one of the operating problems was occurring. The issue facing the works was that the work on the Freightliner sets was not planned in advance. The works only knew what vehicles were coming to the workshops and the work each vehicle in a set needed when the vehicles were shunted into the yard during the night.

The processes applied to individual wagons could not be applied to the maintenance of the Freightliners as they were not individual vehicles but sets of five bogie flat trucks for the carriage of shipping containers. Each set was made up of two end vehicles with couplings and air brake piping,

Hooded Wagon 494534 undergoing maintenance at Temple Mills workshops, 21 June 1975. *Colin J. Marsden*

with three intermediate vehicles with unique couplings and brake piping that could only be coupled to another Freightliner vehicle.

Three inspectors would assess the sets for mechanical or wheel defects and welding faults, after which the set would be shunted into the workshops by locomotive, the set split into its individual vehicles which would then be manhandled into position. Herein lay the trouble. When the set was shunted into the workshops and uncoupled, the five vehicles might need different repairs which could take different times. If the vehicles nearest the door were in need of heavy repairs, then the whole set was blocked into the bay and the capacity could not be used for other vehicles, even though maintenance work had been completed on that part of the set.

A study was undertaken to identify if any improvements could be made in the utilisation of the workshop. The outcome was an overhaul of how the facility operated. From January 1971, the inspections of the vehicles would note what level of repairs was needed and a classification of work given to each vehicle. The vehicles would be arranged in the bays according to the level of work required, regardless of the type of vehicle or the set it had arrived in. The roads in the workshops were classified by the type of work to be undertaken on that road, intermediate repairs, intermediate with attention to wheels and bogies, or general and heavy repairs. The revised way of working was reported to have improved the throughput of Freightliner sets.

Despite the issues that it had inherited, such as the case of Temple Mills, and the work that needed to be undertaken to organise the new company, much was achieved in the first year of its existence and although some challenges still remained to be resolved, the company was able to look forward with optimism toward a future with much promise.

Chapter 4
BREL AND BRE-METRO LIMITED

BREL recognised from the start that its future relied on a more commercial approach to sales outside the company. A budget of £2.767million revenue had been set, but the company had yet to appoint a commercial manager to oversee the function. The company also appreciated that, whilst a serious export drive would be likely to result in large amounts of work from overseas customers, it did not have the expertise or network of overseas offices through which to support a concerted long-term export business. The agency agreement with Arne Glucksman was a good start, but the board understood that more needed to be done to support other territories with sales potential.

BREL needed to look elsewhere for a partner who had the expertise that it lacked, that was already active in the British export trade and which also had an understanding of both the rail industry and the manufacture of railway equipment and vehicles. An approach had already been made and discussions had begun between the BREL board and the board of directors at Metropolitan-Cammell in Birmingham. The negotiations between the two companies proved fruitful, both gaining benefit from the potential venture. BREL would gain the long experience of operating in many countries overseas and the pitfalls of export finance that Metro-Cammell possessed. In return, Metro-Cammell would gain access to the vast resources of BREL's works and the expansion in capacity that offered. A potential joint venture would allow both companies to pursue export orders which it may not have been able to have successfully won and supplied alone.

The BREL directors approved the formation of an export company in May 1970 which was to be a joint venture between the two companies. The new company was to be a jointly owned subsidiary of both BREL and Metro-Cammell, with each holding half of the shares in the new company.

At the same meeting, BREL approved, in principle, the agreement drawn up between the two companies which defined how revenue was to be apportioned and how the workload resulting from orders obtained was to be allocated to Metro-Cammell and BREL's works. A small number of points remained to be clarified but both boards agreed to continue with the creation of the company.

The Publicity Department of the BRB released a press statement on 27 May 1970 announcing 'British Rail Engineering and Metro-Cammell to Merge for Exports', even though the company had not been formally created yet. The press release stated erroneously that the company was to be called BREMET International Limited, but correctly that the company was to be responsible for the exports of rolling stock. The reason for the 'merger' was described, probably fairly, as bringing benefit to both parent companies through 'Metro-Cammell's expertise in world-wide exports' and also that 'BREL's production units allow more competitive delivery times'. The company headquarters were to be established within the Washwood Heath workshops of Metro-Cammell in Birmingham, with an additional office located within BREL's offices at Melbury House in London.

The agreement to form the company was finally ratified at the June 1970 BREL board meeting, with Metro-Cammell's board doing the same. The company was to be called BRE-Metro Limited, with a board of directors consisting partly of directors from the board of BREL and partly from the board of Metro-Cammell. A press release from British Railways' publicity department in November of that year announced the formation of the company, and its nominated directors to the media. Three directors had been appointed by each of the owning companies, with J.M.W. Bosworth (vice chairman of the BRB), A.E. Robson (Managing Director of BREL), and I.D. Gardiner (Commercial Director of BREL) being joined by Sir Thomas Padmore (Director of the Laird Group, the owners of Metro-Cammell), A.H. Sansome (Chairman of Metro-Cammell Limited) and D.B. Whitehouse (Director and General Manager of Metro-Cammell Limited) as the board of directors of the new business, with J.M.W. Bosworth as chairman and Sir Thomas Padmore as deputy chairman.

The agreement between the two companies contained an important clause. The BRB excluded the rights to exploit any new technology from BRE-Metro, the rights remaining with the railway board. The right to exploit all new technologies created in connection with projects such as the Advanced Passenger Train, or any other development on a world-wide royalty basis remained vested in the BRB.

The company was formally launched at a cocktail party held at the Regency Rooms of the Charing Cross Hotel on 12 January 1971. Representatives from forty-nine foreign embassies in London were present at the launch, many of whom were the trade envoys from their respective governments. Some of the notable countries whose governments were represented at the party included the Soviet Union, China, and the United Arab Emirates, with representatives from Finland, Spain, Eire and Greece attending. The majority of the countries at the reception were African and South American, where BRE-Metro saw great potential for trade with the governments of those nations who were modernising and expanding their rail networks.

The working arrangements that had been agreed upon in the contracts which created BRE-Metro saw the export company as being the lead in bidding for overseas work for which BREL and Metro-Cammell would tender to BRE-Metro for. If the order was won, work would be awarded by BRE-Metro to both according to need, expertise and capacity to deliver on time. Financial risk would be vested in BRE-Metro, protecting the parent companies, to some degree, from the vagaries of international finance and the impact of currency valuations over time. BRE-Metro received protection in its own right from the government's Export Credit Guarantee Department from February 1971, giving it the security needed to approach some of the more financially volatile countries across the globe.

The board of BREL identified that the small quantities likely to be ordered by outside parties of the widely different wagon designs then in production for British Rail were unlikely to result in profitable orders. The high costs inherent in small batch manufacture caused by frequent setup for jigs and machine tools and the higher cost to purchase in small quantities of the materials and equipment from suppliers would, in turn, be likely to make BRE-Metro's offers less competitive. In order to maximise the opportunity for BRE-Metro, a new approach would be needed.

A rationalisation of the wagon designs currently available into a smaller number would offer a greater return. BREL's answer to the need to find more commonality within its designs was to look toward a small number of standard bogies which could be used under a variety of wagons, allowing for longer production runs with larger orders using fewer types of equipment for their construction. The use of standard frames upon which different configurable bodies could be mounted to meet customer requirements was pursued for the same reason. The optional bodies could be produced in small quantities if needed as the setup times for welding would hopefully be short and the materials would all be the same gauges of steel sheet allowing for purchase of larger quantities from the steel suppliers resulting in cost savings.

The result of the proposal would, after initial redesign costs, not only result in a cheaper offering for the export and domestic market allowing BREL to compete with other suppliers for the business, but also a more economic offering to British Rail through which the BRB may be able to achieve savings in fleet renewal costs.

BRE-Metro would benefit from the more flexible offering based upon the new standard set of sub-assemblies. The company would be able to approach potential customers with a more coherent offering. It was hoped that this would provide a more compelling purchase for the customer due to the savings which they in turn could achieve through the standardisation of their own rolling stock. BRE-Metro was able to begin creating a 'catalogue' of products and marketing literature to support the creation of awareness in overseas markets of the company. Despite the close relationship between BREL, its subsidiary company and its own parents, the BRB, communication did not always run smoothly.

The public relations department at Euston was surprised to receive a copy of a BRE-Metro brochure which resulted in a flurry of internal memos throughout British Rail, the BRB and BREL, asking if anyone was aware of the brochure and who BRE-Metro was and whether they were allowed to use British Rail's branding in the marketing collateral that had been created. The uncertainty was resolved once the communications reached the BREL board, who clarified the situation, although the BRB was also aware of the situation due to its shared directorate with BREL

Once BRE-Metro began to explore opportunities, it was successful in winning a number of contracts. One of the first orders placed in 1971 was received from the Cayman Islands Leasing Company for 850 shipping containers, which would be manufactured at the container workshops at Derby, the start of a series of orders passing through those workshops over the forthcoming years. The order was followed in August by an order that British Rail's publicity department referred to as 'a valuable order from Northern Ireland Railways', for four three-car diesel-EMUs consisting of a motor coach, non-driving trailer and driving trailer, and for five two-car units without the non-driving trailer. The order was worth £1.6million to the company, with the work being spread across the workshops at York, Derby Locomotive and Derby Litchurch Lane.

The company won an order from Société Gregg d' Europe for four coaches based upon the existing standard Mark IIC design, and consisting of two first class and two second class vehicles to be constructed at Derby Litchurch Lane. The coaches were to be delivered to the Guinea Bauxite Mining Company. The contract specified some particular work that needed to be incorporated into the four vehicles to make them suitable for the location in which they were to work. Each coach was required to be protected against termites and equipped with a pressure ventilation system to prevent ingress of dust from outside. The bogies and brake equipment also had to be partially redesigned to suit local conditions. The work was completed, and the vehicles shipped to West Africa in May.

Later in the year, negotiations with Yugoslav Railways were coming to a conclusion regarding a very large order for special purpose wagons, due to be placed in 1972. The order was finally placed in July 1972 on behalf of Zeljeznicko Transportno Poduzece, Zagreb (Croatian Railways), with the work being allocated to Ashford. The order for 800 covered wagons, to be used for the transport of grain, was worth £6.5million and was due to completed at the rate of 20 wagons per week. The first twenty wagons were delivered to Croatian Railways during a special ceremony at Rijeka in Yugoslavia attended by the Right Honourable Richard Marsh, the Chairman of the BRB.

The efforts made by BRE-Metro to secure export orders continued to yield success in 1974. A contract was secured in March 1974 from the Jordanian Ministry of Transport for the construction and supply of bogie hopper wagons, followed in April by an order for a further seventy to be delivered to the Aqaba Railway Corporation. The 42-ton capacity wagons were to be used for the transport of phosphates between the new mine at El Hassa and the port of Aqaba. The workload resulting from both contracts was assigned to the works at Ashford.

Towards the end of the year, a £155,000 order was won for the construction and supply of thirty-six bolster wagons for the transport of hardwood logs for the 3ft 6in gauge Ghana Railway. The wagons were to be manufactured at Derby Litchurch Lane, but to be sent to Takoradi in Ghana as 'knocked down' kits of parts for assembly by Ghana Railways.

Covered wagons for Yugoslavia under construction at Ashford Works, 5 November 1973.
Colin J. Marsden

As the company went into 1974, its operations had expanded dramatically. BRE-Metro was now a truly multinational company with direct representation in seventeen countries. Representation in other countries was provided through the British Embassy's commercial attaché or through Crown Agents' representation. BREL was involved with the company in negotiations for potential orders for existing locomotive and rolling stock designs across the globe, with some potential customers requesting the involvement of the design to order services now being offered by BRE-Metro using both BREL and Metro-Cammell's design teams.

The overseas market was reported to be growing rapidly towards the end of the 1973, and likely to continue increasing throughout 1974 and into 1975 at least. BRE-Metro saw one particular demand as being particularly attractive. The market for urban rail transport was an ideal hunting ground for British railway vehicle exports. Municipal authorities across the world were embarking on renewal and extension programmes related to their urban railways, with budgets for new rolling stock being quite generous in many cases. This was seen as being extremely promising as BREL had ready-made designs for vehicles ideally suited to prospective customers' needs and which could readily be tailored to the requirements of the local authorities. The only remaining cause for concern was that the production capacity available within the BREL works was slowly diminishing. The reduction in available space in the workshop schedules for potential third party or export work was due to the high volume of work being placed by the BRB at the time. This was likely to result in long lead times for delivery of vehicles. The inability to commit to faster turnaround of orders and delivery of completed new rolling stock was likely to hand the commercial advantage to European and American rail vehicle manufacturers who were more likely to be able to offer a more compelling delivery time to the prospective customer. BREL and Metro-Cammell both began to look into how capacity might be increased without impacting any of the workload already on the books.

Early in 1975, BRE-Metro experienced a problem with an order which had been won for the supply of railway equipment and EMUs to Taiwan as a joint venture with a partner company. The order included thirteen five car EMUs and had run into trouble due to financing and other requirements. The partner company and BRE-Metro had both approached the Department for Trade and Industry for assistance, although BRE-Metro's partner company had taken a fairly uncompromising stance, stating that unless a decision was received that the order would receive support from the government, the electric units would be constructed in South Africa.

A different stance was taken by BRE-Metro, with the support of both BREL and Metro-Cammell, suggesting that since the issues could be resolved by BRE-Metro as the sole contractor for the electric trains, it might be more constructive for the joint bidder to renegotiate the terms of the sale with the Taiwanese Railway Authority, to exclude the EMUs from the joint bid with BRE-Metro continuing as the sole bidder for the trains. The change in terms would impact little on the other bidder as the train construction work was due to be assigned in total to BRE-Metro, who in turn had already accepted the tender from BREL to construct the vehicles. It was believed that this option offered a more amicable solution to the difficulty being experienced with the order. Agreement was reached in May between BRE-Metro, the joint contractor and the Taiwanese Railway Authority, that the provision of EMUs would be undertaken solely by BRE-Metro and BREL from that point.

The demand for rolling stock from railway administrations continued to grow, with BRE-Metro tendering for large amounts of business. The slowdown of work being placed upon BREL by the BRB due to the recession impacting the British economy in the first half of 1975 was proving beneficial to BRE-Metro who were able to take advantage of the shorter lead times on offer. The company was struggling to cope with the amount of opportunity due to the lack of people they had in overseas sales offices. The company embarked on a programme of recruitment across all the territories in which BRE-Metro was active. Despite the plans made to increase the resources of the company to support more activity in the potential export business, there was a growing threat to the future of the company, which suddenly appeared.

Metro-Cammell, the joint partner in BRE-Metro with BREL, announced in late August, that they were to re-enter the export market in their own right, competing directly with BREL rather than continuing to jointly bid for overseas business. The announcement signalled the start of the breakdown of the relationship between the two companies that would become progressively more hostile over the coming years.

At this time, the board of BREL looked at potentially taking the decision to tender directly for overseas business themselves, in the light of Metro-Cammell's decision to do so. The BREL staff working at BRE-Metro could be returned to the parent company, bringing with them the expertise in overseas trade that they had gained. In the meantime, BRE-Metro would continue to function, with difficulty, as the joint export arm of both the parent companies in the short term.

Despite the announcement by Metro-Cammell, BRE-Metro continued to seek export orders, winning two large bids in August 1975. On 8 August, the receipt of an order was announced from Northern Ireland Railways. The order consisted of nine three-car diesel electric multiple units and three two-car units, with a spare motor coach. The work was scheduled to be undertaken at York, Wolverton and both works in Derby. The second order

Northern Ireland Railways' Class 80 Driving Trailer under construction at Derby Litchurch Lane. *Colin J. Marsden*

received in the month was a repeat order from the Jordanian Ministry of Transport on behalf of the Aqaba Railway Corporation. The order consisted of 140 bogie hopper wagons for the 3ft 6in gauge railway. All the wagons were to be constructed at Ashford with standard gauge accommodation bogies to be used to convey them to port.

The company had been actively pursuing a large order from East African Railways for 1,200 wagons, which was worth £19million, during 1976. The negotiations seemed promising at the time as BREL and BRE-Metro had been told that they were the lowest bidder for the business. The order was, however, not awarded to BRE-Metro but to a company in Canada during July. The Canadian company had entered a higher bid, but had offered a complete package which included the wagons, locomotive spares and also a very low interest loan to fund the purchase. BREL and BRE-Metro would continue to be unable to remain competitive in the export market since private competitors were able to undertake commercial bids which included offers and incentives to place the order with them, which the BREL and BRE-Metro were restricted from entering into by the BRB's own policy. The restrictive control placed upon BREL and effectively on to the work being undertaken by BRE-Metro had probably partly caused Metro-Cammell's intention to sever links with the railway and to return to bidding for export work in its own right where its activities would be less restricted.

Representations made to the East African Railways by BRE-Metro resulted in the two companies beginning new negotiations whilst the order placed in Canada was put on hold. Discussions were ongoing through the last months of 1976. Negotiations appeared to be successful, with the wagon and locomotive order being promised to BRE-Metro in late November.

The company, having learned from its experience with the original order for East African Railways (who had now been renamed Kenya Railways), pressed for a quick response for an updated tender for the 1,200 wagons with an additional requirement for 35 diesel shunting locomotives to be shared by BREL and The Hunslet Locomotive Company in Leeds. The new tender documents were sent to BRE-Metro by BREL and Hunslet very quickly, with the bid from BRE-Metro being sent to Kenya soon afterwards. In order to avoid any risk of outside influence from other companies, the sales manager for BRE-Metro travelled to Nairobi to await a summons from the Kenyan authorities to discuss the offer made. The order was finally signed at the beginning of March.

The company embarked on a joint venture with the Egyptian government during 1978 for a replacement programme of new coaches for the Egyptian railway network, all of which were to be built at Derby Litchurch Lane.

The export market had become slack during the second quarter of 1979, and with less demand for low tech wagons from its potential customers, BRE-Metro was struggling to attract business. Many developing countries, which had long been the company's most fertile business territories, now required more advanced and complex railway equipment. A much higher demand was being placed for new, modern locomotives and coaches, and

Export wagons for Kenya under construction at Ashford, 9 October 1977. *Colin J. Marsden*

without an 'export locomotive' or 'export coach' BRE-Metro was finding it hard to compete with American and Korean manufacturers.

The company did secure a wagon order in September. Kenya Railways placed an order for 110 soda ash wagons, worth £4.5million, with the wagons to be built at Shildon and Ashford.

The relationship between BRE-Metro's partners worsened and eventually the company would become dysfunctional, being ignored by BREL who began to bid directly for export work.

Chapter 5
THE EARLY SEVENTIES: 1971–74

The new year, 1971, began with industrial action at various works. Swindon was in the throes of a number of disputes related to the control of work in the erecting and machine shops. The introduction of standard documentation to be completed for each job undertaken in order to improve visibility of progress and to assist in shopfloor planning as well as the payment of staff who were still on piecework caused much discontent. The new system replaced an ad hoc process that had existed previously resulting in little management visibility of progress on the shopfloor, precluding the new planning disciplines which were beginning to spread through all manufacturing sites across Britain. The ad hoc nature of reporting prevented the introduction of computerisation. Similar issues had caused a dispute at Derby Litchurch Lane, although the works committee had agreed on the continuation of piece work on the container shop assembly line with a gradual phasing out of piece work in favour of a wage and productivity bonus scheme. Staff still opposed the changes, with negotiation continuing, whilst replacement of salaried staff with weekly waged staff at Eastleigh had caused a dispute there which had been resolved through negotiation. The disputes around introduction of new work measurement disciplines would eventually be resolved and the workshops returned to normal working.

The year also began with a change at the helm. The BRB appointed R.E.L. Lawrence to the board of the company as immediate successor to J.M.W. Bosworth who would move to another directorial position elsewhere in British Rail. Lawrence would continue as Chairman until the late 1970s, seeing the company through a difficult period. Another change which occurred during the year was a change of headquarters. The company relocated from Melbury Terrace at the end of August to a more central office at 274-280 Bishopsgate, London EC2 close to Liverpool Street station.

The company was attempting to gain clarity from the BRB on the purchases for new stock relating to the Future Workload Programme. BREL was waiting for orders to be confirmed for 600 passenger coaches, and a series of new generation replacement EMUs for London and the South-East for which some of the required equipment and materials had long lead times from the suppliers.

The company was also attempting to ascertain the wagon requirement for the foreseeable future from the railway. The situation had become serious within BREL where lack of visibility of future orders was causing scheduled gaps in production across a number of its workshops. A potential need to reduce capacity to save wasted costs would result in loss of capability and potential job losses. The resulting lower workshop capacity would potentially have cost repercussions later for the BRB when they did actually place orders for new and replacement stock.

The company was provided with a forward plan of locomotive and rolling stock requirement, which included the withdrawal of a number of locomotives and older wagons which would have the impact of reducing the maintenance workload at some works. As a result, a small number of redundancies was necessary to reflect the reduced demand on the maintenance facilities that would occur in 1972 and afterwards.

The lack of clarity and delayed placing of orders upon BREL by the railway threatened the future of York Works specifically in June 1971. The construction of new electrical multiple units at York was coming to an end, with no work placed to succeed it after the completion of the current orders in September 1972. The future of the workshops was in doubt, affecting 800 staff, unless the break in production could be filled.

The potential need for reductions in the workforce was referred to British Rail, making the situation clear and also requesting authorities to order long lead time items which would be needed for any intended work to ensure that the workshops at York could be kept fully utilised. In the meantime, a decision on the future of the works was delayed until the situation could be clarified. Nevertheless, the trade unions were consulted about the possibility of redundancies and rationalisation at a number of works unless there were positive changes in the future workload plan. A provisional plan was presented to the trade unions, which was set against the possibility of receipt of a wagon order from Yugoslav Railways and potential work for the Channel Tunnel project.

The decision to withdraw the diesel-hydraulic fleet by the BRB left BREL with a stock of spares which would no longer be needed, and so the decision was taken to use what was immediately needed for short-term maintenance with the remaining stock of parts to be scrapped and written off. The withdrawn locomotives would then be cannibalized to keep the remainder in service. The costs of writing off the stock of spares had to be borne by BREL. The reduced maintenance workload which resulted from British Rail's decision to withdraw 'non-standard' classes of diesel locomotives and to reduce the number of classes generally had an effect at all of BREL's workshops, but Swindon was particularly hard hit. The reduction in work necessitated a programme of redundancies to be undertaken over the coming years in line with the reducing workloads, specifically salaried clerical staff.

The workshop staff on the shopfloors of all the works were less impacted in the short term due to the number of unplanned repairs which were coming onto the works. These had been increasing due to a higher number of minor accidents occurring on the railway at the time.

Class 52 scrap line at Swindon. Locomotives in the queue for scrapping are D1028 *Western Hussar*, D1057 *Western Chieftain*, D1064 *Western Regent*, D1025 *Western Guardsman* and D1012 *Western Firebrand*. *Laurence Waters*

BREL was generally suffering from the impact of a reduction in traffic that was occurring on the railway specifically in the freight sector. The railway was experiencing a steady erosion of its freight work, which was due in part to small load traffic switching to road. Correspondence between the National Union of Railwaymen (NUR), the Confederation of Shipbuilding and Engineering Unions (CS&EU) and BREL at the time reveals the detail of the reducing levels of work and the resultant industrial unrest that was prevalent. The letters also discussed the actions that had been taken to rationalise the company's workload in accordance with the reduction in maintenance work being received from British Rail.

The reduction in traffic had made 60 locomotives surplus to requirements, with the wagon fleet to also be reduced by 10,000 vehicles, which the unions had been notified of in April of that year. The continuing recession in freight traffic through the second quarter of the year had further reduced mileage within the locomotive fleet, with a reduction of twenty-seven intermediate locomotive repairs being required for the main line diesel locomotive fleet, and electric locomotive repairs reducing by four light repairs, with seven locomotives requiring only light overhaul instead of the scheduled intermediate repairs. The result was a planned reduction in the workforce of the equivalent of 107 employees.

The withdrawals of 66 Clayton Type 1 (Class 17), and 18 North British Locomotive Type 2 (Class 29) from Scottish Region, the majority of the diesel-hydraulic fleet from Western Region (86 Class 35 'Hymek', 34 Class 42 'Warship' and 16 Class 43 'Warship') and 5 Class 76 electric locomotives from London Midland region resulted a planned reduction of the equivalent of 460 men, with the lowered frequency of intermediate repairs resulting in a planned reduction of the equivalent of a further 67 men.

The reduction of 634 men would partially be covered by reduction in overtime working, removing the need for some job losses and explaining the reference to the term 'equivalent' used in the correspondence between BREL and the unions whose members were affected.

As a result of the discussions and the plan agreed, the BRB issued a press release explaining the situation that had led to the problem and the actions that it was felt had to be taken to protect the viability of BREL in the context of events affecting the rail industry in 1971.

The press release, dated 30 July 1971, explained that due to the reallocation of the railway's diesel-electric and diesel-hydraulic fleet caused by the recession in traffic requirements, a number of locomotives had been withdrawn permanently in Western and Scottish Regions. The railway had also experienced a fall in traffic in London Midland Region which had reduced the necessity for repairs since the locomotive fleet was working lower mileages, with a corresponding drop in the frequency of coach repairs. The impact upon BREL was considerable. Four workshops were impacted by the lower workload that resulted from British Rail's traffic contraction. As a result, a reduction in the workforce was deemed to be required, which would be achieved through a programme of voluntary retirements with increased redundancy packages. Hand written notes on the file copy of the press release indicate that the works to have been affected by the job-losses were Swindon (371), Glasgow (50), Crewe (175) and Derby Locomotive (38) works. Job losses at Glasgow Works had been reduced by the transfer of the maintenance of Classes 20, 24 and 25 from Derby and Crewe, causing job losses at those works but reducing the job losses in Scotland.

Notification was given in December 1971 that the remainder of Barassie Works would close on 3 June 1972, and that the repair of locomotives would cease at Swindon with the repair facility to close on the same date. The number of staff at Ashford would be reduced with a possibility that the works would close completely unless adequate future work could be found to utilise the workshops by January 1972. The reduction in staff numbers was to be achieved through voluntary redundancy among those staff close to retirement and through natural wastage of staff where possible.

A glimmer of hope was provided by the Department of the Environment late in 1971, when it was announced that consideration was being given to advancing funding for existing planned projects, which would permit the railway to place orders with BREL, removing the need for many redundancies. The possibility of constructing an additional prototype Advanced Passenger Train set or the construction of pre-production sets earlier, despite faults in the designs being found in trials, was also being considered which would have provided work for both Crewe and Derby. The future of York Works was also guaranteed with the placing of an order with BREL for construction of electric stock for the GNR suburban electrification programme.

The workshops at Derby were experiencing trouble with the new Mark IID passenger coaches which were causing considerable delays in the completion of construction of the vehicles. The delays were not being

Class 08s 08604 and 08693 with Class 46 46044 at Swindon, 22 March 1984. Despite the planned closure of the locomotive maintenance facilities, the workshop required its own resident shunting locomotives. *Laurence Waters*

caused by capacity bottlenecks or industrial action at Litchurch Lane, but rather through problems related to the air-conditioning equipment being installed in the new coaches. The equipment was proving troublesome with numerous failures which required additional work to resolve. The issue had been caused by the decision made by the BRB to continue to use an unproven new air-conditioning system in the coach design before it had been fully developed by the manufacturer. BREL was again being impacted by decisions over which it had no control that would impact upon its reputation outside the railway.

The company did, however, have a problem of its own making that needed to be urgently addressed. The standard of maintenance applied by each workshop was being interpreted differently, often based upon old regional specifications in use before the creation of BREL. The upshot of the different standards adopted by different works was that reliability of locomotives in service was somewhat variable, requiring return to works for repairs before plan. The returns to works caused ongoing delays to other work, keeping locomotives at the works for longer than planned and reducing availability in service. In order to address the issue and improve the quality of the work being performed in the workshops, a common set of standards and quality control programmes was created and disseminated across all the workshops which improved the situation dramatically.

The company was to perform another, ancillary, role for the BRB in 1971. The company provided loans for rolling stock leasing companies, enabling them to purchase rolling stock from BREL for leasing to British Rail, foreshadowing the arrangements adopted by the train operating companies after the privatisation of the railways. The funds were borrowed from merchant banks at an agreed rate of interest for the life of the loan, the first loan being for $50million through a merchant bank, acting as an agent for four American banks, at an interest rate of 0.75 per cent for the first year, followed by 1 per cent thereafter. The monies raised would be loaned to Railway Finance Limited, at a higher rate of interest, who would use the funds for the purchase of rolling stock from BREL for lease to British Rail. As a nationalised company, British Rail was unable to lend public funds to a third party, however BREL as a private company, was able to act as a financial broker as part of its remit as a manufacturer.

The year 1972 dawned with BREL still chasing the Yugoslav wagon order through BRE-Metro. Major design changes necessary in the AM10 stock destined for the GNR electrification impacted the completion of the two prototype units under construction at York which were urgently required for trials. Maintenance workshops were being pressured by the BRB to provide a quicker turnaround of locomotives from the works, even though the maintenance work required was the same. The reduction in the number of locomotives in the diesel fleet undertaken by the railway had resulted in a reduction in coverage for cyclical maintenance. As a result, the BRB was demanding more from BREL to compensate. The number of locomotives arriving at the workshops with minor accident damage was still higher than planned, contributing to the delays in completion of scheduled maintenance on other locomotives. A proposal to provide Crewe diesel depot with inspection pits was adopted, with light repairs and minor fault rectification that did not require a works visit to be undertaken there instead.

The future workload plan was improved with the addition of an order for construction of a large number of 40-ton hopper wagons for the civil engineering department of British Rail, to be constructed at Shildon, and authority for construction of an additional 600 Mark II locomotive hauled coaches to be completed at the rate of seven and a half vehicles per week. The additional order for the coaching stock filled a production gap at Derby Litchurch Lane between the completion of the previous Mark II coach programme, the order for Córas Iompair Éireann and the commencement of construction of the new Mark III coaches due to begin from September 1974. The additional orders provided security for the works at Shildon, for a time, and Derby Litchurch Lane, whilst those at Doncaster, Derby Locomotive and Crewe were being kept utilised by the maintenance and repair workload.

The company was seeking to find other avenues from which the shortfalls in work identified in the future workload plan might be filled. In August 1971, the company won an order from the Ministry of Defence worth £100,000. The order consisted of a contract to manufacture and supply conversion kits for the conversion of Spartan Armoured Personnel Carriers to Samson Armoured Recovery Vehicles. The work was assigned to Derby Litchurch Lane with delivery scheduled for the early part of 1972.

BREL experienced other difficulties early in 1972 which were caused by outside railway contractors being unwilling to take on some work. A major problem occurred at Eastleigh where it was found impossible to find a contractor willing to undertake major repairs of traction motors. The only option that was open to the company was to perform the work itself, which, despite the BRB policy, it proceeded to do. The workshops were provided with new facilities to undertake the work costing £142,000.

The company was becoming concerned at the lack of wagon orders being received from British Rail, which was leaving gaps in the production schedule for 1973. The railway was experiencing a continuing contraction in its freight business due to the switch to road that had been eroding the freight sector for some time, reducing the requirements on the fleet, and removing the need for new vehicles. Despite this, the company had received an order for bogie tippler wagons from the British Steel Corporation, but work was being delayed by the customer who had specified the use of rotary couplers, which were in restricted supply at the time.

In order to keep the works at Shildon viable in the long term, the company asked the BRB to confirm their requirements for freight stock in 1974. In the meantime, BREL looked to transfer existing work to Shildon from other works to maintain at least the workload at the level attained in 1971, with a resulting need to reduce manpower at the works from which work had been transferred. The new policy for Shildon was endorsed by the BREL board in May. Workload was to be reduced in other works with the transfer of wagon construction to Shildon, the labour force at the other sites to be reduced accordingly. The company clearly had faith that Shildon could remain viable, approving the investment of £234,636 for the purchase and installation of two new drop hammers for the works, which was passed by the Investment Committee and in turn by the BRB.

The reduction in wagon repair work also impacted upon the works at Temple Mills. A study was undertaken by the company during October 1972 to rationalise the work that was being undertaken at the site. The aim

General view of Shildon Works, 16 June 1976. *Colin J. Marsden*

was to identify efficiency savings that could potentially be made by rearranging where activities were carried out in the workshops to remove the need for work to be moved unnecessarily around between buildings. As a result, it was determined that no job losses would be required but a small investment of £27,500 to rearrange the workshops would be required.

The workshops were rearranged so that wagon repair would be restricted to the old steel frame and lift shops, with container repairs being undertaken solely in the erstwhile road van shop. The sawmills were to be moved together in what had been the road van fitting shop, with all machining, smithy and maintenance work transferred into the old welding shop. All painting was to be moved into the container shop with the exception of painting of Freightliner wagons which was to be undertaken in the lifting shop outside of normal working hours. As a result, the old 'A' shop could be vacated completely, and the building sold off for other uses. The rearrangement of the workshops was estimated to be able to save the company an estimated £40,000 per year without any job losses.

The manpower required for clerical roles at various works was being decreased slowly, with the downward trend mainly being covered by wastage as employees left the business for other roles outside the rail industry and retirements. The workshop staff at Barassie was decreasing rapidly due to the announced closure, with the same happening at Ashford, even though there was a good chance of a reprieve at the latter site. The rundown of Barassie and Ashford, and part of the works at Swindon had accelerated due to staff opting to take voluntary redundancy, although the company was experiencing more industrial disputes at Swindon as the remaining staff became more militant.

The acceleration of staff leaving Barassie left only a small cadre of staff employed at the site, and so, with agreement from the unions representing the staff there, the closure of Barassie Works was brought forward to 3 July 1972. Following the closure of Barassie, the works at St Rollox was to receive investment and reorganisation in order to accommodate wagon repairs at Glasgow which had previously been allocated to the now closed workshops. BREL allocated £68,888 to the works for the required upgrading of the machine shops and reorganisation.

Investment was also to be made at York. The works at Holgate Road was to receive new traversers to replace the aging and life-expired equipment which also no longer met the requirements of the Factory Acts. The investment of £53,390 was approved by the BREL board as it was within their remit, but also for the new traversers to be made in-house to provide additional work for the machine shops.

Shildon Works was also to receive considerable investment, with the drop forge receiving particular attention. The modernisation of the forges at Shildon allowed the works to receive jobs that would have been performed at Derby Litchurch Lane, facilitating the rationalisation of the forges. The forge at Derby was to cease work on dropforged components with all the work being focused on the modernised dropforge at Shildon.

Staffing levels continued to be reduced at Ashford, although the arrival of the order from Yugoslavia promised to reprieve the majority of the works staff. In order to keep the site utilised, work was transferred from elsewhere to keep the works busy until the first payments were received and work could begin on the order for ZTP Zagreb (Yugoslavian Railways).

As part of the rundown of the locomotive workshops at Swindon, all outstanding work on diesel-mechanical locomotives was to be completed by December 1972, with only a limited amount of component repairs continuing after that time. BREL's relationship with its staff at Swindon remained difficult throughout that time, with more industrial disputes and strikes occurring, specifically by staff involved in manufacture of components and delivery of repairs to locomotives.

The planning of work for Derby and Crewe was experiencing delays due to problems with the trials of the new High Speed Diesel Train. The train could not complete trials due to disputes with the unions. ASLEF was refusing to let its drivers take the prototype trains above 90mph for various reasons during in traffic testing, with negotiations ongoing between the BRB and the union. The lack of progress in the trials programme was inevitably going to cause delay to the commencement of the construction of the fleet at Derby and Crewe. In order to protect jobs and retain the capacity required to build the High Speed Train fleet, BREL had to look to transfer work from other sites to avoid gaps in production at the two works, or for British Rail to place orders for other stock to fill the gaps in the workload caused by the delays.

The company had experienced other delays across its works, both in construction and maintenance activities, not all of which were caused by BREL. A shortfall of locomotives being released back into traffic after maintenance at Crewe had been caused by the need to perform unexpected repair work on a larger than expected number of accident damaged locomotives received during the year. Maintenance work on the electric locomotive fleet had also fallen behind due to the unexpectedly high work content found to be required on the locomotives entering the maintenance shops. Meanwhile, at Doncaster, complications experienced during repairs to the Deltic fleet had caused delays in returning those locomotives back to traffic, although it was expected that backlogs at both works would have been resolved by October and that the plants would both have caught up and returned to the planned schedule by the end of 1972.

The increasing costs of the maintenance of the Deltic fleet were causing concern, particularly as the fleet was forecast to remain in service pending introduction of the High Speed Train fleet into service in late 1976 and into 1977. The delays in the programme were also seen as likely to delay the withdrawal of the Deltics from service, with the inherent increases in maintenance costs at Doncaster. The need to continue supporting the fleet for longer than had been anticipated was to be raised at the BRB meetings by the BREL representatives on the board, with a view to receiving authority for an increased maintenance budget for the Deltics to cover the forecast increases until the new High Speed Train fleet began to come into service.

The workshops at Derby would be particularly impacted by the delays in the testing programme of the new High Speed Diesel Train sets. A gap in continuity of production work was forecast to occur unless an order, that had been promised by the BRB, for additional Mark III vehicles was received by 1 December.

A backlog of work on EMUs at both Eastleigh and Wolverton had been caused by industrial disputes at the works due to pay and efficiency conflicts, but the disputes had been resolved and it was expected that the shortfall would be caught up by the end of the year.

The closure of the diesel-mechanical locomotive maintenance shops at Swindon by BREL had resulted in delays of the company's own making. The maintenance of the Class 08 diesel shunter fleet during 1972 was particularly hit due to the increased workload placed on other centres which were lacking spare capacity to take on the additional work released from Swindon. Maintenance of the class continued at Swindon for a time.

During 1972, a new health and safety concern came to the fore. At the July board meeting, it was reported by the technical director that high levels of industrial noise within certain workshops and the disposal of the effluent and toxic waste created by some of BREL's manufacturing processes were becoming problematic. The issues had the potential to create legal challenges to the company and so needed to be addressed as

Class 08 shunter maintenance was still being undertaken at Swindon as late as 1984. 08 710 in Swindon Works, 11 April 1984. *Laurence Waters*

Class 08 shunter 08 112 outside Swindon Works. *Laurence Waters*

soon as possible. The noise problem, it was reported, related to the lack of cooperation in the use of personal protective equipment, particularly ear protectors, by staff at a number of workshops. The local trade unions had become involved and were lobbying their members to use the provided equipment working alongside the company's medical officers, whilst BREL's legal officers were working on policies designed to resolve the problem in the long term.

The production of effluent and toxic waste was becoming a major problem, with new legislation on the horizon, work was needed to improve disposal facilities and prevention of effluent entering the drains. In order to reduce the company's impact on the local environment and to meet the likely requirements of the new legislation, a programme of improvements to the disposal facilities at all of BREL's workshops was undertaken. The improvements included better toxic waste disposal facilities within the works which were not connected to the drains or watercourses. Whilst the work was being undertaken the construction of new drains was completed. These were fitted with filtration units to prevent any non-toxic waste related to manufacturing processes being released from the works. The drainage works replaced Victorian infrastructure with modern facilities more capable of meeting all of the demands being placed upon them by the workshops.

BREL would perform its role as finance house again in 1972. Two loans were obtained in April, both for a three-year term, the first for £10million from a group of five American banks, and the second for £5million directly from the British arm of an American merchant bank. Both loans would be used to fund Railway Finance Limited on the same terms as the original loan made the previous year. The company would make another loan in 1972, on this occasion to a shipping company for £3.9million for the purchase of a roll-on, roll-off car ferry to be used on the Folkestone to Boulogne route.

The company continued to invest in its works despite the ongoing challenges with reducing workload at some sites. The company agreed a new machine tool investment programme worth £830,000 for 1973 in June 1972, although expenditure to be undertaken in conjunction with the Advanced Passenger Train project were to be segregated from 'normal' expenditure. The 1973 programme was authorised and passed on to the Investment Committee for approval and then for approval by the BRB. The investment programme additionally addressed more pressing needs.

A new 75ft traverser capable of handling vehicles of up to 40 tons in weight was to be provided for Derby Litchurch Lane at a cost of £61,154.

The new traverser would replace a life expired machine but also facilitate the construction and maintenance of new Mark III stock associated with the High Speed Diesel Train programme, the coaches for which were being constructed at Litchurch Lane, whilst the power cars were to be built at Crewe. Deliveries of the power cars were, however, being delayed by continual late supply, from the manufacturer, of the power units to be installed in them. Once in service, the trains were to be maintained at Derby, with Litchurch Lane undertaking coach repairs, and Derby Locomotive power car repairs. The locomotive works at Derby would also receive five new machine tools taking advantage of a grant being made available by the government for investment in factories.

The lease of the ICL 1901A Series computer and peripherals was due to come to an end, and in order to continue its use, the company renewed the lease until February 1975 at a cost of £43,858. The company also began to work with ICL on the production of a shopfloor control system, which would effectively be one of the first manufacturing computer systems, and the forerunner to many of the software industry's manufacturing resource planning systems.

The company had also been trialling a new stock management computer system at Crewe for which the Senior Project Engineer (Computer Systems) from British Rail, C.J. Hudson, had been responsible. Hudson believed that the use of computer systems, if rolled out across BREL, could increase efficiency and reduce costs. The company board agreed that the supply and stock management system should be extended across the works sites and authorised the expenditure that this would involve. The computer systems in use at BREL were to see additional software being introduced during 1973, with the shopping programme for locomotive maintenance at Crewe to be the first to be computerised, with a view that, if successful, the software would be rolled out across the remaining locomotive maintenance sites at Derby, Doncaster, Eastleigh and Glasgow.

At the end of the year, the board's attention became focused on Glasgow. The roof of the container shop had become extremely dangerous and needed replacement. At the same time, the activities associated with container and chain repairs, signal and telegraph relay repairs and the testing and examination facilities available across the works needed to be relocated to alternative locations in the workshops with a more efficient layout. In order to achieve this reorganisation and the repairs on the roof, the BREL board authorised the programme with an expenditure of £82,252.

At the first board meeting of the company in London in 1973, a decision was taken to continue with wagon repairs at Ashford Works alongside new construction work at least for the remainder of the year. The decision provided a reprieve for the remaining staff involved in repair work at the site. Threats to the livelihoods of staff in Derby and Crewe were still a real and present danger in the long term despite the efforts of BREL's senior management. The trials of the High Speed Diesel Train were still experiencing delays, due to faults which typically needed to be ironed out during trials but which were proving more difficult to resolve than might have been anticipated. The trials programme was also being held up due to continued reticence from ASLEF with respect to driver operation of the train at speed. The effect of the delays was a potential work gap at both Derby and Crewe works in the construction workshops.

In order to avoid job losses in both the short and the longer term with the capacity shortfall which would result and impact upon the new train construction programme once trials were completed, the company sought to find a resolution to the temporary lack of full utilisation of staff. The BRB was approached with a request to bring forward the construction of Mark III coaches for the High Speed Train sets whilst trials continued of the prototype trains since the outstanding faults being experienced in the trials were mainly centred on the power cars. Overtime had been temporarily halted in order to delay the appearance of the production gap for as long as possible, but if additional work was not forthcoming, a programme of redundancies at Derby Litchurch Lane would be necessary.

With the High Speed Train programme running nine months behind schedule, BREL pushed both The BRB and the Department of the Environment for an urgent decision about the possibility of placing an order for 150 Mark III coaches immediately to fill the gap in the production schedule which would arise from April 1974. A second order for a further production run of Mark III coaches to fill a further gap that might follow was requested at the same time. In the event that no assistance was forthcoming from British Rail or the government, the only option remaining to the company was to give notice to the unions with members at Derby who would be impacted by a planned series of redundancies to become effective in July 1973. In the meantime, the board would monitor the situation closely, whilst attempting to find other ways to avoid job losses at Derby.

Prototype High Speed Diesel Train undergoing trials between Paddington and Bristol, 14 August 1975. *C.G. Stuart/Great Western Trust*

To a small degree, the situation was inadvertently helped by decisions made in the design team. The number of coaches returning to the works for repairs to upholstery had been increasing, with many vehicles arriving at the works before their scheduled overhauls. The early failure of the upholstery on the coaches was being caused by the inferior materials that had been specified for use during builds and early overhauls. The moquette used proved to be susceptible to wearing through more quickly than was expected and subject to tearing. A better-quality material was used to replace the damaged upholstery and became the standard from that point. The unsuitability of the original material proved fortunate to the staff at Derby Litchurch Lane, with the extra work staving off some job losses and filling gaps in the works schedule.

The continuing delays to the High Speed Diesel Train programme were also being felt at Crewe. The start of construction of power cars planned for the workshops was being held up by the faults being found within the trial programme and, like Derby Litchurch Lane, the workshops at Crewe were likely to experience a shortfall in work as a result. The potential need to embark on a series of redundancies was not viewed favourably by the board of BREL, who attempted to at least defer any need for cuts for as long as possible in the hope that the disputes and issues plaguing the High Speed Diesel Train programme would be resolved and construction of power cars could begin before any job losses became necessary. The shortage of work was not helped by delays in the construction programme for the new Class 87 electric locomotive. The production of the new locomotives was being seriously impacted by industrial action at the supplier of the electric traction equipment, where strikes had stopped production and delayed deliveries. The locomotives were also subject to a series of redesigns and modifications which, whilst delaying the production schedule, was providing work to the shop floor, where rework and the implementation of modifications was at least keeping the staff utilised.

British Rail was asked to move locomotive maintenance and repair work forward, prematurely undertaking scheduled maintenance but providing work for the workshops in the short term. The board also considered the reallocation of locomotive repairs to Crewe from elsewhere, although that was not viewed as ideal due to the redundancies that were likely to result at the workshops from where work had been transferred. The board would continue to monitor the situation, with a second review to be undertaken at the February meeting.

No improvement was seen and as a result of the ongoing disruption of workshop maintenance and production schedules caused by delays in the supply of equipment, in the authorising of the start of High Speed Diesel Train power cars and coaches, the short notice of requirements from the BRB and the uncertainty of employment for the workforce, the BREL board called an additional meeting, which it was requested that senior members of the BRB should attend.

The meeting went ahead on 16 January 1973 at 222 Marylebone Road. The discussion that took place was designed to clarify the strategic options available to BREL to allow the company to build a sustainable future. The hope was that full order books and full utilisation of staff, would guarantee, as far as possible, a long term future upon which the directors could build. It was hoped that, if a clearer picture was available, the BREL board would be able to plan more effectively and invest more strategically in the business than was possible at the time. The main issue that was raised was the relationship between BREL and the BRB which was defined when the company was created in 1969. The main purpose as defined by the BRB was to '… service the railway business using spare capacity for private-party work and addition British Rail requirements'.

The unwritten expectation, which had however been voiced during the BRB meetings, was that BREL would ensure that capacity reserved for the railway to meet future needs as outlined in the Future Rail Plan in each iteration would be available if and when the railway decided to use it. The BREL directors were unhappy to continue in this manner as the capacity required to meet the Future Rail Plan requirements could not be used for any other purpose, and the authorisation of the quotations for the work outlined in the plan were often late, reduced or did not appear at all. The unreliability of the British Rail requirements forecast was creating gaps in the continuity of production required for continuous utilisation of the workshop facilities and staff, jeopardising jobs. The underutilised capacity could often not be filled with third party work due to the short lead times in discovering that production gaps would be created by changes in The BRB's schedule.

The relationship as it stood was preventing BREL from building a sustainably full order book over the long term. A full order book would support a production plan which would make best use of the company's resources, allow it to reinvest profits and to grow as a successful international railway and general engineering company.

The BREL board also expressed concerns at the BRB's decision to approach the outside industry with a view to placing orders for urgently needed locomotives, when capacity at BREL was not being fully used.

The board informed the BRB that BREL required a rolling programme of firm requirements from British Rail which had been fully authorised by the Railway Investment Committee and the BRB. The company directors made it clear to the railway board at an extraordinary meeting in January 1973 that it could no longer be expected that BREL would refuse third-party work on any assumption that British Rail would be placing orders at some time in the future.

The board of the company would be true to its word. In early January, the company had accepted an order from Winn International Containers Limited for the construction of sixty 30ft shipping containers and forty 40ft containers. All the containers were to be built in the container works at Derby Litchurch Lane. The month proved productive for rolling stock construction, with third party orders accepted by the company for a variety of stock. The company announced that it had won a contract to build eleven battery locomotives for London Transport at a cost of £600,000, the locomotives to be built at Doncaster, with the first delivery due in November 1973.

British Portland Cement Manufacturers Limited placed an order for 136 two axle bulk cement wagons, which BREL announced would be built at the wagon works at Doncaster and Shildon. In March, the company accepted an order from Tilling Construction for thirty-three two axle, 50-ton hopper wagons for aggregate traffic, to be constructed at Shildon, with deliveries due between October and November.

Despite the differences which were developing between the BREL and the railway board, orders were placed for new stock in late January and early February. The works at York was assigned a large proportion of the work as it related to the production of EMU sets, which the works was becoming something of a specialist in constructing. The new vehicles would need new facilities and equipment, and the volume of work now being offered by the railway would require the creation of a new production line. The improvement works and investment in new equipment was authorised by BREL at a cost of £133,400, which in turn was approved by the Railway Investment Committee as the cost was above the £100,000 limit available to the BREL directors at the time. Horwich Foundry was still in need of further modernisation works and the costs to be incurred in the project had now risen to £1.5million. The return on investment available from the modernisation was still attractive and the investment was approved for submission of the business plan to the Railway Investment Committee.

The situation at both Derby Litchurch Lane and Crewe improved to a degree in February when the railway and ASLEF had come to an agreement whereby the drivers involved in the High Speed Diesel Train programme would be prepared to operate the prototype units at up to 100mph speeds. Negotiations regarding the operation of the trains up to their maximum speed of 125mph were proceeding well but not yet agreed. A revised High Speed Train production programme had been supplied to BREL as a result of the progress now being made in the testing of the prototype train which assumed that no further trouble would be found with the new bogie design that had been implemented for the production units. The programme, while at least now in place, still left a shortfall of work at Crewe.

The request to fill the schedule through the bringing forward of locomotive maintenance was not agreed upon, the Executive Director of Systems and Operations on the railway board not being prepared to release locomotives from traffic for premature maintenance. There was an opportunity for some modification work to some of the locomotive fleet to be undertaken earlier than might have otherwise been necessary. The shortfall at Crewe was still to cause a short-term issue, but with the capacity being needed for the High Speed Train power cars in the near future, the staffing levels and facilities at the works had to be protected. The only option left to the BREL board was to transfer repair work to Crewe from other works. The impact of supporting Crewe was the need for planned redundancies in other works.

The blow would be softened a little at Glasgow with the authorisation for repairs to restart on the Class 24 fleet and the allocation of additional

Construction of the entire HST power car fleet was carried out at Crewe Works, 6 April 1982. No. 43193 is under construction in the main erecting shop. *Colin J Marsden*

locomotive repairs to the works. The authorisation to begin work on heavy body repairs on an additional 3,000 mineral wagons prevented major job losses at the plant.

Unreliability in the supply chain would continue to cause delays within BREL's workshops. In April, it was reported that work had slowed considerably at Derby Litchurch Lane, due to late and short deliveries of seat components for locomotive hauled Mark IIF coaches. It was believed though, that the delay could be caught up with in less than six months if the supply delay could be resolved. At York, the production of EMUs was being delayed by the supplier being unable to deliver the required volume of electrical equipment, although the situation had been worsened further by industrial action at the works by BREL electricians.

The construction of the new Class 87 electric locomotive fleet was still behind schedule, the issue with supply of electrical equipment having still not having been resolved. The supply difficulties relating to seat components for Mark IIF coaches and electrical equipment for the Class 87 fleet still remained unresolved at the time of the BREL board meeting in July.

In order to resolve the situation, the BREL board took the decision to use the plastic moulding shop at Swindon to make the seat mouldings in house. Whilst Swindon was unable to produce the full quantity required to meet production needs on the Mark IIF programme, construction had at least begun to move forward once more. The supply problem was finally resolved in October 1973 with the flow of components meeting demand. Swindon continued to contribute, despite the supplier having resolved their own issues which proved a good decision as the problem arose once more in November. The delays being experienced with supplies of electrical equipment for the Class 87 programme had also still not been resolved by the time of the November board meeting.

The workshops were also experiencing delays in production caused by industrial action. Some industrial disputes existed outside the rail industry, but impacted upon the supply of equipment and materials, whilst other disputes effected BREL directly. At Wolverton and Eastleigh, strikes were delaying the completion of electrical multiple unit repairs, with the situation at Wolverton being complicated by the loss of large numbers of staff to the Milton Keynes Development Project, where higher wages were on offer. BREL was unable to compete with higher wages on offer in other companies, as despite being an autonomous company, its sole ownership by the Railways Board left it having to work within salary and wage bands used on the railway and defined by government ministries. The lack of flexibility to define its own wage structures would be a cause of staff retention and hiring issues from the middle of 1973 until its sale.

A new challenge with which BREL was now having to deal, was related to the safe removal and handling of asbestos, which had been commonly used as insulation in older stock and which was now recognised as a major health hazard. The repair of sleeping coaches at York was one of the first programmes to experience serious delay due to the new methods required to safely remove and dispose of the material. The staff working on removing the asbestos insulation were to be provided with a new state of the art facility which would protect them from the dangers associated with inhaling asbestos fibres. New methods of working with the hazardous material were to be implemented in connection with the new building, whilst both BREL and British Rail Research at Derby also investigated novel methods for safe handling of the material through saturation with glycerine or other materials which would prevent the asbestos fibres being released into the air in the new workshop.

Despite the discussion and agreements reached earlier in the year with regard to the future work from British Rail, delays to the firm placing of orders for new stock by May was causing concern at BREL with respect to the work load for Derby Locomotive and Litchurch Lane, Shildon and York in the medium term. The absence of firm orders was concerning the purchasing department who were, yet again, unable to place orders for long lead time materials, jeopardising the timely completion of work when the production orders were finally placed. The situation at Shildon was viewed as being particularly serious as the lack of a planned production schedule from May onwards was resulting in a visible production gap during 1974. The gap inevitably led to idle manpower and increased costs, although future work was already on hand which would secure the jobs of the staff in the works in the longer term.

The issues with workload at Derby and Crewe were resolved in June 1973, with agreement reached between British Rail and ASLEF for full speed trials of the High Speed Train to go ahead. The programme of trials was now due to be complete by August, with a pre-production programme of High Speed Train sets to follow immediately. The news was greeted with relief within BREL as planning could now go ahead and workshop production gaps could be filled. The new schedule was

Derby Locomotive Works cab preparation workshop, 19 November 1973. *Colin J. Marsden*

to also include an additional quantity of Mark III coaches to cover other possible gaps in production.

The company received a further boost with the announcement of orders from British Rail for forty-five four-car EMUs for the new 'Great Northern Outer', and 'Great Eastern Inner' electric suburban services. The units were all assigned to York with construction due to start in April 1974. At the same time, a further order was announced for 100 two-axle vans and 350 32-ton high capacity hopper wagons for coal Merry-Go-Round services for power stations, both batches of vehicles being assigned to Shildon.

Third party work also helped resolve the potential shortfalls in production work, through an order from Associated Portland Cement Manufacturers Limited for 174 50-ton bulk cement wagons for use in their block train workings. The new contract added to the earlier order of 136 identical wagons.

The company was beginning to see a steady build-up of delay in the construction of new Freightliner vehicles at Temple Mills Works. Once again, the difficulty was not one of BREL's making. The delay was caused by incomplete vehicles having to be stored in the yards at Temple Mills awaiting braking equipment from the supplier. Elsewhere, the repairs being undertaken on wagons was being impacted by the deteriorating situation in regard to the supply of steel, with ongoing industrial action in the steel industry reducing the availability of the required gauges of steel sheet, with the situation continuing to deteriorate.

The late summer of 1973 saw BREL having to look toward a major investment programme in its buildings at Swindon and Horwich. Decisions taken to defer maintenance to save costs both within BREL and British Rail's civil engineering department had resulted in repairs now becoming critical, with some buildings beginning to become unsafe and no longer meeting statutory health and safety requirements. In order to address the impending problem, the company authorised a proposal to be put to the Railway Investment Committee for the combined expenditure of £1.18million on buildings at both sites to bring them up to standard.

The company continued to experience short periods of industrial unrest as the autumn approached. The works at Horwich and Wolverton both experienced stoppages which were caused by some of the staff at both works having relatively low earnings due to the existing pay and incentive schemes then in place. The dispute was resolved with the three unions involved at Horwich. The pay situation was improved and in return the unions agreed that more flexibility was required on the shopfloor to help BREL protect jobs by varying the type of work undertaken. At Wolverton, the dispute over pay was still ongoing in September but negotiations were reported to be progressing constructively, with both sides gaining from the compromises being tabled.

At the same time, BREL was experiencing difficulty in recruitment. The company reported that recruiting electricians was proving particularly difficult as wages available outside the rail industry were generally higher for the same work, and BREL was constrained by the wage structure that was being imposed by the BRB. The resolution of the problems with the High Speed Diesel Train test programme, and the more regular confirmation of future demand for rolling stock and locomotives by British Rail which had been requested in January had created a short-term shortage of 505 staff, with the work load envisaged for 1974 requiring an increase of a further 840 staff to meet the workload.

The workload for British Rail, for which the company had quoted and was expecting to be awarded, was likely to consume a large proportion of the capacity available at all of BREL's workshops through the last three months of 1973 and a large part of 1974. The company had submitted quotations for a large number of locomotives, High Speed Train units, high density commuter trains and other rolling stock. The board was pleased that communication with the railway had improved and that all of the delayed orders were now being placed, but the workload was likely to preclude the acceptance of third-party orders in the short term which were more profitable. The BREL board agreed to be more selective in the short term, but also to plan how more capacity could be made available to third party and export orders to generate revenue for the company.

The potential for private-party work in 1974 was greater than it had been for some time, with the company having negotiations in progress with a number of parties. The company had tendered for the supply of vehicles to both the Manchester and Merseyside Passenger Transport Executives. The futures of Shildon and Ashford seemed more secure than for some time due to the volume of potential work being discussed with leasing companies for freight vehicles, whilst British Rail was looking to increase the number of Freightliner and high-capacity wagons in its fleet to meet improving traffic trends.

The risk of redundancies reported to the BRB earlier in the year had been resolved by the better communications which were now occurring between the railway and BREL coupled with the resurgence of the private market where more potential could be seen. The restrictions placed on the company by the BRB, however, were still causing the company to be unable to respond to changes in the economy. The lack of autonomy allowed was once more giving the BREL board challenges to address which need not have been necessary.

The company embarked on a programme of machine tool replacement both as part of the continual improvement programme the company had in place for the machine shops in all works, but also as a means to create additional and more flexible capacity through the use of more modern and more capable machinery. One of the first recipients of new machinery to expand capacity was the Locomotive Works at Derby, with a budget of £62,000 being signed off by the BREL board for the purchase and installation of a new combined horizontal boring, milling and drilling machine. As the budget was within the sign-off limits permitted to the board, the company was able to immediately sign the purchase order and acquire the new machine in October 1973.

BREL continued to be able to keep the container workshop at Derby Litchurch Lane busy throughout 1974 and into 1975. The company won a large order from Bell Lines in December for the supply of 500 20ft shipping containers, to be delivered in Bell's own in-house livery. The order brought the total number of containers to be supplied to Bell Lines to 1,250, at a total cost of over £1million. The work was to be undertaken purely at Derby with a scheduled delivery of thirty containers per week agreed upon.

The company relied not only upon BRE-Metro for outside work through its export drive, but also through its own commercial arm sourcing additional work from British customers. The company had won a contract to supply London Transport with locomotives for its maintenance division during 1973. The power on the lines would typically be switched out whilst maintenance was being undertaken on the London Underground and an independently powered locomotive for works trains was required. Demand for a new fleet of locomotives was also being driven by the works associated with the new 'Fleet Line' (later renamed the Jubilee Line) and the Piccadilly Line extension to Heathrow Airport.

London Transport designed a battery-electric locomotive to meet the need. The locomotive was to be capable of working in the London tunnels from its own power supply or from the main line supply where power remained available from the supply rails. The design involved a heavily rivetted construction, which required a workshop with steam locomotive construction experience and the relevant plant and machinery for their construction. BREL won the tender and London Transport ordered eleven of their locomotives. The locomotives were built at BREL's Doncaster Works. The bogies, frames, bodysides and roof were fabricated in the relevant workshops, with the assemblies being collected in the erecting shops where the locomotive final assembly was undertaken around the installation of the electrical equipment. The traction equipment included 160 lead acid battery cells as well as other equipment. The locomotives

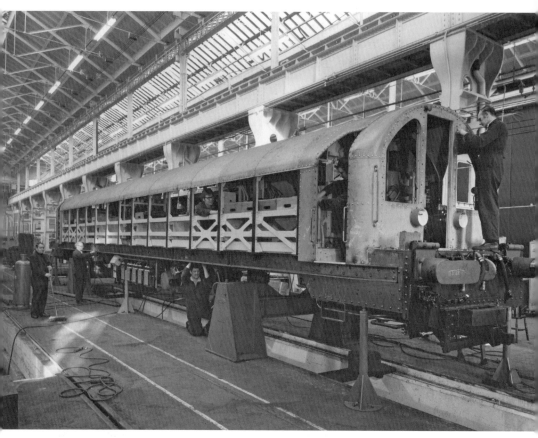

London Underground battery locomotive under construction at Doncaster, 21 November 1973. *Colin J. Marsden*

were finished in London Transport maroon with brown roof and black frames in the paint shop at Doncaster before delivery to the customer.

The works buildings across the company's estate had become unfit for purpose in places, and in 1974 BREL began construction of new facilities at some of its works to provide more modern accommodation for some of its staff. The flagship construction programme undertaken that year was the construction of a new office block at Crewe which opened in September. The new building replaced the London and North Western Railway's office building, which at 100 years old had become tired and unfit for BREL's future needs. The building was a three-floor structure which could accommodate 430 administration and clerical staff. The building was equipped with modern air conditioning based upon a state-of-the-art heat recovery system using heat generated in the building by machinery and people to warm the structure throughout. The structure had been designed in-house by the BRB's Chief Architect with outside contractors performing the building work.

The year ended with the supply chain remaining unreliable. The lack of timely deliveries from suppliers resulted in delays for which BREL was often blamed by the media, although the reality was very different. Steel supplies were likely to cause problems for the new year with availability of steel sheet and plate likely to dimmish by around 30 per cent and spring steel forecast to be extremely hard to procure. The company looked to resolve the shortfall by sourcing 5,000 tons of various types of steel from Europe to make up the shortfall from British suppliers.

The end of 1973 also saw the beginning of the programmed closure of parts of Swindon Works with £245,000 allocated to the reorganisation of the facilities. 'A' shop was to be vacated and abandoned, with all the equipment removed and relocated to the building on the east side of the works site. The reason for the abandonment of 'A' shop was that the company viewed the building as being unsuitable for its current needs with more modern facilities being available at other works, such as Crewe and Doncaster.

The works at Wolverton also received investment at the end of the year. The battery workshops were allocated £85,110 for improvements. The aim was to make the working environment better for staff whilst also putting improvements in place to enable the works to produce lead-acid batteries with a longer operating life. Derby Litchurch Lane was also due to receive additional investment. Despite not being involved in the High Speed Train power car construction programme, the works were to manufacture the cab units for the power cars. The units were to be created using glass reinforced plastic, for which £61,102 was provided to fund the creation of new facilities in Derby.

The year ended with a turnaround in fortunes of the company, after two difficult years. The BREL directors and management looked forward with renewed optimism to 1974 and onwards, with order books looking the healthiest they had for some time, and export opportunities promising much. The company attempted to embark of a programme of recruitment to grow the workforce to a level which could support the company's plans. The personnel department, in association with the public relations team and British Rail, created a series of television, radio and press advertisements aimed at attracting new recruits to the industry. Meanwhile, concerted efforts were made in the works themselves to find new skilled employees through the staff that were already employed by BREL. The efforts to recruit large numbers of new staff would remain difficult due to the ongoing differential in wages being offered by BREL against those being offered by outside industry.

At the same time, the company embarked on a series of initiatives designed to reassure staff that, after a period of contraction, the future of the company looked more promising and job security was improving. A statement of intent was also shared with all of the trade unions with members employed in BREL's workshops and offices. The statement spoke of a plan for expansion to reverse the trends of the last few years, with recruitment rather than redundancy being the new normal. Some degree of rationalisation was still required but would be minimised as much as possible. The personnel team finished the year with one final announcement. The employment records at BREL would be computerised in the next twelve months, with the introduction of a new computer system, MANIS.

The new year dawned with BREL making firm decisions on how the company should operate commercially. Despite the improved visibility of British Rail's plans and the increased promised workload, the company was not prepared to accept that the railway would definitely place orders for new locomotives and rolling stock at the dates in their plan. The company also viewed maintenance plans as being subject to change at the whim of the operations department of British Rail. In order to reduce the work gaps that had been seen in previous years which created threats to job security, reduced revenues for the company and frequent industrial disputes and reorganisation, the company would seek to fill their own order books. Private work would be actively sought to ensure the maximum possible utilisation of workshops and staff.

The BRB was also to be constantly lobbied for confirmation of future workload forecasts in order that long lead time items could be ordered, ensuring that parts and materials were available at the works when needed for construction or maintenance activities to proceed on schedule. The company wanted the railway operation arm and BRB to provide a fully authorised five year rolling programme of work which would allow detailed planning of the workloads and capacity requirements at all its works. BREL was hopeful that British Rail would at least be able to provide a confirmed series of orders to cover all of their requirements for 1975, 1976 and 1977. The planning that would result would give a clear picture of when and what type of capacity in works was available over that time period, allowing this to be communicated to BRE-Metro. BRE-Metro could then reach out to the market to acquire orders from overseas to match the capacity that would be available with knowledge of potential lead times for completion of that work by the workshops. BREL would also be in a better situation commercially, with sales to British customers of general engineering services being much simpler to manage.

An incident occurred at Glasgow Works at the end of 1973 which was being investigated by the police in Glasgow. It was raised at the January 1974 board meeting as changes needed to be made to prevent a reoccurrence. An armed robbery had occurred on 21 December as the week's wages were being provided to staff. The practice in BREL's works at the time was for the wage envelopes containing cash to be taken to the shop floor and given to the employees rather than have them come to a finance office to collect them. The robbery had resulted in the death of an employee who had attempted to intervene. Glasgow Police had advised the BREL management that the raid had followed a number of local raids on banks, post offices and other workshops on pay days. The police's advice was also to stop paying by cash, and move to cheque or post office giro as soon as possible. The board had been advised accordingly and it was envisaged that a pilot scheme should be undertaken immediately. The Chief Constable of Glasgow Police attended the board meeting and advised the company that a more secure method of paying wages should be adopted even if cash payments were to continue. The attempt to pay by cheque or post office giro proved unacceptable to staff who threatened industrial action in some places if payment by cash was not to continue. The situation was eventually resolved when BREL adopted a new procedure where employees came to a secure office to collect their wages rather than their being taken to the shop floor.

The dawning of 1974 saw the continuing recession being experienced by the British economy result in the three-day week. Whilst BREL was not impacted directly by the recession, the three-day week caused problems with the purchase of materials and parts from the outside trade, for which the company had to plan more in advance, reinforcing their requests from the railway that forecasts requirements needed to be confirmed with BREL much earlier.

The increasing workload planned for the BREL works resulted in a reprieve for Swindon in April 1974. The reorganisation of the works site would be reappraised due to the need to retain space that had become surplus to requirements, but which was now likely to have a part to play once more to support the timely completion of the new projects that were about to begin. Investment was also being made in other works.

The company had identified the need to provide more facilities for the removal of asbestos, as the number of vehicles coming into the works for major overhauls, particular DMUs and EMUs, was increasing, with more asbestos likely to become exposed. In order to provide a safe working environment for those involved in removing the material from locomotives and rolling stock, specialist facilities were to be built at the works at Derby Litchurch Lane, Doncaster, Eastleigh, Glasgow and Wolverton where the work was being undertaken. A total budget of £648,500 would be required.

The locomotive works at Crewe and Derby were to be re-equipped with new bogie manufacturing facilities to handle the forecast demand related

Class 08 D3261 under overhaul at Swindon Works. The locomotive is notable for still carrying the older crest and the locomotive green livery whilst its companions in the works are in rail blue with TOPS numbers. *Laurence Waters*

to construction programmes for the High Speed Train, Mark III coaches, electrical multiple units, new locomotives and the Advanced Passenger Train, as well as planned modifications needed to bogies on the DMU fleets for which a budget of £440,500 was requested from the Railway Investment Committee who approved the expenditure. Horwich Works was to gain a new facility for the production of laminated springs on site to support the increased maintenance workload related to the heavy repair programme being undertaken on the wagon fleet.

Horwich received further investment during the summer with further modernisation work to be undertaken on the mechanical foundry at the works. An additional budget of £884,000 being made available by the Railway Investment Committee to accomplish the next phase of the modernisation work. The same investment period saw new facilities being created at both Crewe and Derby locomotive works, specifically for the heavy maintenance of engines and electrical systems on British Rail's fleet of Class 47 locomotives. A budget of £312,695 was approved for the provision of specialist tool and equipment at the works, which was increased to £414,663 in July. Enquiries had been made by BREL offering the work to outside contractors, but the June 1974 board meeting reported that, despite trading conditions in the British economy being hard, all the companies approached indicated that they were not interested in the work.

Shildon wagon works benefitted from investment during the summer of 1974. The existing construction workshops were to be expanded at a cost of £210,150 to meet new wagon construction orders that were filling the order books. The works site was also to be reorganised to assist in the flow of work around the workshops. The steel stock yard cranes and gantries had come to the end of their operational life and were to be decommissioned and scrapped. The opportunity was to be taken to relocate the steel store to a better location in the works. The costs of improving the steel handling facilities at Shildon would require a budget of £260,000, which the Investment Committee approved. Lastly, Shildon was to receive an additional wheel lathe to remove a bottleneck which had restricted the capacity of the works in general. The investment of an additional £177,460 was seen as offering the potential of a good return as a result of increased throughput of work at the works.

An upshot of the increasing need to improve and invest in workshop facilities was the increase in the delegation of authority to the Managing Director of BREL who was able, after the June board meeting, to approve up to £100,000 of expenditure without board approval. The BREL board's authority was also increased by the BRB, allowing them more autonomy in purchase decisions.

Investment was planned for Derby Locomotive Works. The upcoming programme of Advanced Passenger Train construction for the prototype and production sets expected to begin in the near future would see the construction of power cars for the train sets located at Derby's works, the first new locomotive construction to have been undertaken at the site since 1967. The specialist skills that would be required were not completely available in the workshops and so a programme of recruitment to attract staff to fill the skills gaps was to be undertaken. Construction of bogies for the Advanced Passenger Train prototype vehicles had already been authorised by the BRB and had begun at Derby alongside increased bogie construction for conventional passenger and freight stock.

The company of course did not have the benefit of foresight and could not envisage the ultimate fate of the Advanced Passenger Train programme, with the BRB also placing great hopes in the revolution of Britain's passenger train services that the project offered. The flaws that had effected the prototypes were viewed as being possible to resolve and in June 1974 no one in the rail industry had any thought that the project would not succeed, other than perhaps the handful of engineers and technicians at British Rail Research who were struggling to overcome the faults in the experimental APT-E that would eventually partly be the cause of the cancellation of the project, alongside lack of support from the media, in 1986 as a result of the continuing failures of the prototype APT-P sets during trials.

BREL invested in other new technology for their own use during 1974. In July, the lease of the ICL computer was renewed for another two years at a cost of £31,888 after the imminent expiry of the contract in 1975. Additional disc units for storage were also hired for £4,584. The software being tested at Crewe for stock control was found to be satisfactory and a planned roll out across all the other works was to be begun. The project would involve the conversion of 400,000 stock records from paper to electronic form. The 2.5million stock issue and receipt paper forms being processed annually could be dispensed with and replaced by electronic transactions. The Finance Director recommended to the BREL board that all the necessary terminals and communications equipment required should be purchased as soon as possible. At the same time,

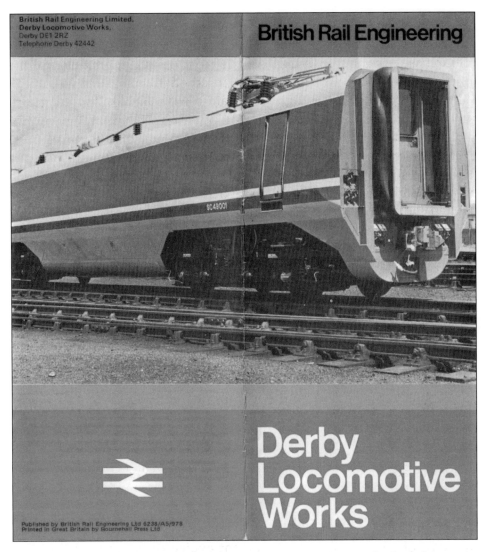

British Rail Engineering Limited,
Derby Locomotive Works,
Derby DE1 2RZ
Telephone Derby 42442

British Rail Engineering

SC49001

Published by British Rail Engineering Ltd 6238/A5/978.
Printed in Great Britain by Bournehall Press Ltd

**Derby
Locomotive
Works**

Cover of BREL open day guide for Derby Locomotive Works showing the first of the prototype APT power cars. *Author's collection*

consultation with staff affected began in order to begin training them on the new system, and also to notify them that the automation of the stores might result in a small number of job-losses. The roll-out would be undertaken at the works in Derby, Glasgow, Eastleigh, Wolverton, and finally Horwich, with Ashford, Doncaster, Shildon, Swindon and Crewe to follow later.

Glasgow Works, 21 June 1974. *Colin J. Marsden*

Third party work progressed well over the year, with the workshops at Wolverton undertaking a contract for the Ministry of Defence to build armoured bodies for the army's Spartan Armoured Personnel Carriers. BREL was keen to remain a contractor to the Ministry of Defence and sought regular work from the armed forces to enable to company to ringfence capacity for work related to defence contracts.

Wolverton had experienced some industrial disputes in other parts of the works. The staff involved in railway coach body repairs had long running complaints relating to working conditions and pay which had resulted in a number of periods of industrial action. The disputes had manifested through periods of working to rule, withdrawal of overtime, or short strikes. Efforts were being made to resolve the disagreement, with negotiations being undertaken between BREL and the trade unions involved, but no consensus had been reached by September 1974, although normal working resuming the following month once an acceptable solution had been found.

As the autumn approached, the company began to plan for its investment programmes for 1975. The investment programme for the works buildings and infrastructure was set at £1.48million. The budgeted programme was restricted to performing only work which was necessary to keep the buildings in a satisfactory condition, or to meet legal health and safety standards. The recruitment of apprentices was to increase however. The company set a target of recruiting double the number of engineering apprentices in 1975, looking to resolve the shortages in skilled staff that were prevalent in all works as a result of recruitment difficulties by training their own. The company also looked to recruit a number of qualified engineers across a broad range of engineering specialties from the universities.

Increased demand from British Rail for laminated springs for vehicle repairs was causing an issue at Horwich, where existing capacity in the spring workshop was insufficient to meet the workload. In response the BREL board and the Railway Investment Committee authorised an additional production line for the works at a cost of £393,122 to meet the railway's current and future need for laminated springs.

BREL had been able to plan their future capacity and staffing levels because the BRB had produced their Third Future Rail Plan which covered their intentions for the railway between 1976 and 1981, with projections out until the end of 1985 and consulted BREL about the content of the plan as had been requested. The new plan reversed the decline in railway investment which had been causing so much trouble with BREL's workload planning and the uneasiness among workshop staff about the future of their jobs.

The tentative plans for a reduction in workshop capacity and potential closures that BREL senior management had been discussing was abandoned, with an upsurge in work already beginning to be seen across all works. Training schools were being filled to capacity as apprentice recruitment increased, and for which there seemed to be an appetite among school leavers. The increase in work in the immediate future was offset by the gradual reduction in rolling stock investment in the longer term British Rail plan. The management of BREL was not overly concerned in regard to the planned reduction in investment in new rolling stock by the railway, the plan allowed the company visibility of the production capacity that would be required at any point and thus they felt comfortable to bid on export and third party work to fill any shortfall in work being received from British Rail.

The evidence seemed to suggest that the board was right to think so. Private party work was increasing, with Shildon being particularly busy. Forge work was increasing with investment being planned at Shildon to increase the capacity of the foundry there to meet the demand, whilst the wagon repair workshops were extremely busy, workload having increased by 50 per cent over the equivalent time in 1970.

There were, however, still problems with the supply chain that the works managers were having to work around to keep deliveries of both new construction and repair and maintenance activities on time. The supply of brake systems was difficult and was particularly impacting upon the completion of new high capacity coal wagons being built at Shildon. Derby Litchurch Lane was also experiencing trouble with parts supply. Windows, pipe fittings and cabling for the Mark III builds were proving troublesome and causing delays to the completion of the new coaches.

The year ended on a high, although British Rail were beginning to discuss the need to embark on a programme of productivity reviews since railway expenditure and income were becoming widely separated, which in the long term could threaten the work load being promised to BREL in the future rail plan. The railway created the Railway Productivity Group Committee to which it had invited a firm of consultants to contribute. The aim of the group from the outset was to look to reduce manpower across the railway, although BREL was not included in that aim since the group was looking purely at rail operations. One aim of the group that would have a knock-on effect at BREL was the Railway Productivity Group's desire to achieve greater utilisation of railway rolling stock, with programmes to reduce the frequency of maintenance to be considered.

BREL remained busy and looked forward to the new year. Discussions were underway with the BRB about the potential to supply cast iron shoulders for concrete sleepers to the railway. The railway forecast that it would need around 6million of these per year each year over the coming twenty years. The railway had experienced difficulty in sourcing these from the railway trade and so had approached BREL with a view to allocating the work to them. The suggestion was for BREL to undertake to manufacture around 4million sleeper shoulders per year, with the remaining 2million to be acquired from private foundries. BREL responded positively to the proposal from British Railway Board, suggesting a new facility to be built alongside the existing plant at Horwich. The new facility was estimated to require three years to build and commission with production starting early in 1978.

The situation was by no means perfect at the close of 1974, with the supply of parts and materials from the outside manufacturers still causing delays despite constant efforts from BREL to improve the situation through embedding staff within the works of the suppliers of parts to monitor quality and production rates, activation of penalty clauses in supply contracts, and provision of part manufacturing facilities in house at various workshops. Recruitment was still proving difficult in some areas due to the difference between BREL's wage offers and those of local engineering businesses. The works at Glasgow was impacted particularly by the wage discrepancy, finding it difficult to recruit welders and electricians due to the high wages being offered by the North Sea Oil companies and the supporting engineering companies. Despite the difficulties with recruiting experienced staff in Glasgow, the recruitment of new craft apprentices was higher than in previous years.

Industrial relations were also beginning to improve across the business. The personnel department had begun to run a series of industrial relations training course for both management and staff, which seemed to be having a positive effect by the turn of the year. Events in the new year would, however, see a return to dissatisfaction and industrial action.

The years 1973 and 1974 ended with the annual reports and accounts stating that the company had made a small profit in both years. In 1973, BREL had achieved a modest operating profit of £414,000 after interest payable of £4.28million against outstanding loans made to the company. The operating revenues had been much healthier than the final retained profit may have suggested. The company achieved a profit of £2.72million from £105.5million of work from the BRB, with an addition profit of £1.97million made on third party work worth £21.7million. Third party work being undertaken that year had been divided between £21million of business from British customers and £704,000 for export.

In 1974, the company made a profit of £524,000 after interest payable of £4.32million to finance loans outstanding. The company had achieved healthy operating revenues once again with £3.04million profit made on £133million of work completed for the BRB and £1.79million profit on £21.12million of outside work. The third-party work undertaken by the company that year amounted to £16.46million for British customers with £4.64million of overseas orders.

In both years, the interest payable was mainly on the loans made by the BRB in 1970 to fund the setup of the company, for which allowance was made in the costs for work charged to the railway. In effect, the interest payable figures had already been covered by British Rail in the payments made for work undertaken, which BREL then effectively paid back to the parent company to cover the financing costs of the company. The arrangements for financing Railway Finance Limited and various shipping companies in the Sealink portfolio had changed during 1973 at the insistence of the Department of the Environment and HM Treasury.

It had been decided that the arrangements by which BREL obtained finance from merchant banks at favourable interest rates, due to the guarantee of the loan by the BRB would cease, with only the outstanding projects being funded, no new projects to be considered. The monies required were to be made available through treasury funds made available to the BRB for the purpose. The railway would in turn lend the capital to BREL at 9 per cent interest, BREL in turn loaning the money to Railway Finance and the shipping companies at the rate of 10 per cent.

The 1974 annual report indicated that the loan arrangements that had been made to fund the purchase of rolling stock from BREL for lease to the BRB were to cease at the end of the year. During the year, however,

BREL had borrowed an additional £6million from the railway board to fund loans to leasing companies for purchase of rolling stock for leasing back to British Rail. The liability of debt owed to the BRB at the end of 1974 amounted to £62million.

The number of employees had increased slightly in 1974 from the number in 1973. In the 1973, the company had employed an average of 32,567 people across the business in all roles, which had increased to an average weekly figure of 32,710 staff. Wages had also increased with a total of £72.17million being paid in wages and salaries, compared to £58.69million in 1973.

Chapter 6

INDUSTRIAL DISRUPTION AND SUPPLY ISSUES: 1975 AND 1976

The new year dawned in an atmosphere of optimism at BREL The previous year had ended with a promising order book, and better industrial relations. Communication between the company, the BRB and the railway's operational management was improving and BREL's commercial activities seemed likely to bear fruit, despite an achieved shortfall of £6.8million against the sales budget for 1974. Expenditure authorities had been the highest since the formation of the company at £8.85million, reflecting the higher quantity of work undertaken over the year.

The production programme for the Mark III coach was now proceeding well with five completed vehicles leaving the coach works at Derby Litchurch Lane every week. The company began to look at the repair facilities that would be required now that the vehicles were beginning to enter service. The planned repair workload determined by the BRB was for an average twelve and a half vehicles to be released from Derby after the completion of maintenance and repair work each week.

In order to achieve the output expected, it was deemed necessary to improve the facilities at the works to facilitate the work required. The traversers used in the coach works were unable to accommodate the longer Mark III coaches, being limited to the movement of 70ft long vehicles due to the constraints present within the scale of the machinery. In order to handle the new 75ft long Mark III coach, it was necessary to replace a number of traversers in the works. BREL's board approved a total investment of £1.152million in Derby Litchurch Lane's workshops, which was also approved by the Railway Investment Committee.

Investment was not only being made at Derby, with Doncaster the recipient of £194,406 for new equipment required for the construction of the new Class 56 diesel main line freight locomotive fleet, which was to be allocated to that works, although some bogies were to be constructed at Crewe. BREL also approached the Railway Investment Committee for authority to undertake additional expenditure at Doncaster to provide the longer term maintenance facilities that would be needed, assuming that the work would be allocated to the same works in which the class had been built.

The improvement in industrial relations that seemed to be being achieved at the end of 1974 soon deteriorated once more. In February, the unions officially rejected a pay offer made to workshop supervisory staff, opting to either put the offer to arbitration or to undertake industrial action. The situation had not improved by March, with the unions involved having instructed their members to operate a ban on overtime working and to work to rule from the 24th of the month.

Crewe Loco Works bogie assembly and overhaul shop, with a new Class 56 bogie awaiting testing, 6 April 1982. *Colin J. Marsden*

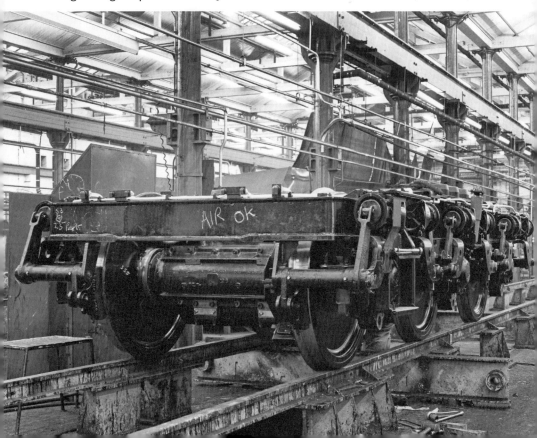

The introduction of the Total Operations Processing System (TOPS) by British Rail in 1974 had been of assistance to BREL particularly in the improvements being achieved in the quicker turnaround of wagon repairs. The wagon workshops across BREL were still requesting one last improvement to the new reports being provided by TOPS which listed what types of wagons were coming to the works and the identification number of the vehicle. The problem was that the workshops still did not know why the vehicle was being sent to them. British Railways' computer centre was contacted with a view to having the software reprogrammed to include the reason for the works visit, which would enable to the workshops to use the capacity more effectively.

The industrial dispute with the workshop supervisors continued into April, although an improved offer from BREL was under consideration by the unions. The work to rule and overtime ban had a dramatic effect on repair work going through the works, which had been exacerbated by the lack of input of vehicles by the regions due to lower mileage resulting from the steady decline in freight traffic.

Cab side panels from scrapped locomotives showing the TOPs number and data panels. *Laurence Waters*

The company was also experiencing delays not of its own making once more. Strike action at the manufacturers of the braking systems used on wagons was seriously delaying production of new freight vehicles. Thirty-six new Freightliner vehicles had been constructed without brakes and were now stored until the equipment was delivered. Steel bogie wagons being built had been completed but had to be kept on accommodation bogies in the works as the variable load valves for the airbrakes on their own bogies were not being delivered. At Crewe, power car construction for the High Speed Train fleet were being delayed by late deliveries of power and traction equipment from the manufacturers. At Shildon, issues were being found with the design of the hopper wagons for Jordan and with lime hopper wagons being built for British Steel Corporation. The designs for both types of vehicles, whilst sound operationally, had proven difficult to construct. The workshops had resolved the problem by adopting different welding and other construction techniques by April and were now catching up the delays.

Some good news had been received by the company. The energy crisis that was striking Britain as 1975 dawned had resulted in the need for a dramatic increase in the production of coal in British collieries which was destined for power stations. The current fleet of coal wagons in British Rail's fleet would be insufficient to cover the increased traffic that would result and so the BRB notified BREL of a plan to increase the fleet by 2,000 new 45-ton GLW air-braked mineral wagons, at a total cost of around £14.5million. The work would be undertaken at Shildon, Swindon and Ashford, protecting jobs and the workshops for the short term. A memo was sent to the Railway Investment Committee accordingly on 27 January.

Coach construction had not been immune to delays caused by both external factors and industrial action within BREL's workshops. The production of locomotive hauled Mark III coaches had been delayed by a shortfall in deliveries of braking systems from outside manufacturers. Staff in the works being unwilling to work overtime during industrial action and the late introduction of incentive schemes designed to improve pay had both contributed to further delays and lower production of new coaches, a shortfall of forty coaches being forecast as a result. The implementation of modifications and late specification changes was causing further delay as rework to implement the required changes on part complete coaches was delaying the start of construction of the next batch of coaches in the programme. Construction of new EMU sets had been delayed at York by continuing unavailability of components when needed for production, which was being caused by late deliveries of materials and equipment from suppliers.

The situation had been made worse by the industrial action being taken across BREL, and staffing issues being experienced at the works due to lack of faith in the forward workload plan. The pessimism of the workforce was resulting in staff seeking alternative employment elsewhere, whilst recruitment of skilled staff to expand the capacity of the workshops was proving challenging. Pay differentials between other engineering companies and the wages that BREL was able to offer under the restrictions placed upon it by the BRB policy on grading and pay for jobs was preventing recruitment. In May, one factor causing delay was resolved with the ending of the strike at the manufacturer of the braking systems which saw supplies beginning to flow into the works once more, although that only lasted until June when the company's employees were once more on strike.

BREL was not immune to the increasing industrial unrest to be seen across British industry during the early summer of 1975. In June, the workshops supervisors were still banning overtime, and working to rule. Clerical staff at the majority of the company's works were banning overtime due to a dispute over pay, whilst there was considerable discontent among management staff, particularly among workshop superintendents. The situation within the workshops and offices at Doncaster was particularly bad with discontent being reported as being rife across the whole works at the meeting of the BREL board in June. The situation was expected to be generally resolved by the imminent 1975 pay award which had been approved by both the BRB and the Ministry of the Environment. The resolution of the differences in levels of pay which had arisen between workshop supervisors and management staff was also in the process of being resolved, agreement having been reached on most points with negotiation due to be completed in the near future.

Despite the ongoing industrial relations challenges the company was undergoing and the difficulties being experienced throughout the supply chain, BREL was still willing to embark on investment programmes to address capacity issues and the changing needs of the railway. In June, the company authorised a programme of investment in new facilities for the heavy overhaul of diesel-electric traction electrical equipment at the locomotive works in Derby. The traction motors on Class 45 locomotives and the generators on Classes 24, 25, 45 and 46 were increasingly in need of heavy maintenance as the locomotives aged and the traction equipment began to wear out, increasing the workload being placed upon Derby. The new investment programme was designed to create additional capacity with the provision of new machine tools and improved facilities.

The ongoing trouble with supplies of materials from outside manufacturers was still causing delays in July. Six items were in short supply at York which were required for the construction of EMU vehicles for the Great Northern Suburban electrification programme. The shortage of materials was preventing the completion of the first vehicle on time, and it was envisaged that of the sixty-eight vehicles due for delivery by the end of the year, at best a figure of thirty-six might be achieved. The Freightliner wagons had still not received the valves needed to complete their own bogies, and were still stored on accommodation bogies at the workshops where they had been built.

In August, the financial director reported that the company had made an operating loss of £573,000 for the year up to 14 June. The loss had been caused by a shortfall in work completion that could be invoiced to the BRB and the private sector due to industrial action and supply chain delays. The revenue achieved by the company to that point had been £69.47 million against a budgeted figure of £84.57 million, which would have resulted in a profit of £671,000 for the half year. The numbers reported to the BREL board show what small margins were available to the company due to their inability to build a profit into the work undertaken for the BRB.

The rail industry was experiencing the impacts of the recession being felt elsewhere in the British economy by the late summer. British Rail's requirements had been reduced with private firms being less willing to place orders, some deferring their order until later in the year. To make up the shortfall, BREL had tendered with the Ministry of Defence for general engineering work to make up the shortfall in workload that was beginning to appear in the production and maintenance plans. The company's tenders to the Ministry of Defence proved successful. An announcement was made in July 1975 that the company had been awarded a contract to construct thirty-nine bogie flat wagons for the transport of armoured fighting vehicles for the army. The vehicles were to be constructed at Shildon using bogies built by the Gloucester Railway, Carriage and Wagon Company.

An opportunity had arisen for a new source of work for BREL, with British Rail informing all the companies who had their own freight stock that all of the privately owned wagon fleet must be converted to air-braking by 1981 at the latest when provision of vacuum braking on locomotives would cease.

The recession being felt by the railway in Britain was being offset by demand for new rolling stock from overseas, with increasing demand from railway authorities likely to provide work for BREL.

At their July meeting, the board took the decision to look to the implementation of further computer systems following the success of the stock control software in use at Crewe. The system was being rolled out across the stores in the other works and was proceeding on schedule. In order to achieve savings, a joint British Rail and BREL Computer Steering Group was to be formed to investigate the opportunities computerisation offered. The committee was tasked with identifying where computerisation of BREL's operations was possible, both to reduce costs, and to reduce the amount of time the workshops wasted in recreating shopfloor paper work by hand every time a change was made to a process or design. The group was also asked to investigate what additional information was needed by the workshops across the country with a view to requesting that be added to the systems by British Rail's in house programmers as well as those at the software vendors.

An independent BREL Computer Steering Group was also to be formed to work on computer systems which would only be of use to the company. The joint group would investigate the software packages in the market through existing computer and software suppliers, whilst also looking into the possibility of the programmers already employed by British Rail creating a series of software packages in house. The BREL group was to investigate the capabilities of the software packages already in use within British Rail to assess if they might offer value to the company. The BREL group was also tasked with extending the use of the manufacturing production control system *NIMMS* ('*Nineteen Hundred Integrated Modular Management System*' produced by ICL and designed to run on their Nineteen Hundred series mainframe computers) across all of the workshops as soon as possible following trials at Crewe.

The issues that the company was experiencing with the recruitment of staff were still ongoing in September with the company reporting a shortfall of 146 skilled staff. Industrial unrest was still also a serious problem with relations between the company and its workshop staff being described as 'uneasy'. The trade unions were campaigning for a change to the system under which waged staff were being paid. The workshop staff now wanted pay to be measured on day work, effectively the wage plus productivity bonus which many in the workforce had protested against in the past. There was also growing unrest reported among clerical staff who, according to the reports from management staff, were unhappy at what they viewed as an 'erosion of their status and conditions'.

The company continued to invest in its workshops, despite the decline being felt in the rail industry as a result of the ongoing recession. In October, the BREL board approved a project costing £117,050 for improvements to the works at Glasgow. The project was aimed at addressing a shortage of capacity at the works in the maintenance facilities for electric traction equipment on locomotives in Scotland. The increasing heavy maintenance required on the traction equipment on the aging Type 2 fleet was creating a demand for more capacity in the workshops. The investment in Glasgow would make it suitable not only for the Type 2 classes in Scotland but also for other locomotive classes. The investment would allow the expanded workshops to take on work for the rest of the locomotive fleet in case British Rail decided to withdraw the Type 2 fleet. Investment was authorised to make improvements at Wolverton as well. The traverser in the traction maintenance shop at the works had been identified as life expired and in need of urgent replacement. Investigations by the works manager had identified that the machinery would cost more to repair than to replace with a new traverser unit and so the BREL board authorised £134,919 for its replacement.

The annual report presented to the BREL directors at the October board meeting outlined that there had been a shortfall in completion of both maintenance and construction work during the year. The majority of the reduction in productivity had been caused by failure to deliver materials, parts and equipment by the manufacturers and suppliers of those items. Unavailability of materials in the workshops had particularly impacted the installation of brake gear of all types as both major suppliers had experienced challenges during 1975. The delivery of wheel sets from the suppliers' foundries had been delayed on a number of occasions during the year so far, as had electrical equipment from the manufacturer. The issues being experienced in the supply chain were causing delays in BREL's works which were not of their making, and which were ongoing despite the intervention of the board who had been discussing the situation with their counterparts in the trade with a view to finding a resolution to the problem.

The works at Eastleigh was experiencing difficulty with the maintenance of EMUs for Southern Region. The workshops were experiencing problems in the overhaul of those units due to the diversity and age of the trains coming into the works. The different designs and maintenance requirements for different types of vehicles meant setup time delays each time a new vehicle entered the works due to the need to set up different jigs and different tools. A major cause for concern being experienced in the maintenance programme at the time was the frequent discovery of asbestos insulation in the stock which required stripping. Each vehicle had to be checked and made safe before any work could be undertaken in the works, which was causing bottlenecks due to lack of capacity in the asbestos removal workshop.

The workshops were undertaking a project which had the potential to provide long term security for Eastleigh. The overhaul and refurbishment of a prototype four car EMU set for the Kent Coast route services was underway. If approved by British Rail after trials, the refurbishment of further electric sets for the Kent Coast would provide ongoing work for the site with a plan to complete the refurbishment and overhaul of one four car set per week between 1977 and 1980.

The workshops at Eastleigh provide an interesting example of how BREL's inability to respond to changing rates of pay within engineering companies outside of the railway caused shortfalls in skilled staff who were desperately needed towards the end of the 1970s and into the early 1980s. It can be seen throughout this book that BREL was, at times, finding it difficult to retain skilled staff, or to recruit from outside the rail industry. The challenges facing the management at Eastleigh were particularly difficult. The works were located in an area of high employment, with demands for the same skills within local aerospace and defence engineering companies who were able to pay considerably higher rates of pay. BREL lagged behind its job market competitors in being able to provide a compelling offer to its staff and thus it struggled to maintain the staff levels needed to meet the workload it had. The management team at Eastleigh knew that the wages on offer from local firms around Eastleigh and Southampton were generally higher than BREL was permitted to offer by the BRB pay policy in force, but were unable to respond due to the BRB's lack of flexibility.

The year ended with more investment being approved for the workshops. The carriage works at York was to receive a new, state of the art, pre-commissioning test facility for EMUs. The new facility was to be used initially for the testing of new electric sets for the Great Northern Inner Suburban Electrification project. It was intended to provide more advanced testing capability as well as greater capacity, which would speed up to completion of trains.

The loan that had been provided to Carpass (Shipping) Limited had been repaid in full by December 1975 before the company ceased trading. A repayment of £3million plus interest had been made to BREL and the outstanding loan which had been taken out to finance the loan to Carpass had also been repaid. The funds could not be used for increased wages though.

The recruitment position was easing as the year closed, partly due to a reduction in the hiring of new staff due to future uncertainty. The company had, however, increased the overall number of employees by 153 waged, and 13 salaried clerical staff to meet immediate shortages across the business. The overall increase in staffing offset a small number of planned job losses which had resulted from the implementation of computer systems in the stores across the business during the year.

Despite ongoing industrial unrest and the industrial action that had been occurring at the beginning of the year, the personnel director reported that the number of hours lost due to industrial action during 1975 had been the lowest for many years. Disputes had been resolved much more quickly and the relationship between the company and the trade unions seemed to be improving slightly, although some disputes remained to be resolved going into the new year. The main outstanding cause of discontent which had not yet been resolved related to the demarcation dispute at York which had been resolved at national level with the trade unions involved, but not within the workshops at York. The shopfloor staff within the works had refused to accept the agreement made by their unions and negotiation was still ongoing between the unions and the employees affected.

The annual report and accounts for 1975 showed that despite difficulties that had been experienced during the year, and initial losses, the company had performed reasonably for the financial year. Sales totalling £183.4million had been achieved for the year, which consisted of £176million of orders from the BRB, the remainder from third parties. Against the revenue achieved, the company made an operating profit of £6.14million with £5.69million profit achieved against British Rail work, and £451,000 on third party work. Interest of £5.87million was payable against outstanding loans, which was covered by allowances made in prices quoted to the railway. A retained profit for the year of £262,000 was achieved after interest deductions.

Third party sales for 1975 were made up of £3.8million of orders from Britain, and £3.6million of export orders. The difficult trading conditions for the year were obvious, the previous year's achieved third party sales being £16.4million for British companies and £4.6million of export orders. Despite the industrial and economic challenges faced by the company, the average number of employees working at BREL per week over the year had increased to 34,516 from 32,710 in 1974, with £97.68million expenditure for salaries and wages.

The new year 1976, dawned with the demarcation dispute at York being settled by the two unions involved. The two unions had reached out to the Trades Union Congress for arbitration since the members of both unions working at York had not been prepared to accept the agreements reached by their union representatives. The TUC Dispute Committee made a number of recommendations which the members of the unions accepted, ending the dispute.

The company received what it believed would be its first two external orders for the year in February and March, the orders placed directly through Brush Traction. Letters of intent were received for a small batch of diesel shunting locomotives worth £697,000, and 250 coal hopper wagons, both of which were destined for export to the Nigerian Railway Company. The orders had been placed directly without the involvement of BRE-Metro.

The order for the shunting locomotives was initially rescheduled by between six and eight weeks, but in April was reported to the BREL board as being less likely, due to the demands being made for delivery times, despite the delay in placing the firm order. In June, the Nigerian Railway attempted to cancel the letter of intent relating to the coal hopper wagons which had been raised on Brush and on to BREL, who made efforts to prevent the Nigerians from cancelling the planned order, although it was not deemed hopeful that the decision could be reversed.

The new year saw new investment, with £213,288 authorised for new repair facilities at Derby Litchurch Lane in February. The new facilities were to be used initially for repair work on the three Advanced Passenger Train prototypes (APT-P) that were to be built there. The facilities would support the fitting and exchange of both bogies and underfloor equipment modules.

Doncaster Works would also receive increased investment. The additional funding authorised for Doncaster related to maintenance of the new Class 56 fleet. The authorised fleet of ninety locomotives, for which construction was underway, would require dedicated facilities due to the unique features which had been included in the designs. The intended work diagrams for the fleet had been shared with BREL by the railway's operations department, which confirmed the locations where the locomotives would mainly be based and work. The plans for the use of the new fleet confirmed that the best location for maintenance facilities was Doncaster, and thus the additional expenditure of £140,150 related to a dedicated maintenance facility could be justified.

The steel sheet works at Horwich and Worcester were facing an uncertain future in 1976. A paper had been submitted to the BREL board which suggested that rationalisation of the facilities related to sheet steel work at both sites was required. The paper was accepted for discussion at the BRB subsidiary chairmen's conference. The foundry at Horwich continued to receive potential investment despite the uncertainty at the steel sheet workshops on the site.

A budget of £2.18million was approved in principle for submission to the Railway Investment Committee, although the submission depended upon whether the British Rail Supply Committee continued to support the requirement under discussion for the supply of concrete sleeper shoulder castings from the foundry. The committee had advised BREL that the required quantity per year had reduced to around 4million, but that it did not want to place the entire order with BREL as it was seen to be advantageous to future supplies of other castings if a source of supply was preserved in the outside trade. The minimum viable quantity that would utilise the works profitably was 3million castings per year. Discussions were ongoing about the intentions of the railway and so the authorised investment budget to support the new workload was placed on hold pending confirmation back from the BRB.

Additional funding was also provided for Crewe Works. The machine shop was granted a budget of £101,640 for the replacement of four life expired lathes with a single modern numerically controlled chucking lathe. The new machine was programmable and had a quicker tool exchange option through a chuck rather than using a preloaded turret into which all the tools needed had to loaded before production started. The new machine would be faster and more flexible that the existing obsolete machines.

In May, a major health concern had arisen at Doncaster Works. The amount of blue asbestos being found in DMU vehicles entering the works was becoming a serious problem. Many of the vehicles had been built with blue asbestos sprayed into the void between internal and external panels to form insulation but no records had been kept at the time of which vehicles in the fleet had been treated in this way. There was thus no way of telling whether a vehicle entering the works had been contaminated with dangerous blue asbestos, which had been identified as the most hazardous form of the mineral. Staff at Doncaster did not feel that it was safe to be working on the multiple unit fleet.

It was decided that all of the fleet returning to the works for maintenance would, without exception, be put through the new asbestos removal house for checking and, as necessary, removal and disposal of all blue asbestos found onboard. This would include all areas of the vehicles, including guard's compartments and also driving cabs.

The new asbestos removal facility involved staff working in an air tight workshop which prevented the fibres released into the air escaping into the wider environment. All staff working with asbestos in the facility had to wear a sealed PVC suit connected to an air hose which provided a supply of fresh air from outside the building, preventing any risk of the inhalation of asbestos fibre. Staff who regularly worked in the asbestos removal facilities received an extra 10p per hour operating allowance to compensate for wearing the suits. A complaint had been raised with the unions that supervisory staff who didn't work full time within the asbestos house but who had reason to occasionally enter the facility were not compensated for the time they spent in the suits. It was widely felt that they should be. The Board of BREL agreed and the oversight in the pay conditions of the staff impacted was amended.

The issues which had been causing so much trouble throughout 1975 and in to 1976 had convinced the BREL board that something need to be done to address the situation and secure the supply of material, equipment and parts going forward. In order to start the process, the board authorised the investigation into the creation of a facility at Swindon which would make braking systems to be used in new construction and spares to be used in maintenance work. The manufacturer had agreed a licencing arrangement with BREL which allowed them to manufacture a range of systems and their spare parts in house.

The project was not deemed appropriate by the Supply Committee which reported to the BRB who still had a policy of sourcing materials and equipment from external companies. BREL was once again unable to bring work in-house. BREL's relationship with its owner prevented it from responding to events in the wider engineering industry which may have proved of benefit in the short term whilst making the company potentially more viable in the long term. The manufacturer of the braking systems used by the railway, after negotiations with BREL, offered to guarantee to hold six months stock of spares and full systems in stock at their own works which BREL could call on as they needed. The board agreed this would be an acceptable solution to the problem.

The agreement foreshadowed an arrangement between manufacturer and supplier which became common in the late 1990s where the same arrangement would exist and which would become referred to as 'Just In Time Logistics'. In many ways, the company was ahead of its time and perhaps without the interference from the BRB, BREL may have been capable of achieving so much more.

In August, the first signs of recovery were being seen in the British economy and the railway began to see its traffic begin to increase accordingly. The impact of the new optimism that was spreading due to the perceived turnaround of the economy could be seen within the work being undertaken by BREL across all most of its maintenance workshops. The regions began to send more passenger stock and locomotives for repair and as a result locomotive repairs had increased by 6 per cent, with coach repairs increasing by just over 1.5 per cent. The company was experiencing a shortage of men in the workshops as a result of the increasing workloads, with 210 vacancies being created within the locomotive workshops and 84 in carriage workshops.

The work undertaken in wagon repair shops had dropped dramatically throughout the year due to the lack of freight traffic on the railway. The wagon fleet had a much lower mileage for the year so far due to the lack of utilisation and as a result scheduled maintenance was being deferred by the railway as it believed that it was not necessary. The wagon works at Ashford, Doncaster, Horwich and Shildon had seen an overall decrease of 14 per cent. The decline in work left all four works effectively overmanned for the workload which they had, putting 300 jobs at risk.

The paper that had been submitted earlier in the year regarding the futures of the steel sheet works at Horwich and Worcester had been debated by the BREL board and at the BRB subsidiaries Chairmen's Conference. The result was the decision to close the facility at Worcester. The decision was met with strong opposition from the NUR, who represented most of the workforce at Worcester.

As a result of the drop in workload across the company's works and the difficult trading conditions which reduced the volume of third party work available, the company reported a loss of £768,000 for the half year up to June 1976. The loss was made despite sales of £104.46million for the same period.

In September, BRELs intake of third party work started to recover as industry began to have more optimism about the immediate future. Two orders were placed for the manufacture and supply of shipping containers. Overseas Containers Limited placed a firm order for 200 20ft containers with Bell Lines Limited placing an order for up to 2,000 40ft containers to be manufactured over the next two years. The company also seemed to be well placed in the wagon and general engineering market with tenders being reported to be extremely competitive by potential customers. It was hoped that orders would be received in the near future for a number of wagon construction projects, among which were tenders for 50 bogie fertiliser wagons for Shell Star Limited and 100 hopper wagons for the British Steel Corporation.

Work had also begun to arrive at the workshops for the breaking up of withdrawn Class 24 locomotives, although problems had been encountered with the scrapping programme due to asbestos contamination and other unexpected difficulties inherent in the disposal of some older parts. BREL directors were in discussion with the BRB as to the company's ability to meet the disposal requirements that would result from the accelerating locomotive withdrawal programme being undertaken by the railway.

The BRB informed the BREL board in September that it had been discussing both the Advanced Passenger Train and the High Speed Diesel Train with their peers in the Federal Railroad Administration in the United States and the AMTRAK company which operated passenger services in all but two of the states in America on behalf of the Federal government. The Federal Railroad Administration were extremely interested in the High Speed Diesel Train with a view to using it within their programme to improve passenger services on the railways whilst also reducing journey times to compete with domestic airlines. AMTRAK were interested in the Advanced Passenger Train. BREL was informed that the Federal Railroad Administration and AMTRAK were sending teams over to Britain in October to evaluate both trains and that BREL should be involved in the process particularly since both the American organisations had expressed an interest in purchasing completed vehicles from Britain rather than taking on manufacture in the United States through a licence agreement.

The meetings and evaluations went ahead as planned with representatives from both the BRB and BREL present throughout, with all parties agreeing that the visit had been a success. The head of the American delegation committed to provide more detail of the Federal government's plans to improve inter-city passenger services once he arrived back in the United States, in order that discussions could continue. In the meantime, the Federal Railroad Administration wished to undertake further evaluation of the High Speed Diesel Train in the United Kingdom.

As the year drew to a close, problems were being reported with the production programme associated with the new Class 56 fleet. The construction of the new locomotives had fallen behind schedule by October with industrial disputes and staff shortages causing the main delays. There were also serious delays being caused by the continual need to implement design changes on the shop floor with the resulting disruption caused by the required rework to part built locomotives and the withdrawal of old drawings and work instructions.

Similar challenges were being seen at York throughout the year which worsened in the weeks leading up to the start of October. The number of design changes and the modifications being applied to the stock, coupled with the need to ensure that the correct current drawings and work instructions were being used was causing more delay to the construction of the EMUs for use on the electrified GNR suburban lines around North London. Elsewhere, delays were being caused on the production of new 46-ton mineral wagons for British Rail by a delay in the introduction of a work incentive scheme caused by non-acceptance of the scheme by staff and a decision to work to rule as a result.

Asbestos had already been flagged to the board and senior management as an increasing health risk, but an increasing number of other health and safety incidents began to occur towards the end of 1976. The number of accidents occurring in BREL's workshops began to increase, reversing a trend of decreasing number of incidents which had been seen over the previous five years. The number of accidents that were occurring in all works was causing concern but particularly at Doncaster, where the

Due to capacity issues at BREL Doncaster who had been given the design and assembly project for the Class 58s, the final twenty Class 56s to be built were transferred to BREL Crewe Works, who had capacity as it was at the end of the HST power car construction project. Class 56 No. 56116 (the second of the Crewe build) is seen in the main assembly shop, 6 April 1982. *Colin J. Marsden*

number of incidents that were being reported was exceptionally high. The board tasked the personnel director with ascertaining why the incident rate was rising and what was causing the excessive number of reports from Doncaster. The result of investigations led to a programme of health and safety education being undertaken by the company across all of its works with changes to operating procedures being introduced.

The steel sheet works at Worcester was nominated for closure in November with a six month notice of closure issued to the workforce. In a letter to the board of directors at BREL, the NUR notified the company that it was totally opposed to the closure and that a period of industrial action across BREL would be undertaken in protest.

The workshops at Eastleigh also gained the attention of the company. The wheel workshop had not seen investment for some time, but in December a proposal was put to the board to invest in the modernisation of the workshop. The project was to replace a number of obsolete machine tools with new modern machines capable of meeting the tolerances that the workshops now demanded. The machines would also be more efficient allowing more work to be put through the workshop than was currently possible. The opportunity would also be taken to reorganise the workshop to allow for a more efficient workflow of jobs passing through, replacing the current layout which had resulted from ad hoc changes made over many years. The workshop modernisation would result in the reduction of the workforce of twelve men and the equivalent of overtime for eighteen men. The proposal was approved for submission to the Railway Investment Committee with a planned budget of £467,000. The Investment Committee approved the expenditure on 14 December.

Industrial action began to seem likely at other workshops, for different reasons as the year ended. The relationship between the company and its workforce at both Crewe and Horwich was reported to the December board meeting as being concerning with a strong likelihood of industrial action in 1977. Relations with the workforce at Doncaster had been deteriorating as well, with it being likely that the works would be on strike in the new year. Representations made to the unions and discussion over improved conditions resulted in a calming of the discontent being felt, and by the December board meeting, the situation at Doncaster was reported as having been 'contained'.

The new year seemed to be approaching with some degree of uncertainty at BREL

Chapter 7

INDUSTRIAL RELATIONS AND RAIL DECLINE: 1977–79

The year 1977 began with a new chairman being appointed to the BREL board, I.M. Campbell being elected as the new chairman at the board's first meeting of the year at the Bishopsgate office.

The industrial relations difficulties at Crewe and Horwich still simmered, but no action had been taken on behalf of the unions until February when the situation at Crewe worsened. The discontent at Crewe had occurred as a result of a disagreement between the NUR and the AEF over the planned upgrading of roles by BREL which would protect the jobs of the men, and result in a pay increase. The new roles would however cause a demarcation issue between the two unions since the work to be undertaken by the new upgraded job roles would cover tasks typically undertaken separately by members of both unions. The two unions were unable to settle their differences and only two options remained open. The first was to refer the dispute to ACAS for conciliation, whilst the second was confrontation between the two unions. The situation entered a period of uneasy peace between the two unions despite the lack of agreement.

Industrial unrest was not the only staffing problem facing BREL in early 1977. Retention of skilled staff had become extremely difficult, the personnel director summarising the cause as being related to the lower wages the company was able to offer compared to other engineering companies at the time. As has already been seen, at some workshops the wage question was even more of a problem where BREL had to compete with other well established engineering companies who were simply able to offer better packages to their employees.

The workshops in York began the year by informing the BREL board that the start of production of the Class 312 EMU sets for the Great

Northern Outer services had been delayed but that the works management believed that twenty-four of the twenty-six sets would be delivered to the regional depot by 17 September. The company board thought that the delivery promise was too optimistic and informed British Rail that the full complement of twenty-six sets would not be completed until November.

Investment in the workshops began early in the new year with plans to provide five additional workshop sites with new asbestos removal facilities to deal with the increasing number of vehicles being returned for maintenance and repairs. Approval was sought for an investment of £1.5million from the Railway Investment Committee to provide the facilities needed, which followed shortly afterwards. Construction and equipping of the facilities began as soon as each site was able to begin work. An unplanned investment was required as a result of a fire that had broken out in the paint shop at Eastleigh, which spread to an adjacent building. The roofs of both buildings had been badly damaged and needed replacement estimated to cost in the region of £75,000.

The discussions between British Rail, BREL, AMTRAK and the Federal Railroad Administration had reached a hiatus towards the end of 1975 with the head of the delegation not providing the information that he had promised and not responding to letters and telegrams from the BRB. In an effort to push the potential project forward, both British Rail and BREL invited the American team to come back to Britain to undertake the phase one evaluation of the High Speed Diesel and Advanced Passenger Trains. The delegation did not respond.

Eastleigh Works received more investment with a view to improving the workshops in April. The component cleaning facilities that were used to clean parts for locomotives, EMUs and coaches were scattered across six different locations on the site. The process of cleaning parts to be reused during maintenance was time consuming, as a number of parts needed to be treated in more than one of the cleaning shops. BREL authorised an expenditure of £191,000 to centralise and modernise the cleaning facilities provided at Eastleigh. The improvement would improve working conditions in the cleaning plants which were aging. The investment was also forecast to save £35,000 per year, reducing staffing by nine men and reducing overtime requirements related to component cleaning by around 160 hours per week.

The dispute at Crewe between the NUR and the AEF was still smouldering at Crewe in April 1977 despite ongoing negotiations involving BREL and both unions. The unrest caused delays to the completion of locomotive repairs at Crewe, resulting in locomotives spending longer in the works than was planned and creating a backlog of repairs, with locomotives being stored in the yards or kept in traffic past the date of the scheduled overhaul. Delays had also been occurring at York due to ongoing materials shortages caused by suppliers missing delivery dates. The delay mainly impacted upon the EMUs destined for the Great Northern Suburban services around North London, which caused a delay in the commencement of the new timetable.

The relationship between British Rail and BREL had been improving regarding the communications around rolling stock requirements, but a production gap appeared likely to occur at Derby Litchurch Lane at the end of the current High Speed Train construction programme. The lack of work appearing in Derby's production plan was being caused by the late authorisation of High Speed Trains destined for West Country services from Paddington. The delay was not, on this occasion, caused by the BRB but by delays in the Department of Transport giving authority to the railway to proceed with the programme. Delayed authority from the ministry was also likely to cause production gaps at the works between the West Country High Speed Train build, and the programme to construct High Speed Trains for the north-east and south-west. BREL was anxious to fill the gap in the schedule with export orders to protect jobs and preserve capacity for the later High Speed Train construction programmes when finally authorised.

The company had identified the need to look at the possibility of creating a new design for an export coach. The Mark III coach was proving difficult to sell abroad, with feedback from BRE-Metro indicating that the design was not suitable for the markets in which they were most actively pursuing rolling stock orders. The lack of success in selling the Mark III overseas and the possibility of embarking on a project to create an 'international' coach were discussed at the BREL board meeting held at Wolverton Works in April. The cost associated with the design work needed to create the new vehicle was estimated to be around £100,000. The design costs were agreed to be a good investment and authority was given for the design teams at Derby to proceed, with input being provided by BRE-Metro on the general requirements the coach would need to meet to be successful. The board also agreed on the development of a new standard narrow gauge freight bogie for the export market.

The bogie was to be designed as part of a joint venture between BREL and Gloucester Railway, Carriage and Wagon Company. BREL was looking to establish new relationships for overseas work due to the souring of the relationship with Metro-Cammell and had begun discussions with the Gloucester company with regard to sharing capacity and joint marketing. The joint venture was to be on a less formal basis than with Metro-Cammell under BRE-Metro.

Cover of BREL Open Day guide for Wolverton Works showing one of the Class 304 Electric Multiple Units, originally built at the works, and then maintained there. *Author's collection*

The April board meeting also discussed the current issues with general industrial unrest across the workshops and delays in production which were becoming common. The personnel director reported that the high levels of discontent were mainly being caused by pay. The current pay and efficiency schemes were reaching the end of their useful life. Staff in the works had discovered that it was easier to increase earnings by not cooperating with the work measurement programmes than by increasing output. Unmeasured work being reported to the shop superintendents accounted for a quarter of the work being completed. A replacement pay programme was required which would increase staff pay whilst also increasing output.

The workshop wage schemes were to be replaced with a simpler system based upon an improved base rate of hourly pay, with two substantial fixed bonuses paid each week in return for achieving and then exceeding the weekly production schedule. Payments to pensions and for overtime were to be increased accordingly.

The new pay award was partly designed to assist staff retention and recruitment which was still a problem across the company. The works' manager from Wolverton, W.E. Levett, attended part of the board meeting, as had become the norm when the board was meeting in one of the works. He reported that staff retention was still a problem there and was particularly due to higher wages being offered from local caravan and boat builders. On a positive note, the works manager reported that the skills available in Wolverton enabled the workshops to successfully continue to construct Spartan Armoured Personnel Carrier bodies for the Ministry of Defence.

The company received an unexpected response from the American Federal Railway Administration in June. An outline agreement for supply of both High Speed Diesel Train, and Advanced Passenger Train units was presented to BREL with the promise of a formal agreement to follow. The outline agreement was deemed to be unacceptable by the company, but an opportunity to discuss the content would be available in July when the president of AMTRAK was due to visit Britain and had already scheduled a meeting with the chairmen of both the BRB and BREL

The workshop machine tool investment programme for the following year was decided upon at the June board meeting. One hundred and twelve machine tools had been identified as being life expired and in need of replacement during 1978, which could be achieved through the purchase of eighty-one modern machines. A budget of £2.8million was

Two 25-ton overhead cranes lift a Mark II coach off its accommodation bogies for lowering onto its refurbished bogies at Wolverton. *Author's collection*

agreed upon and passed for consideration by the Railway Investment Committee, who approved the entire programme in July. At the same time, an investment of £320,000 was approved for consideration by the Investment Committee for York to replace an obsolete wheel lathe. The current lathe was incapable of meeting British Rail standards due to its condition. A new lathe was to be sourced from Germany as at the time no British manufacturer was producing a wheel lathe.

Interior views of Wolverton Works. Clockwise from top left: Spindle Moulding shaping components in the Timber Shop; Repair of invertors in the Electric Repair Shop; Assembly of lead acid batteries in the Cell Shop; Trainees under instruction in the Works Training School; Rewinding coach dynamo armatures in the Electric Shop. From Open Day guide. *Author's collection*

Further investment was agreed in July when £230,000 was authorised for the urgent replacement of two workshop traversers at Wolverton which were incapable of transporting the Mark III coach and were also in very poor condition and beyond economic repair, having been installed in 1896

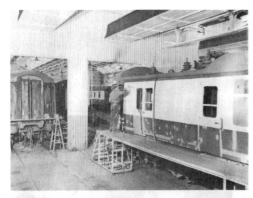

Interior views of Wolverton Works. Clockwise from top left: Brush painting a coach; Repair of coach seat back in the Trimming Shop; Laying glass fibre on a large mould; Exterior body repairs in the West Repair Shop. From Open Day guide. *Author's collection*

and 1901. An investment of £159,760 was approved for the replacement of three machines with one modern programmable turning and boring machine at Crewe. The replacement by a single more capable machine would result in a change to the manning requirements in that part of the machine shop, with the four men on two shifts with an extra man on the day shift for hand finishing work produced by the old machines being replaced by two single man shifts, making seven men redundant with an accompanying reduction in overtime.

Swindon continued to receive investment with £154,000 allocated for the replacement of two overhead cranes which had been built in 1903 by the Great Western Railway. The cranes were now proving difficult to maintain as they became more worn out and less reliable. The two new cranes were required for the EMU repair work which was to be assigned to the works once British Rail had approved the refurbishment of the Class 410 and 411 EMUs for the Southern Region.

Retention of staff was becoming an even more serious problem than ever before within BREL by June 1977. The company was seeing an extremely concerning decline in staff numbers with the workshops seeing a tidal wave of resignations at times. The company's management were completely helpless and despite their best efforts to try to improve the situation and to look after their staff were neither able to respond or even to offer short term incentives to encourage staff to remain with the company nor were they able to offer improvements to stave off industrial action.

Discussions held at board level indicated the frustration that the senior management of the company were feeling at the time, which was unlikely to be visible to the workforce outside of headquarters. The board had attempted many times to approach the BRB for more autonomy in awarding necessary and desperately needed pay increases and improved employment packages, but had been unsuccessful on each occasion. The BRB was unprepared to make the necessary compromises, since they were in turn constrained by the government as part of their counter inflation policy. With staff being unaware of the attempts being made by BREL's board and senior management to improve their lot, morale among the workforce was deteriorating rapidly with the situation at Crewe, Doncaster and Horwich becoming particularly volatile and likely to explode into full-scale national strikes at any moment.

Industrial relations continued to be difficult, although some progress was being made by August. The dispute at Crewe between the two unions was reaching a conclusion, with agreement being reached on most of the points of difference, although the rift between the two unions would still not be completely resolved until the end of the year. A new dispute had broken out over redundancy arrangements in the machine shops at Crewe to add to the unrest at the works. The boiler makers were undertaking industrial action at Doncaster, although the union president had offered to mediate by talking to the men and asking them to cooperate with the company. Industrial unrest continued, however, with ongoing disputes at Crewe, Doncaster and Horwich added to by a new dispute at Eastleigh.

September 1977 saw a further £2.32million allocated to the provision of asbestos handling facilities across all of the BREL workshops. Doncaster received an increase in the previously allocated expenditure dedicated to creating new asbestos handling facilities on the site, with Doncaster's project to cost £2.14million alone. At the same time, Ashford received investment for the first time in five years. Investment had been stopped due to the uncertainty over the future of the works, but an order from Kenya and the likelihood of winning other export wagon orders justified reinvesting in the workshops. A total of £662,000 was authorised for the modernisation of the workshops and replacement of obsolete machines and cranes. Shildon also received new investment during the September board meeting, with £192,918 allocated for the replacement of a number of obsolete and worn-out machine tools across the works. The new machines would, however, result in the loss of eleven machine operators' jobs.

November saw a change in the board of directors with James Rigg being appointed a director of BREL by the BRB, although on this occasion the appointment was made from outside the rail industry. James Rigg had been a director and the general manager of Rolls Royce Limited's Aero Division.

Discussions with British Rail were ongoing regarding the work to be carried out on the refurbishment programme on the Class 410 and 411 units. In anticipation of commencement of the work, BREL requested authority from the Railway Investment Committee for an investment of £664,000 for modernisation of the facilities at Swindon. The works had been chosen to undertake the work due to there being better potential for recruitment of new staff and retraining of existing employees working there. The works also had reserves of unused space which could potentially be brought back into use very quickly, and so the proposed abandonment of the workshop site east of Rodman Road was stopped. Approval for the work on the Southern Region units was received in March with approval for the proposed reinvestment following, securing the future of Swindon Works for a little longer.

More investment followed in December, with Derby Litchurch Lane receiving £1.036million in funding subject to approval by the Railway Investment Committee. The investment was to be used for a major overhaul of plant and machinery at the works and an increase in capacity to allow an increased Mark III coach repair workload to be taken on. The increased capability would be for both locomotive hauled and High Speed Train coaches, with an expected completion rate of twenty-five vehicles a week leaving the works at the completion of repairs.

Wolverton was to receive £1.36million of investment, again subject to Railway Investment Committee approval, for a reorganisation and refit of the lifting and wheel shops designed to alleviate severe congestion in the works. The project would involve the relocation of the wheel workshop into two redundant bays of the vehicle repair shop, with bogie repairs being transferred to the space vacated by the relocation of the wheel shop. Finally, a complete reorganisation of the lifting bay would be undertaken. The reorganisation would sadly result in the loss of seventeen staff and a reduction in overtime of 350 hours a week. Approval was received from the Railway Investment Committee for all three projects in January 1978.

The year ended with an unusual project under discussion by the company. The project would involve BREL purchasing seventy-five surplus Freightliner wagons from British Rail, with a view to overhauling and converting the vehicles for sale to British Leyland for the transport of their motor vehicles from the factories. The traffic arrangements for the car transporter trains had not been agreed between the BRB and British Leyland in January, so the project was placed on hold pending developments in the negotiations.

Investment became necessary at Eastleigh early in 1978 due to a change in procedures relating to Southern Region EMUs. Prior to the new year, asbestos had not been removed from drivers cabs and guards' compartments as this had been undertaken in regional train depots, with Eastleigh only making vehicles safe in passenger carrying areas. The works was now to undertake complete removal of asbestos from all areas of train units prior to them entering the repair line. An investment of £911,000 was required to expand and re-equip the asbestos handling facilities at the works.

The year 1978 began badly for BREL, particularly in relation to deliveries of the new High Speed Train sets. BREL had mostly succeeded on meeting the delivery schedules set by the BRB for its new trains during 1977, however deliveries of the remaining train sets in early 1978 had started badly. Industrial action at the manufacturers had stopped supply of power units and spares, whilst strikes at the suppler of gear wheels to BREL had prevented completion of power car number thirty-three onwards at Crewe. No solution existed to either shortfall at the time, although the manufacturer of the power units had promised that forty-four units would be available to Crewe during 1978. One issue could however potentially be resolved quickly.

The manufacturer of the braking systems used on the High Speed Train sets was experiencing a strike which prevented supplies of any equipment reaching Crewe or Derby Litchurch Lane, but BREL had an option. It was possible to bring forward the supply of braking systems which had been ordered for the Western Region High Speed Train sets, as the equipment was to a different design from a separate manufacturer. As work had not yet started on the Western Region sets at either works, the equipment could be used to progress the existing construction programme. The manufacturer was willing and able to expedite the order and so BREL took up the option.

The company undertook a further programme of investment in its works, approving a number of projects to be submitted to the Railway Investment Committee in March. One of the most important was a programme of extensions to the works training schools. The Future Rail Plan for 1981 to 1985 received from the BRB early in 1978, coupled with the firm orders placed on BREL, left the company requiring an increase of 2,000 skilled staff. The company adopted a policy to address the shortfall. Half the number of vacancies were to be filled through the retraining of existing staff, particularly those whose jobs were at risk of redundancy. The other half would be filled through the company's apprentice training schemes.

To meet the demand for upskilling staff and training new apprentices, the schools at Derby Litchurch Lane, Doncaster, Wolverton and York would need to be extended, with a new school to be created at Glasgow. Proposals for expansion at Doncaster (£111,640), Wolverton (£159,803) and York (£154,613) were immediately sent on to the Railway Investment Committee for approval. Proposals for Derby, and Glasgow would follow. The proposals were approved by the committee very quickly.

Meanwhile, industrial relations had not improved a great deal during the first quarter of the new year. Four separate disputes were occurring at Crewe by the end of March. Resistance to the proposed changes to pay and the introduction of a re-incentive scheme aimed to improve staff retention had been totally rejected by staff at Doncaster with selective industrial action being taken, followed by a complete strike undertaken by all the unions at Doncaster.

Pickets from Doncaster visited York and all waged staff at the works undertook a one week strike in support of Doncaster. At Crewe, staff were balloted on industrial action, with strike action being rejected by three to one in the ballot, although the option to undertake work to rule action was supported. Seven hundred and seventy-three electricians and fitters ignored the result of the ballot and went on strike. At Derby, 430 vehicle builders voted in favour of strike action at Litchurch Lane, while staff at Horwich also walked out.

The dispute at Horwich was resolved by early April with staff returning to work and a method of introducing the re-incentive scheme across the works agreed by all staff. The disputes at the other workshops continued for slightly longer, although negotiation and compromise resulted in the majority of staff at least returning to work, although some continued to work to rule. Once the re-incentive scheme had been introduced across the works in conjunction with the 1978 pay award, the trend of staff leaving was noticeably reversed.

Relations with staff did not remain calm for long, however. Supervisory staff at six works began to file grievances over differentials and began working to rule and banning overtime. The Workshop Supervisory Committee which represented all supervisors recommended that all works supervisory staff undertook the same action if the grievance had not been resolved by 17 March, with full strike action to take place from 7 August. Strikes were avoided with the grievances resolved across all works.

The plan for a new training centre for the works at Glasgow progressed well with the company making an offer of £410,000 to the owners of a large property that was for sale in Charles Street. The property was viewed as perfect for conversion into a training school and stores. The owners accepted the offer in September. Once the buildings were in BREL's possession, the board approached the Railway Investment Committee for the allocation of £666,500 to cover the costs of conversion and equipping the new site, which received authorisation almost immediately. The existing stores in the works were fragmented across the site, with a quarter of the stores in condemned buildings, with another third located in buildings earmarked for conversion to production. The new site would be much easier to manage and would locate the stores in one place, reducing the need for multiple handling of parts and materials.

The new school was to replace the current arrangement whereby apprentices from Glasgow Works attended the local engineering college full time. The new arrangements would see the apprentices attend the BREL training centre for four days a week, working in a workshop environment and to BREL standards of discipline. The remaining day would be spent at the college undertaking further education courses. The new school would create twelve jobs for new teaching staff to run the school.

Derby Litchurch Lane was to receive an extension to the existing training centre by the construction of a new annexe within the works boundaries designed to accommodate an additional 120 apprentices a year. Construction was authorised and was due to start in September.

Relations with staff at Crewe had not improved and retention of staff had become a problem once more following a pay award made by Rolls Royce Motors Limited. Industrial relations were deteriorating at BREL's Crewe workshops due to a grievance related to the interpretation of conditions relating to the re-incentive scheme, in response to which staff had begun working to rule and adopting a ban of any overtime working. The national officers of the unions representing the staff undertaking industrial action agreed with the Company's position, but the works staff insisted on the removal of conditions which they disagreed with and continued to take unofficial action. BREL management found the removal of the conditions unacceptable and so an impasse was reached where neither side would make compromises. The dispute was eventually resolved in October with all staff working normally.

Management development in the company was becoming increasingly difficult towards the end of the year. Management staff were no longer prepared to relocate to other workshops for promotions due to difficulty with getting mortgages, and the financial loss that the move would incur, since BREL was unable to pay relocation costs due to the BRB policies. The company found that its most talented young engineers were leaving the company to join outside firms due to the lack of viable promotion opportunity within BREL.

The ongoing difficulties being experienced in recruitment, and opportunity for engineering staff left a forecast shortfall of between 1,700 and 2,700 skilled staff anticipated for 1979 and 1980, despite the improvement in staff retention that had been achieved during 1978. The problem was becoming less due to the discrepancies between the wages and salaries offered by outside industry compared to those which BREL was able to offer as the decade ended, although that situation was not helpful. The difficulty was more aspirational among the British workforce as the 1980s dawned. The railways and other heavy engineering careers were viewed among graduate engineers and younger experienced workshop staff as old and 'boring' and not the future whilst the new electronics, computer, and aerospace industries were seen as more exciting and the way forward. The opportunity elsewhere to work on what were seen as more exciting projects and products was difficult for BREL and many other traditional heavy engineering companies to address. The shortfall would impact maintenance activities and it was suggested that some light repairs may need to be undertaken in regional depots. The suggestion would sow the seeds for the railway to rethink its maintenance operations which would have implications for the future of BREL during the late 1980s.

The company ended the year by proposing a further series of investment activities partly aimed at reducing the staffing gap that was being anticipated. The wheel shop and bogie cleaning facilities at Glasgow were to be reorganised at a cost of £1.09million. The current wheel shop was laid out in a haphazard manner which caused inefficiency, whilst the bogie cleaning facility was old and inefficient, and produced a low standard of cleaning and was to be replaced.

At Eastleigh, problems were being found with the condition of the bodywork on EMUs being delivered to the works for maintenance. The panels were found to be deteriorating more quickly than anticipated, resulting in the need for the units to undergo heavy body repairs at the next visit to the works. Anticipation of heavy workload in the near future and the current layout of the works flowlines resulted in a need to upgrade much of the equipment at the works, as well as a reorganisation of the flowline to reduce the time vehicles were being held in the workshops awaiting progression to the next operation in the maintenance regime.

The year would end, as it had begun, with a series of industrial disputes. The workforce at York opted to take industrial action in opposition to the changes in work measurement being rolled out in the workshops linked to the new pay and re-incentive schemes, whilst some staff at Derby Litchurch Lane took various forms of industrial action in response to the increased intake of apprentices. A separate industrial issue arose at the end of the year, related to health and safety in previous years.

In December 1978, the company received a series of claims for compensation for industrial deafness, despite the unwillingness of some staff to wear ear protection provided by BREL discussed in an earlier chapter. Of the 629 claims received, 88 had already been settled at a total cost of £258,453. The remaining 541 claims left the company with a potential liability of over £2million.

The year 1979 began badly for the company. Container orders became harder to win due to competition from Korean and Northern Irish manufacturers. Freightliner was contemplating placing orders for its containers with external suppliers in these countries in preference to BREL. With the workload dwindling, the board took the decision to cease tendering for container construction and to withdraw from the activity as soon as possible. The NUR was informally advised of the decision, and that the company was planning to give notice that the container plants were to close by the end of March with a view to closure being undertaken at the end of the existing workload in September of 1979. The situation did not improve and so the company continued with its decision to withdraw from the manufacture of shipping containers, with the workshops at Derby Litchurch Lane closing at the end of September with all the remaining staff being made redundant.

Attempts to computerise BREL's facilities were being delayed in the early part of the year. Reduced staffing in the Computing Services and Operational Research Department at British Rail, which was undertaking the work on behalf of the company, had created bottlenecks and delays. The ICL computer in use at BREL was due to be phased out with all of the software used transferred to the more powerful ICL 2980 computer located in the British Rail Computer Centre in Nottingham, however a national shortage of programmers had resulted in delays to the rewriting of the software to make it work on the different machine. Industrial relations grievances related to the use of computer systems within BREL's works were also delaying the introduction of the NIMMS production system.

The poor start to the year did not prevent the company continuing to invest in the works which it believed, at the time, had a long term future. Swindon received a further programme of investment, approved in March, for the creation of new facilities for the maintenance and overhaul of electric traction equipment. The investment of £280,310 was to support the transfer of Class 08 shunting locomotive electrical traction equipment back to Swindon due to lack of capacity elsewhere.

The industrial relations question at Derby continued to worsen throughout the spring and into the early summer. The opposition to the increased intake of apprentices then spread to Wolverton where industrial action was also threatened in response to the new apprenticeship schemes. Claims for industrial hearing loss continued to be received and by June had risen to 2,256, with 400 settled at a cost of £96,000.

The ongoing investment that had been made into the foundry within Horwich Works was beginning to come to fruition in the summer of 1979,

Queue of Class 08 locomotives awaiting maintenance, 22 March 1984. *Laurence Waters*

with the new machinery beginning production. It was envisaged that the foundry would be working at full capacity during 1980, at which point a reduction in the number of staff working in production and maintenance of the foundry was expected. The changes made to the foundry would not impact the maintenance workshops at Horwich.

The board had been working to define the machine tool replacement programme for 1980, and in June the final programme was put forward to the Railway Investment Committee for approval. A budget of £3.85million was requested for the replacement of 106 machines that were coming to the end of their useful life by 78 more modern and more capable machines across all of BREL's machine shops. A more immediate need was identified at Doncaster, where a new programmable turret punch machine was needed, to be able secure the contract with International Harvesters for the production of combine harvester parts that had been ongoing for a

Horwich maintenance workshops with Class 313 undergoing overhaul, 11 July 1979.
Colin J. Marsden

number of years. An investment of £226,000 was approved to ensure the continuation of this profitable work.

The company continued to have a difficult year. In August, it was reported that the Electrical Multiple Unit refurbishment programme for Kent Coast services was being delayed by late design changes, whilst work on High Speed Train power cars at Crewe was being delayed by shortages of materials, parts and traction equipment caused by late deliveries from the suppliers. The problem with late deliveries of parts was also preventing the completion of the expected number of power cars undergoing repairs at Derby Locomotive Works. At York construction of EMUs was being delayed by the same problems in the supply chain. Management visits to all the suppliers involved were arranged in order that an attempt could be made to find a resolution to the ongoing problem.

A management visit was also scheduled for late November. The Commercial Director was due to travel to the United States to visit the Federal Railroad Authority and AMTRAK to negotiate a contract for five 'Leyland' lightweight coaches from the federal authority and to attempt to close a contract for 400 mainline coaches from AMTRAK. BREL was also looking at beginning a serious sales drive in South-East Asia towards the end of the year with a view to obtaining wagon and bogie coach orders. The new marketing campaign was to be undertaken as purely BREL initiative with no involvement from BRE-Metro.

The year ended with British Rail announcing a programme of mandatory shopping of locomotives for maintenance at the scheduled date, designed to improve the in-service availability of the locomotive fleet. The announcement was enthusiastically received within BREL, who would now be able to plan in detail the work that was to be undertaken by their maintenance shops. Finally, the works would know what type of locomotives were due, how many and whether the visit was an intermediate repair or a heavy overhaul.

Chapter 8

INTO THE 1980s

The new decade dawned with BREL seemingly well placed to recover from the issues that it had experienced during the last year of the 1970s. The supply chain challenges seemed to have been resolved following dialogue between the company's directors and their peers on the boards of the companies involved in supplying materials, parts and equipment to the workshops. The sales figures for December 1979 had been 2 per cent above the budgeted expectation and the future work load notification for maintenance seemed to indicate that the new decade offered much to the company. Despite the cautious optimism the new year brought with it, the company recognised that a degree of rationalisation of its works was required to ensure that they were fit for the demands of the 1980s. No one in BREL knew that by the end of the decade the company, in its current form, would have ceased to exist.

In the climate of rationalisation that existed within the senior management a programme of continued investment in the workshops was agreed for 1980 to prepare the works for the future. The first site to receive investment was Derby Litchurch Lane. A programme was authorised which would reorganise the stores facilities at the works. The works stores were spread over nineteen locations spread over the site with an additional facility in a rented warehouse, 2 miles away from the works.

The rented accommodation amounted to a quarter of the total floor space dedicated to parts and materials storage for Litchurch Lane, and cost BREL £81,000 per year in rent. Authorisation was given for an investment of £586,887 to convert the old container manufacturing workshops into a dedicated purpose built stores facility for the works, allowing the company to terminate the lease of the outside warehouse. At the same time the smaller stores in the workshops would be reorganised to reduce the total number of locations to eleven. The rationalisation exercise would result in sixteen men being made redundant and a reduction in overtime.

The workshops at York were to be involved in the construction of the new Class 317 EMU which had been specifically designed to take advantage of automatic and semi-automatic welding procedures which allowed long weld runs. The works at York did not possess welding machines capable of performing these required lengths of welds and so investment of £458,085 was authorised for the purchase and installation of the required welding machines. The implementation of new welding processes made seventeen men surplus to requirements in the erection shops who were made redundant and achieved a saving of an additional 140 hours of overtime per month.

The company began to experience a decline in export work early in 1980, with BRE-Metro becoming less relevant as BREL began to look for export work directly. The company won an order for twelve modified withdrawn British Rail Mark II coaches worth £700,000 in late January, but experienced disappointment with a number of tenders it had placed with prospective customers, all of whom opted to place the orders with other companies. An example of the problems being experienced in the export markets can

Class 317 Driving Trailer Standard under construction at York, 5 February 1986.
Colin J. Marsden

be seen in a tender for the construction and supply of wagons to Zambia. The bid was made for the business by BREL at a cost of £36,000 per vehicle which was lost, the order being placed with a company in Belgium who had bid the lowest cost among all of the bidders for the work, at a mere £19,000 per vehicle.

Hawker Siddeley approached BREL asking them to quote for the manufacture of thirty-six of a potential order though Brush Locomotives (who were owned by Hawker Siddeley) for seventy-two diesel mechanical locomotives for Iranian Railways. Hawker Siddeley responded to the quote, stating that the price offered by BREL was twice the price quoted by a locomotive manufacturer in Germany.

BREL reported the outcome of both tenders to the Department of Trade asking them to intervene, as the board believed that the Belgian and German companies were receiving unfair government subsidy which had allowed them to bid so low for the work. The question of potentially unfair competitive tendering against BREL by European manufacturers remained unresolved.

BREL's attempts to rationalise the workshops for the 1980s caused a number of industrial disputes in the first half of the year. The company sought to retrain its workforce to be able to undertake a wider range of work, with employees who were surplus to requirements in one skill area being the first to receive training to allow them to transition into a role for which there was still work. The declining amount of work in the wagon repair shops as a result of the contraction in British Rail's wagon fleet was likely to cause job losses there.

The company believed that by embarking on a programme of retraining which would allow the affected staff to transition into another area, such as coach repairs, where demand was still high, it would be able to protect jobs, preserve skills and avoid redundancies. It was expected that the unions would support such a scheme. This was not the case.

At the same time, the company undertook a review of its engineering graduate staff. In order to retain their knowledge and experience, and in light of recent trouble with staff retention, the company promoted a number of the most talented engineers or those who were showing great potential in the work they had been undertaking. At the same time, however, those who were viewed as being less capable were made redundant. The apprenticeship programme was also expanded with an intake of 1,312 expected during 1980.

The future looked even more bleak for parts of BREL's business activities. Freight traffic on British Rail was continuing to decline and, as a result, the BRB shared a proposal with BREL, in May 1980, related to their plans for the freight rolling stock and locomotive fleet. The railway was considering reducing the number of wagons that were being sent to the workshops for maintenance by around 3,000 vehicles a year due to lack of utilisation of the fleet. The number of freight locomotives undergoing scheduled classified repairs was also potentially to be reduced because of the lower mileage that each locomotive was covering each year. In response, BREL began to consider whether it was viable to continue construction of new freight locomotives and wagons.

The company took action to save cost and protect jobs during the early summer. Overtime was stopped at the repairs facilities at the wagon works with staff transferred on to new build work that was in progress. BREL reached an agreement on the maintenance of freight locomotives which resulted in a reduction of sixty locomotives from the repair schedule which were not in need of maintenance due to low utilisation levels. The reduction in workload did not result in any redundancies in the locomotive repair shops, instead there was an agreement that overtime working was to be halved. The managing director reported to the BREL board at the June 1980 meeting that the possibility of halting construction of freight locomotives and wagons would result in no savings that year. Savings could be made in future years with an estimated £20million saving in 1981, with a £40million saving every year thereafter. Ashford works was viewed as being particularly at risk of closure if the recession in railway freight continued but the board agreed to postpone any decision until more information had been received from British Rail regarding their future plans.

In the meantime, the company directors encouraged the creation of a 'catalogue' of export vehicles which could be used to potentially win orders to fill the impending loss of maintenance work. The range of export vehicles would include the completion of the development of the 'export coach' already underway in the design offices at Derby. The coach was to be joined by a range of export multiple units, both diesel and electric, as well as a range of railbuses. The company believed that a series of 'export bogies' would potentially be a profitable product line, particularly if the range could cover a variety of track gauges that would meet the demands of most railway companies across the world. The final addition to the new export range was to be an export locomotive, which it was hoped could either be, or be based upon, the new Class 58 freight locomotive upon which construction was about to begin.

Staffing of the works was proving problematic with both recruitment and staff retention becoming more difficult due to wage restrictions being imposed on the company. The nationally negotiated wage rates were reported by the Derby Locomotive Works manager as worsening industrial relations and putting the workshops into a non-competitive situation when compared to the other manufacturing and engineering companies. The situation at Derby Locomotive Works had been improved slightly by the works being able to recruit from staff that had been made redundant when the steel works at Corby had closed. This was only a short term solution to the staffing needs at Derby and was not an option that every workshop could take advantage of.

Staff shortages were not being helped at Derby Litchurch Lane by the refusal of staff to accept a reasonable allocation of apprentices, who had completed their training, to the shopfloor. The works staff also refused to accept time measurement for job completions and normal working for the removal of asbestos from vehicles coming into the works. The refusal was made despite assurances from independent medical doctors and health and safety experts that the working practices in the asbestos house at the works were in accordance with health and safety executive standards and perfectly safe. The likelihood of industrial action in the carriage works seemed to be increasing.

The situation with railway freight operations had not improved by July, with the proposal for a reduction in freight locomotive and wagon repairs now becoming confirmed by the BRB. In response, BREL considered its options, with the future of Ashford Works becoming more doubtful due to the downward revision of workload due for the remainder of the year and through 1981.

The company board requested that options for cost reductions without loss of employment at Ashford, as well at other works be investigated by works managers who were to report back to the board as soon as possible. An option to change costing methods used at Ashford to make tenders for overseas work more attractive was explored. The savings found resulted in a reduction in costs of between 10 and 15 per cent, but a saving of 25 per cent needed to be found to allow the workshop to compete with European manufacturers. A detailed study was embarked upon to establish if any more savings could be achieved that would allow Ashford to remain viable, with a minimum of job losses.

In the meantime, the company proposed a possible reduction of the workforce at Ashford from 871 to 428. The job losses, if necessary were to be undertaken by the beginning of October 1981. The unions were to be informed through an announcement to be made at the Ashford Shopmen's Council on 31 August 1980.

The situation had not improved by August. After discussion between BREL, the Chief Mechanical and Electrical Engineer at British Rail and the BRB, the workload for maintenance of freight locomotives and wagons was agreed. Overtime was stopped completely to cover the shortfall without the necessity of job cuts, with both the Chief Engineer and the BRB informed that any further reduction in the agreed workload would result in necessary job losses.

Despite the agreements with the railway, BREL was put in a position where the workload being received into the maintenance workshops was likely to continue to contract. Management was working to reduce all working expenses. Overtime on all wagon repairs was ceased, and stock and work in progress levels were being reduced. Capital investment programmes were re-evaluated with a view to cancelling or deferring them until the prospects for the company improved.

The company also planned for a worst case situation, where job losses would be necessary to preserve the viability of the company. It was estimated that, if the current decline in work levels continued, the company would need to reduce the workforce employed in its wagon repair facilities from 2,243 staff to 1,604 by the end of October 1981, with the majority of the job losses likely to occur at Ashford. The possible redundancy programme was disclosed to the National Shopmen's Council at the end of August 1980, with all staff representatives at Ashford also being informed.

Meanwhile a new threat to the health of workers at Derby had been identified and reported to the board. The threat related, once again, to the handling of asbestos in BREL's works. Asbestos contamination reported by the workforce at Derby Litchurch Lane related to remnants of the material, which were still trapped behind certain panels, dropping from vehicles under maintenance when the panels were removed. It was investigated further during July and in August the company called in the Trades Union Congresses' industrial disease specialist. The specialist, Dr Owen, and the

BRB's own industrial disease specialist, produced a joint report covering the risks associated with droppage of asbestos in small quantities from vehicles in the works.

The report was circulated to both the trade unions and BREL management. Both men recommended that a further period of tests would be necessary, which was agreed by all parties. The tests would take place over an agreed eight-week period during which time any asbestos falls were to be noted. An immediate test of the atmosphere in the location of the fall was to be undertaken by the resident scientific services officer. All tests were to be observed by a representative from the TUC and from management.

Delays were still being experienced in the High Speed Train power car build programme, caused by lack of deliveries of power units from the suppliers, while construction of new wagons had been delayed by a failure in the supply of wheelsets caused by a steel workers strike. An export order for new wagons to Bangladesh was particularly affected by the wheelset delays.

The recession in traffic that was affecting the railway was not being seen by the BRB, or by BREL as impacting upon the Advanced Passenger Train Programme. The plan for construction of the fleet of new trains was still expected to go ahead despite continuing problems being found within the design of the experimental (APT-E) and prototype trains (APT-P). In order to undertake the build programme, BREL requested additional investment in the works which were to be involved in both construction and maintenance of the new trains. BREL estimated that the cost of the new facilities would amount to around £23.4million.

Crewe required an estimated £1.26million investment to make the works ready for construction of power cars and driving trailer vehicles. The construction of trailer cars for the new trains at Derby Litchurch Lane would require an investment of £6.71million, whilst Derby Locomotive Works would need £2.26million to support the construction of the new type of bogies. The last investment requested from British Rail was for Glasgow, which was estimated to need £13.21million for the creation of maintenance facilities to repair the trains once they were in service. The entire build programme was estimated to cost £250million for the fleet of trains for the West Coast Main Line, from which BREL requested an advance of £34.5million to be used for the advance purchase of long lead time materials.

Repairs of High Speed Train power cars and main line locomotives in the erecting shop at Derby Locomotive Works. From open day guide. *Author's collection*

Investment was still being approved for replacement of life expired machinery at locomotive workshops where replacement was necessary to keep the workshops functioning. An investment of £285,000 was approved for purchase of a new traverser for Crewe, with the existing one to be repaired as it was in poor condition.

BREL's difficulty in competing with European locomotive and rolling stock manufacturers arose once again in September 1980. The company lost a bid for 200 coaches for Córas Iompair Éireann which had been awarded to a French company. The bid from the company had been exceedingly low with the BREL directors believing that it was at less

Views inside Derby Locomotive Works. Clockwise from top left: Testing a 150hp Diesel engine in the Diesel Railcar Test House; General view of the heavy machine shop; Rewinding the main generator armature from a Diesel Electric Locomotive; Machining aluminium links an a numerically controlled milling machine in the erecting shop. From open day guide. *Author's collection*

than cost. The BREL board also believed that the company was receiving subsidies from the French government which was against free trade laws. The finance package that was being offered by the French company was also exceedingly generous. The board referred the order to the Department of Transport and the Foreign Office, as BRE-Metro had previously done with other orders lost to European manufacturers.

The political pressure applied on BREL's behalf resulted in the company being asked to go to Republic of Ireland to present their tender to Córas Iompair Éireann's senior management team. The meeting was scheduled for December, with BREL discussing options for financial support from the government to offset the advantages that European manufacturers possessed at the time. Fiscal support was also requested to offset the disadvantage being experienced by BREL due to inflation and high interest rates, as well as the strong pound.

The Commercial Director presented the revised tender and a brochure for the Mark III coach. The BREL delegation specifically pointed out the benefits that the coach would bring to the Irish railway and how it fitted their operational needs much more closely than the competitor's offering.

The future of Ashford Works was being discussed further. A meeting had taken place with trade union representatives on 20 August to discuss options for the works, the NUR and CS&EU both opposing redundancies as being necessary at the works. The works' future looked bleak; with no major export orders on the horizon for wagons that could be allocated to there, and the cancellation of 100 BBA steel carrying flat trucks by British Rail, the current production schedule would end in early 1981.

The options remaining to the company with regard to the workshops at Ashford were to reduce the workforce as had been proposed, or to mothball the works for a period of time in the hope that the commercial situation would improve. Two further options existed that BREL were exploring. The first was to investigate if the Chief Mechanical and Electrical Engineer's Department or the Chief Signal and Telegraph Engineer's Office at British Rail was letting out fabrication work externally that could be undertaken at Ashford. The second option that the company explored was whether it would be viable to transfer a proportion of coach repair work to the works from other sites, although the knock on impact of doing so on job security at those works also needed to be reviewed.

Computerisation of all of BREL's workshops was proceeding on schedule, with the company proposing to the BRB that the company should have its own team of dedicated computer programmers to undertake maintenance and modification of their software systems. British Rail was considering the potential to redeploy some of its programmers to BREL's staff. In September, the company began to look into the possibility of computerizing time and attendance and production documentation across its workshops. BREL conducted a joint consultation exercise with all the unions that represented staff across its locomotive works with a view to running a pilot scheme. The unions made it very clear that they were not prepared to cooperate with the scheme and would be instructing their members to refuse to support the pilot. The unions, rightly, believed that the computerisation of paper production documents and the computerisation of time and attendance records may result in future redundancies as a result of automation.

The year ended with more bad news for the company from the BRB. The recession being experienced by the British economy was impacting upon the railway. The railway informed BREL that it no longer needed nor was it able to afford the full output of railway vehicles from BREL's workshops. The company responded by cutting back all overtime but for the time being continued to support the full forty-hour working week. The majority of British industry had implemented a three-day week due to reduced demand, but BREL did not yet feel the need to do so. The company remained committed to protecting, as best it could, the livelihoods of all its staff.

The last board meeting of 1980 discussed the position that the company was in as the year drew to a close. The reduction of overtime achieved during the year had amounted to an equivalent of 1,750 full time staff and was viewed by the directors as not ideal but beneficial in preventing a large number of job losses. Despite the savings made in the year, the company still had a surplus of 550 staff whose roles were not supported by the reduced workload being received from the railway and had become surplus to BREL's staffing needs for the foreseeable future.

The staff impacted were to be offered a voluntary redundancy package, with those who were coming up to retirement age being offered an additional early retirement package. The trade unions had been involved in discussions with the BREL board and senior management as to the future of staffing at all of BREL's works and had accepted in principle the necessity for continued short time working, subject to further discussion, in order that jobs could be protected as much as possible and that potential capacity for taking on additional outside work would also be preserved.

The company was actively seeking additional work from outside British Rail and had continued to support the creation of a range of products aimed at export markets. The design team in Derby had been working on a standard design for an export coach which would be suitable for different climates across the world. A range of standard freight wagons from covered vans to hopper and mineral wagons had been developed, as had a standard 'export' bogie which could be provided for various gauges of track in use in Africa and across Asia.

The company had also been working with British Leyland on a joint venture for the provision of a new series of railbus trains to replace some of the first generation DMUs, specifically aimed at initially replacing those in use on lightly used branch lines and rural routes, which we will return to later. The provision of a new series of railbus vehicles began with the single Class 140 (R3) prototype would eventually evolve into the Class 141 Pacer built partly by BREL (chassis and mechanical elements) and partly by British Leyland (body, seating and control desks). An export version was also being developed and the Class 140 (R3) model was to be demonstrated in the Republic of Ireland in May 1981.

The BREL management and design team in Derby were also looking at providing a standard export diesel locomotive suitable for use in a variety of situations. The Class 58 locomotive was viewed as being ideal, although the manufacturing costs were currently too high and so an investigation was being undertaken within BREL to establish how costs could be reduced without impacting upon the quality of the completed locomotive, whilst achieving a commercially attractive price for potential export customers. The plan to base an export locomotive upon the Class 58 seems at first to have been a reasonable strategy, however, when compared to comparably priced locomotives from American manufacturers the Class 58 proved a little underpowered.

The last effort that was being made by the company to establish a regular intake of orders from abroad was being developed during the last few months of 1980. The company was in the process of developing a series of cross-braced standalone bogies which could be used with other manufacturers' stock as maintenance replacements or as part of newly purchased stock for overseas railway companies. The BREL management team believed that they may be able to secure work on part vehicle production where perhaps the whole vehicle was not likely to be ordered from them. Discussions were also being undertaken with the Gloucester Railway Carriage and Wagon Company about potentially forming a joint venture to handle this kind of work.

The end of 1980 saw the storm clouds begin to appear over Ashford Works. In a restricted circulation confidential minute included in the board minutes for the December board meeting, the directors discussed the

Most years under the BREL banner, one or more of the sites opened its doors to the public with an open day. This was seen as a good way to attract interest in the business, encourage younger people to follow the railway and share work opportunities with teenagers. Wolverton held such an event on 17 August 1985 with one of the main loco attractions being BREL-built Class 58 No. 58026 alongside the replica of Locomotion. *Colin J. Marsden*

future of the workshops in Kent. The board announced that following long consideration of all the options open to the company that would possibly enable the workshops to remain open, unfortunately no viable option remained. In accordance with this, the board had decided that notice would have to be given to staff at Ashford that the works would be closed, and that an action plan should be produced that would aim to close the works for the final time by the end of 1981. Provision was to be made for the required redundancy payments which would amount to an estimated £2.5million. The site was to be sold as soon as possible after closure as the value of the land and buildings was assessed to be currently greater than the written down book value in BREL's accounts.

The new year started in much the same vein, with 270 staff expected to have left the company from across all the workshops as part of the redundancy plan related to the need to reduce staffing levels by 550. The whole of the group leaving were aged over 64 and had accepted the company's offer of a combined early retirement and redundancy settlement.

The workshops in Derby and Crewe were still awaiting news of when construction of the planned fleet of Advanced Passenger Trains would begin. The order had yet to be placed by the BRB due to further delays in the programme caused by continuing issues with the tilt mechanism on the prototype trains which had not been resolved. The unresolved faults had resulted in an anticipated delay to the programme of a further two years before construction of the train was likely. In order to fill the gap in production that would result in the immediate short term, and to avoid penalty charges being levied upon the BRB by BREL, the railway was considering giving authority for the construction of four additional High Speed Train power cars at Crewe and 270 Mark III coaches at Derby, although no definite commitment had yet been made by the BRB.

The situation became progressively worse as the Advanced Passenger Train project fell further behind schedule in February. The BRB announced that the unresolved technical problems with the prototype trains and the recently agreed necessary alterations to the design of the production 'APT Squadron' were now likely to delay the start of construction of the train fleet by between two and three years. The trouble being experienced with the trains was to have a huge knock on effect within BREL. The delays were causing a production gap in the work schedules at both Crewe and Derby Litchurch Lane. The BREL board raised this with the British Rail Board and advised them that they required authority for alternate work which could be allocated to both sites to protect jobs and preserve production capacity for the start of construction of the 'APT Squadron'. They required that work should be authorised by the end of December 1981 for locomotive work, to fill the gap at Crewe, and by June 1981 for additional locomotive hauled Mark III and High Speed Train coaches to be allocated to Derby.

The BRB was informed that if this was not to be forthcoming or was delayed, then BREL would be obliged to levy underutilisation charges on the railway which would amount to £15million per year. The charges would not be made if outside work could be obtained to fill the void in the production plan. The company would also not need to levy the charges

HST power car No. 43190 in the HST test area at Crewe, 6 April 1982. *Colin J. Marsden*

if 'drastic de-manning' were undertaken. The latter option was viewed as very much less than desirable as it would impact upon the livelihoods of the men and women working in the affected workshops, a point made at a board meeting where this was discussed. The longer-term impact of a reduction in the workforce would be a serious short term delay in the eventual production of the train units once the issue was resolved and construction was authorised by the BRB, as well as unnecessary recruitment and training costs that would have to be incurred by BREL in order to restaff the workshops to meet the demand. These costs, it was felt, ought to be passed on to the BRB as part of the price of the new trains should the latter course of action have to be undertaken.

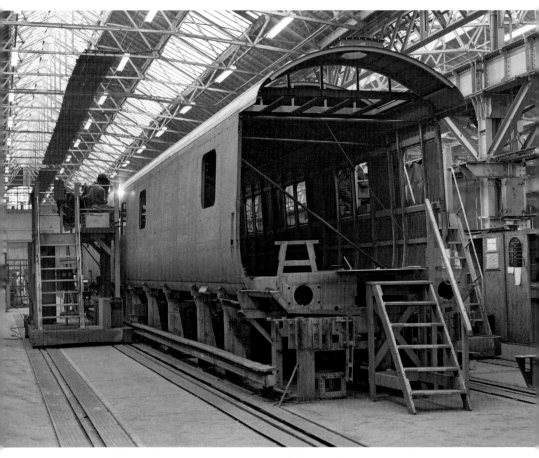

The entire fleet of loco-hauled Mk3 vehicles including the two types of sleeper coaches (SLE and SLEP) were assembled at Derby Litchurch Lane. Here on 2 April 1982 a SLE vehicle is seen in the fabrication shop. *Colin J. Marsden*

The likelihood of winning contracts from outside British Rail for work which could be undertaken to fill the production gaps was low at the time, however. Whilst 212 tenders had been submitted to a range of potential customers, totalling around £48million, BREL believed they would struggle to win many of the bids. Adverse trading conditions being experienced at the beginning of 1981 were making winning orders difficult for British exporters generally. The high inflation in the United Kingdom at the time, coupled with high interest rates and a strong pound were making British tenders less attractive against those from their European and American competitors.

The BREL board shared their concerns about the way in which overseas competitors were entering into railway equipment tenders with both the Foreign and Commonwealth Office and the Department for Trade and Industry in February, which was minuted in the board meeting for that month. The directors raised a complaint with the government that European railway equipment manufacturers were receiving an unfair commercial advantage because their governments were underwriting attractive financing packages, despite free trade rules, that the companies could offer as incentives to potential customers if they were to place their orders with them.

BREL anticipated that the shortfall in work being seen in the forward production plans was likely to mean an excess staffing in the workshops of around 650 employees. Voluntary redundancy plans had already been offered and had been taken up by 250 staff, with the workshop's staff being encouraged to continue to take up the offer of voluntary redundancy in place to meet the necessary reductions in manning levels without the need to embark of a programme of compulsory redundancies. The offer was improved in March with a view to making it more attractive and it was hoped would reduce overmanning from 650 to 120.

A tender for ten train sets in partnership with the General Electric Company (GEC), for export to Taiwan, was hoped to bring some work in which could be allocated to Derby Litchurch Lane, reducing the need for some redundancies if the order were won. BREL had also been working on redeploying work to avoid short term redundancies. The attempt to reallocate work had resulted in an industrial demarcation dispute between electricians and vehicle builders at York working on the Class 317 construction programme which had arisen during early March. The company was also seriously considering adopting short time working to attempt to protect jobs in the long term if they could.

The company was also struggling with the need to balance existing workload with apprentice intake. The staff surplus was likely to increase to around 400 due to an intake of 300 new apprentices. The apprentice intake had already been reduced by 400 from 1,130, the original planned intake. The company was struggling to balance the need to keep the apprentice schools occupied and the need to preserve skills in the workshops, against the lack of work currently passing through the shops. The company also had to take on a minimum number of apprentices each year or risk losing their exemption from the levy payable to the Engineering Industry Training Board by companies not investing in future skills.

Short time working was introduced at Horwich Foundry in May with consent from the trade unions representing staff working there. The foundry was closed for one week in five, although the maintenance facilities remained unaffected. The work involved in overhauling electric stock for Southern Region was shared between Horwich and Eastleigh, providing work for both sites. Horwich was also busy overhauling stock for Merseyrail.

The Managing Director of BREL reported that the further decreases in work being received from the railway and lack of outside orders being received was worsening the situation. He reported that, by the end of the year, the lack of work and the number of apprentices who were due to complete their training was likely to result in the overmanning of the

Horwich assisted Eastleigh with an overhaul project to increase the number of 4EPBs on the Southern Region. This was done by overhauling existing four-car sets and augmenting a number of two EPB sets to four vehicles by coupling modified SUB TS coaches between DMBS EPB coaches. A vehicle from 5234 receives attention at Horwich, 3 October 1981. *Colin J. Marsden*

Above: **Gutted interior** on intermediate coach from 5234 at Horwich in 1981. *Colin J. Marsden*

Below: **Class 503** Merseyrail Driving Trailer Second M29151M, undergoing a classified overhaul. Horwich Works, 3 October 1981. *Colin J. Marsden*

Electric Multiple Unit 5234 receives attention at Horwich as part of the project to provide more 4EPB units for Southern Region, 3 October 1981. *Colin J. Marsden*

workshops by around 1,400 staff and as a result compulsory redundancies were likely to be necessary unless the situation improved.

In June, the trade unions were consulted with an information paper being circulated to the NUR and CS&EU. The paper outlined BREL's plans for 1982, which included a reduction of 850 staff, the closure of Ashford Works, retraining of staff at Derby Litchurch Lane to enable them to undertake a wider variety of work, thus preserving their jobs, and the potential need to introduce four day working at some of their workshops. The NUR informed BREL in July that a motion had been passed at the recent NUR conference that if the planned closure of Ashford Works was to go ahead with compulsory redundancies, an official national NUR strike would result.

A different view of Electric Multiple Unit 5234 at Horwich in 1981 showing the extent of the workshop. *Colin J. Marsden*

As the summer progressed, the situation looked more hopeful. Export work was expected to be received to fill some of the excess capacity in the workshops. A tender to Córas Iompair Éireann for 124 mainline coaches in kit form worth £12million had been submitted in late May which was favourably received in the Republic of Ireland. Discussions were also ongoing with Northern Ireland Railways which had a similar requirement and were looking to base their new stock on that being proposed for the railways in the Republic of Ireland.

Firm commitment was received from Peru during early July for an order of 200 complete wagons and 200 cross braced export bogies, following intervention by Cecil Parkinson MP in his role as Minster of State for Trade after a letter of intent had initially been placed with an Argentinian company. An order was also received from Malaya for 40 cross braced export bogies with discussions underway for a follow-on order for a further 780 export bogies. BREL was expecting to receive a large order for 180 new bogies, with a further 156 to follow from the London Transport Executive for the refurbishment of tube stock, which senior management at London Transport were advising the London Transport Executive Board to accept. Discussions were underway with Iranian Railways for the supply of locomotives protected against dust and sandstorms for delivery within three months. BREL was proposing to meet the requirement with forty modified and refurbished redundant Class 46 locomotives and had tendered accordingly.

The order from the Republic of Ireland was, however, not forthcoming. The Irish government in Dublin suspended investment in its railways due to an increasingly worsening economic situation in the country. The order from Iran was not received, the tender expiring with no indication from the Iranian Railway of an intention to proceed with a purchase. The Argentinians were also working hard to try and retrieve the order from Peru but by August the Peruvian Railway was still continuing with BREL as the supplier of its wagons and bogies. A firm order had been received from London Transport for 180 replacement bogies for its tube fleet but the order for Malaya was looking increasing unlikely to be received. The Malayan government was putting political pressure on Malayan Railways to place the order on a Malayan owned company with technical assistance being supplied by a South Korean manufacturer.

The low workload was still causing overmanning at a number of workshops in September. A surplus of 604 skilled staff was estimated, but at the same time the company was short of 107 vehicle builders and electricians. The company proposed retraining to address the shortages and preserve some jobs, mainly at Derby Litchurch Lane. The proposal was rejected by the vehicle builders at Derby, and consequently the company was forced to announce 120 redundancies in other trades for whom there was no work available. At the same time, BREL reallocated a quarter of the carriage repair work from Derby to other works, with surplus staff at Derby being given the option of transferring to fill vacancies at other sites, undertaking retraining, or otherwise being encouraged to accept voluntary redundancy. In September, the company also found it necessary to reduce headcount in its accounts department as continuing advances in computerisation of clerical work had reduced the need for staff and thus twelve management and sixty clerical posts would be eliminated during 1982.

Relations with Peruvian Railways remained good as the year came to an end with BREL discussing potential sales of the joint venture BRE-Leyland Railbus as part of the joint venture's exploitation of the potential they saw in the new train. As a result it was agreed with both British Rail and the BRB that the R3 Railbus prototype should be withdrawn from British Rail service and returned to BREL for refurbishment prior to being sent to Peru for trials. Discussions were still ongoing in December with Peruvian Railways about where the railway would prefer to conduct the trials of the train.

The year ended with a mixed outlook for the company. Workload was down but overseas orders seemed to be more likely than earlier in the year. Industrial relations were shaky at some locations with the threat of a national NUR strike in the new year if Ashford Works was to close, although at other locations industrial relations were as good as they had been for some time. The new year would however bring new challenges.

Chapter 9
HARD TIMES

The year 1982 began with more bad news for BREL with the announcement from the BRB that they had imposed a £250million ceiling for locomotives and rolling stock which would impact the company's workshops dramatically. Sales had already been down by 8 per cent against the 1981 budget at a total of £443million. The potential loss of half of BREL's income from work undertaken for the railway was potentially disastrous. As a result of the disruption to the production and maintenance plans caused by the dramatic reduction of the work that could be expected from British Rail, BREL management prepared a proposal for a complete reorganisation of the workshops for submission to the BREL board for discussion. The plan to close the works at Ashford went ahead, there being no work available for the workshops, and despite the threat of a national strike by the NUR.

The BREL board informed the British Railways Joint Consultative Council that the overcapacity that would result from British Rail's decision to dramatically reduce investment in stock and maintenance would have serious implications for the company and its staff. The company also informed the General Secretaries of the Transport Salaried Staffs' Association (TSSA) and British Transport Officers' Guild (BTOG) unions of the potential redundancies that would arise should the railway continue to reduce investment by letter on 21 April 1982. The unions informed BREL that the planned reductions in workload would be discussed at the meeting of the Informal Liaison Committee of the Railway Shopmen's National Council on 22 April.

In an internal BREL memo dated 28 April 1982 to T.B. Reid and C.A. Rose, R.H. Wilcox (all on the BREL Board) discussed the responses from the unions. The TSSA had informed BREL that they wished to discuss the situation directly with British Rail at the next meeting of the British Rail Joint Consultative Committee which was due to take place on 30 April. A second letter sent to the unions further clarifying the situation with regard to the salaried staff employed by BREL and the impact of the reductions in workload from the railway sent on 21 April had not arrived until the 26th, after the Liaison Committee had met and thus the unions had not had chance to discuss the impending reductions with CS&EU and the NUR.

Wilcox also suggested that it would be a good time for the BREL Joint Consultative Committee to meet for the first time since November 1980 in order that an action plan could be formulated both internally and with the trade unions to present a joint protest to the BRB explaining the impact on jobs and capacity, with a view to protecting as many jobs as possible and also lobbying British Rail not to reduce investment in the railway. The reductions in workload were calculated to potentially mean a reduction in staff by half at Swindon, with Horwich (with the exception of the foundry) and Shildon facing complete closure according to Wilcox's calculations, with 789 salaried positions being surplus to the company's requirements, across all of BREL's workshop sites, if the workload reduction were to go ahead.

A large number of, 'Flat Top' conversions were undertaken at Horwich from GUV vans for use on London Midland electrification. They provided a flat roof from which work could be undertaken on the 25kV ac overhead. Access was by way of a roof hatch. The sets operated in rakes of six to eight vehicles. *Colin J. Marsden*

Meanwhile the BREL directors had approached both the BRB and all the trade unions with a view to establishing how BREL's works capacity could be preserved. Efforts were being made to secure a viable future for the workshops in the current difficult financial climate being experienced by British Rail. Discussions were undertaken at board level within BREL to establish what could be done to protect jobs, preserve capacity to allow future work to be bid for, whilst keeping the company and the workshops viable. BREL asked the railway to provide financial support for the development of new coaches and lightweight DMUs for export. The railway was also asked to invest in new stock, refurbishment of existing stock and repairs to stock in order to reduce underutilisation within the works. The unions were consulted and informed that the future was somewhat dependent upon investment within British Rail and the knock on work for BREL, but also that a programme of cost reductions and efficiency improvements would need to be undertaken to allow the company to be competitive on export work, but also to allow it to justify retaining its share of British Rail work.

BREL proposed an investment of £3.6million for a new 'International Coach' based upon the existing Mark III design, but with features and options more attractive to an export customer. The coach was to be lightweight, but high strength allowing it to be used on more lightly built railways in parts of Africa and South America as well as the more heavily engineered lines in other parts of Africa and Asia. The proposed coach was to be designed to be built in flexible jigs allowing different requirements to be easily and cost effectively met, making the proposed new coach more attractive to the widest possible export markets.

The landscape had changed for BREL in the early 1980s. The company no longer had a monopoly on work from British Rail and government drives to enforce competitive tendering in the public sector also impacted on the nationalised railway. The open tendering for business in the rail industry was also being driven by companies like Metro-Cammell. BREL's erstwhile partner in the export business was now demanding equal access to railway business and a share of work available from British Rail. Metro-Cammell frequently demanded that work be allocated to them to keep their own workshops fully utilised, often at the expense of the BREL workshops. The division of the available work from the railway to other manufacturers would have a huge ongoing impact upon BREL.

The close control of BREL by the BRB caused more trouble for the company in the 1980s than it had in the 1970s. Whilst the private companies like Metro-Cammell and Gloucester Railway Carriage and Wagon had complete business autonomy to make their own decisions based upon business needs, BREL was restricted by the demands placed upon it by the BRB which prevented the business responding to market needs and changing engineering requirements in the 1980s.

In view of the difficult situation BREL found itself in, plans were being made to reorganise the company as outlined in the proposals received earlier in the year from management. A restricted minute in the March 1982 board meeting minutes referred to a provision made in the accounts for 1982 for potential redundancy payments relating to planned closures of workshops as agreed by the directors of the company, but the closure plans made in March were not stated in the main minutes for obvious reasons, and it did not mention the names of the works that might be impacted should the plans need to be implemented.

A British Railway Board memo dated March 1982 gives more detail of the planned restricting of BREL related to the declining need for its services by the railway. The memo described in detail the options that were being considered by the BREL board in order to restructure the company in line with future requirements. It was anticipated that the company would need to reduce its staff levels by one fifth, but this was dependent upon whether planned British Rail new build programmes were to be authorised, or whether they were to be delayed or abandoned entirely. The reduction was also dependent upon future investment to be made by the railway, specifically proposals for electrification and the related need for new electric locomotives and multiple units, and the Advanced Passenger Train programme, which was experiencing considerable delays.

In order to retain capacity at some workshops, it was proposed to transfer work to works which were to remain open. Wagon construction was planned to be transferred from Shildon to Doncaster, with wagon repairs being transferred away from Swindon to Doncaster, Temple Mills and Derby Litchurch Lane. Shildon Works would therefore close once the remaining in progress work had been completed. Construction of the Class 58 fleet was potentially to be transferred to Crewe, while some of the EMU refurbishments planned to be undertaken at Swindon would be transferred to Derby Litchurch Lane. The repair work being undertaken on coaches and wagons at Horwich would be transferred away to Wolverton and Eastleigh, and to Wolverton and Temple Mills respectively. It was planned that Horwich's maintenance facilities would then be closed, but the foundry would remain open.

A second stage of rationalisation had been included in the proposals given to the BRB. The forecast workload for 1984 to 1986 would leave BREL with excess capacity from the middle of 1984, even after the closure of Shildon, Horwich and the run-down of Swindon. Swindon was chosen to be run down as the layout of its workshops was proving difficult to manage with a lot of manual handling of work being required as it needed to be moved between buildings in different parts of the site. Efficiency programmes had been implemented to attempt to save the workshops from job losses and contraction but the arrangement of buildings and workshops on the site had proved to be impossible to implement effective changes.

The reducing workloads anticipated by BREL in relation to the forecast requirements being supplied by the railway meant that it would be

The west end of the main Crewe erecting shop was used to strip locos arriving for repair. Class 47 No. 47214 is seen in the stripping area, 6 April 1982. *Colin J. Marsden*

necessary for Swindon to close completely, with one other medium sized works to be closed with it by the end of 1984. At the time, indications were that this would affect Derby Locomotive Works, although Derby Litchurch Lane would remain unaffected. British Rail's policy on its wagon load business, as indicated at the time, would be likely to reduce the requirement for repairs on a smaller fleet. It was envisaged that Temple Mills was likely to have run out of work and have to be closed by the end of 1985.

BREL had informed the BRB that the planned rationalisation was at proposal stage only and the planned changes were dependent upon British Rail's major investment policy over the coming few years. The company needed more detailed forecasts of the railway's requirements and the timely authorisation of construction and maintenance programmes. The company also needed to be informed of the BRB's plans with respect to the Advanced Passenger Train (R) programme, its plans for electrification of other routes, and likely needs for new electric stock, as well as more visibility of the railway's intended DMU replacement policy. If these were forthcoming, the company believed that most closures and job losses could be avoided.

Derby Locomotive Works was one of BREL's main locomotive repair facilities, 30 September 1985. 'Peak' 45115, is captured during a light overhaul. *Colin J. Marsden*

There was more hope coming from the company's export drive. In March, an order was won from Córas Iompair Éireann for seventy-two Mark III coaches with an option for a further fifty-two. Discussions with Kenyan Railways regarding a potential order for coaches was proceeding well, with the company also being invited to tender for rolling stock for the Nigerian railway worth up to £100million.

Spring saw some respite for the company. The BRB approved an order for construction of twenty railbuses in two car sets, although the order still had to be approved by the Department of Transport. The export drive in Africa was beginning to yield potential results with an order promised for mid-April from Kenya for seventy-four coaches worth £24million, which was eventually signed in May. BREL's request for financial assistance for the development of the International Coach was progressing well, the funding being granted by the Railway Investment Committee, final approval being needed only from the BRB who were indicating a favourable outcome. The Department of Transport indicated that the creation of a coach purely for export and not for use by British Rail did not breach the terms of the Transport Act under which BREL had been created. The Department of Trade and Industry also indicated that the company qualified for a government grant for research related to the new coach.

Export orders appeared to offer more hope as the year progressed. Balfour Beatty, as the main contractor for engineering and infrastructure programmes being undertaken by Panamanian Railways, had approached BREL with an invitation to tender for ten coaches and fifty-six wagons.

The long term future was not looking so good though. The work placed on BREL by the railway and likely outside contracts left a discrepancy between the capacity available and the production schedule for 1983. It was estimated that the company had an excess of 3,600 staff for the year with the order book as it stood.

The company was also losing staff to private engineering firms who were paying higher wages, BREL being restricted by the BRB in responding to competitive wages being paid outside the railway. BREL was only able to pay salaries and wages which had been approved by the BRB in their pay scales, and even though BREL was nominally an independent company, its sole ownership by the railway restricted its ability to make commercially necessary decisions such as these. As a result, the company was forecasting to be 714 waged staff and 125 salaried staff short of the budgeted required staffing level by the end of 1982. The overstaffing forecast to be seen by the end of 1983 might be offset by the continued haemorrhaging of skilled and experienced staff to other companies, although the skills loss was beginning to be felt within some parts of the business.

The BRB delayed the implementation of the capacity reduction programme being proposed by BREL in response to the workload being provided by the railway. The BREL board required authorisation from the BRB to undertake such a programme, which was refused in June. Instead, a joint working party was set up to review the distribution of the 1983 workload on a twelve workshop basis, meaning one more works would be expected to close, since Ashford had already closed, to meet the twelve intended to go forward.

The committee also involved the Manpower Services Commission with a view to keeping the Works Training School at Swindon open for another twelve months instead of closing it as had been planned in the proposals to rationalise BREL's workshops. The number of apprentices being recruited by BREL in 1982 had reduced to 539, the lowest for eight years. The spare capacity for engineering training was taken up by the Manpower Services Commission for one year courses for unemployed school leavers. The apprentice schools at Derby, Horwich and Swindon all filled the excess space through school leaver courses, for which the Manpower Services Commission provided funding delaying the need to close the schools due to the lack of apprentices.

The company was experiencing difficulty and delay in the construction programme in May for the Class 510 EMUs at York, but as in the past, the setbacks were not of its making. Trouble in the supply chain was delaying completion of units due to the unavailability of satisfactory traction equipment from the manufacturer. Discussions were being undertaken between the directors of the manufacturer and BREL directors with a view to resolving the situation as soon as possible. The companies agreed that the problem could be resolved by seconding a BREL engineer to the company from June. The resident BREL engineer would be responsible for liaising between the two companies and ensuring quality and delivery requirements were met.

The inability of the company to be competitive with its export pricing continued to trouble the company. A tender for 575 wagons to Saudi Arabia was, for example, purely lost on price, as the design and delivery times were said to be perfectly acceptable to the Saudi Railway authorities. The competing bid which won the order had been presented at what BREL management believed to be cost price with only the materials costs being covered by the price being offered. To BREL, this indicated considerable unfair government subsidy for foreign companies competing for the same business BREL was bidding for and with this in mind, all future tenders were being prepared to be as competitive as possible with only a small allowance made to cover surplus capacity fixed costs in the price. A tender for a further 850 wagons and 100 brake vans for Saudi Arabia as well as a new tender for 287 coaches for Nigerian Railways had been submitted with this in mind. Nigerian Railways invited BREL to tender for more work amounting to 650 covered goods wagons, 200 container wagons, 100 bogie brake vans, 160 generator coaches, 63 'de-luxe' coaches and 64 suburban coaches.

The chances of winning business from Nigeria did not seem good, though. In July, BREL was informed by the Nigerians that they were tenth out of twelve bidders for the wagons and brake vans order on price and fourth out of seven on the bid for the coach order. The tender for the new coaches from BREL, at £49million was double that of the bid from Korea, and 50 per cent higher than the bid from Japan.

The middle of the year saw BREL suffering the impact of industrial action both within BREL and on the railway. The industrial action undertaken by ASLEF that summer affected output of repair work since the trains were not being delivered to the workshops for maintenance, or maintenance had been delayed due to the lower mileages being run. Strikes within BREL had cost the company the equivalent of just under 26,000 man hours due to a stoppage at Glasgow whilst ongoing disputes with the NUR had cost the company over £1.5million worth of output.

At the same time that the industrial action was disrupting production and maintenance activities within BREL, the company was discussing the future of the workshops at Swindon. A meeting that took place at Swindon on 10 May 1982 involved senior management from Swindon and BREL directors. The meeting had been called to discuss the possible options for the future at the works.

Improvements in productivity and utilisation of trains on the railway had led to a reduction in the train fleets by British Rail with a knock on effect on maintenance work coming to the workshops across BREL where the fewer trains in service impacted upon the need for large repair facilities. The reduction in the railway's train fleet had in turn resulted in a requirement for fewer new trains and other rolling stock. As a result, the number of construction orders being received from the BRB had steadily reduced.

The lack of repair jobs and purchases of new rolling stock meant that the work available was not sufficient to keep all of BREL's workshops utilised to a level where costs were absorbed by the revenue being generated.

Workload was not improving during the summer either. The authorisation from the Department of Transport for the twenty two-car Class 141 railbuses was still awaited in August, whilst the railway had informed BREL that the anticipated 300 service wagon order to be constructed at Shildon was now not going to be placed. Construction of Mark III coaches at Derby Litchurch Lane was also showing an anticipated gap of three months between batches of coaches which could not be filled with other work. Export orders were, however, being won. Kenya Railways had placed an order for seventy-four coaches worth £23.8million, and Northern Ireland Railways had agreed to purchase the R3 Railbus for its branch line and lightly used services.

The picture looked no better in September. The BRB was still unable to authorise BREL to begin construction of the 180 Mark III coaches which had been promised to fill the workshops at Derby, whilst authorisation was still awaited for thirty-three long welded rail carrying wagons and

The entire fleet of Mark III HST vehicles, with the exception of the power cars were built at Derby Litchurch Lane. TSO 42316 is seen after completion, 2 April 1982. *Colin J. Marsden*

confirmation of requirements had not arrived from the Parcels division of the railway with regard to their new vehicle needs. The authorisation for the twenty Class 141 sets that had been delayed at the Department of Transport had finally been received verbally, although BREL was still waiting for the BRB to decide upon timings.

The company undertook a rationalisation of its management staff in August based upon anticipated future structure, with BREL headquarters in Derby being the first to see reductions in management. The production department reduced its management headcount by four, with technical staff also losing three management posts, and four supervisors, personnel losing four managers, whilst the purchasing and supplies department lost eight management roles.

The steadily decreasing workload in the workshops going into September 1982 and on into the new year, meant that the company was now expecting a surplus of 4,894 staff in a variety of roles across all its sites by the end of 1983.

Derby Litchurch Lane undertook overhauls on Motorail flat wagons. B749134 is seen in the yard at Derby on 2 April 1982. *Colin J. Marsden*

Motorail flat FVV B745643 is seen under repair at BREL Derby Litchurch Lane, 2 April 1982. *Colin J. Marsden*

It was hoped to avoid compulsory redundancies through a programme of voluntary redundancy which had already begun. Five hundred and thirty-one staff had already taken voluntary redundancy and left the business, with another 1,928 staff having requested to leave voluntarily with the settlements having been agreed and termination dates in place. The personnel department at BREL headquarters had another 3,100 requests for voluntary redundancy package estimates, although the company felt that not everyone who had requested voluntary redundancy could be allowed to leave due to a shortage of skills in some areas of the business.

The company was concerned that the staff who had volunteered to leave the business could cause an imbalance in shifts. A number of semi-skilled vacancies existed which could potentially be filled by some of the skilled grades, protecting their jobs whilst meeting the company's need to downsize in some areas, and possibly rebalancing the shift manpower. The NUR was opposed to the redeployment of skilled staff into semi-skilled roles which caused concern among the company's directors as around 1,400 staff would be impacted and would have to be made redundant if they couldn't be redeployed elsewhere in the workshops.

The end of the year saw all of the works, with the exception of Horwich, having reduced the manpower employed to the budgeted numbers, although it was envisaged that a small number of compulsory redundancies would be required early in 1983. The company now employed 5,083 salaried staff (down from 5,391 in January), and 27,192 waged staff (down from 27,767 in January). The reductions and redeployment of staff during the year was envisaged to have met the company's needs in the short term with a second phase of additional compulsory redundancies to be needed after January 1983.

The company was disadvantaged by the move towards more competitive tendering for railway business in the 1980s. The impact of the new policy within British Rail can be clearly seen in the case of the new Class 89 locomotive. The BRB had opted to reject the tender for the construction of the locomotive from BREL, instead opting for the joint tender from Brush and GEC. The tenders from the two companies, ironically included BREL as sub-contractor in the construction of the locomotive which meant that the work would be undertaken by the company anyway but probably at a cost premium due to the margins which both Brush and GEC would need to make on the price quoted to them by BREL. The strange situation was made even more unfathomable to all concerned in the project by the BRB's refusal to enter into correspondence directly with BREL regarding any queries or problems that arose in the construction programme, only being prepared to deal with Brush or GEC who would have to act as intermediary.

A similarly bizarre decision was made by the BRB, to the detriment of BREL, in November with the placing of the order for four prototype three car lightweight DMUs for Provincial Services. The BRB split the tender, placing orders for two prototypes of the same vehicles with both BREL and Metro-Cammell. BREL did receive a complete order from the railway late in the year. Authorisation was given for construction of twenty-three-car Class 510 sets for Southern Region in November, worth £10.5million to the company.

The international coach project was, however, making good progress by November 1982. The initial designs were complete and the body shell of the prototype was due to be completed by October 1983 for testing, with a complete demonstration vehicle, built to British gauge, due to be ready for use by January 1985, although this would ultimately be delayed until 1986.

The new year saw a milestone for BREL with the handover of the first completed Class 58 locomotive to British Rail. The locomotive was still seen as being a promising basis for a successful export locomotive, even though that never transpired, but at the time, BREL were placing great hopes in it. The company also began to look abroad for new sources of business, a proposal being put to the board for the creation of a sales office in the United States, although this time the company would go it alone after its experiences with BRE-Metro and the acrimonious split with Metro-Cammell. It was proposed that the office in America would be staffed with personnel seconded from the United Kingdom rather than employing local people.

A lot of optimism was connected to the Class 58 despite no export orders being on hand for the locomotive, and no final dedicated designs having been produced for an international version. The company, despite the great hope that was being placed in the Class 58, still needed to reduce its workforce in accordance with the work available to the workshops in the current maintenance and production plans. Notices of displacement were sent out accordingly with 53 staff at Doncaster, 134 at Shildon and 251 at Wolverton being placed at risk of redundancy in January. A further 438 staff at the three workshop sites were informed that they were facing redundancy with the formal notices being sent to those concerned in February. The company was, at the same time, in discussion with the unions hoping that they would consider downgrading some of the roles and leasing between trades to allow a reduction in the number of redundancies that would be needed across all three of the sites.

Despite the efforts being made within BREL and by the trade unions, the company ultimately needed to reduce its capacity due to the continuing reduction in work from the railway, and the likelihood that the workload would remain low for the foreseeable future. The excess capacity compared to the existing and future workload created the need to reduce the company's workshops by a fifth. The planned contraction created a need to make 3,000 of the workforce redundant, which was planned to be achieved initially by voluntary redundancy offers followed, if necessary, by compulsory redundancies.

The new year had started with the company possessing twelve works and employing a total of 31,100 staff. The company had already downsized its operations due to decreasing workloads, resulting in the loss of 5,500 jobs during 1981 and 1982. The BREL board had proposed a series of additional staff reductions and workshop rationalisation as a result of the discussions that had been undertaken at various board meetings, which in turn led to the restricted meeting minute from March 1982. The proposals were initially deferred by the BRB in June 1982, but were finally authorised by the board at their meeting on 10 February 1983. A press release was issued by the BRB in February 1983.

The resulting programme involved the reallocation of all rolling stock maintenance work from Horwich to other workshops with the resulting closure of all the workshops there with the exception of the foundry. The works at Temple Mills was to close completely as soon as possible. The works at Shildon was to be gradually run down with complete closure to be achieved during 1984. The intention was announced to the unions at those workshops, with notices of closure sent out to the staff at Temple Mills and Shildon and also those working in the maintenance workshops at Horwich, whilst the staff in the Horwich Foundry were reassured that their jobs were safe on 1 August. Closure of the workshops at Temple Mills and the parts of Horwich that were to shut down finally occurred on 31 December 1983. The works at Shildon followed, with the gates closing for the last time in June 1984. BREL would start 1985 with nine workshop sites and the foundry at Horwich.

The closures and other rationalisation of workshops which were to remain open was envisaged to have reduced the workforce to 26,700 in total by the end of 1983, a reduction of 4,398. The company was aware that the closure of Shildon would cause immense hardship in that area as the railway workshops were the only employer in the area. The company took action to soften the blow as best they could, which will be returned to later.

The workshops that were being reallocated work which had originally been planned for Horwich, Shildon and Temple Mills found that the workforce refused to undertake any of the transferred activities. At the same time, the trade unions which represented staff at the three works which were to close approached BREL's directors with a proposal to keep the works open. The BREL committee set up to work through the closure of the works and any options that remained to keep them open welcomed the proposals but after working them through decided that they did not reduce costs or provide better utilisation within the three sites and so the proposals were rejected, and the decision made that the three sites would need to be closed. Final notices were consequently given to the 2,743 staff affected, to take effect on 1 August.

The NUR and CS&EU responded to the announcements with a number of instructions to its members. The unions instructed all staff that had been issued with a notice of redundancy to reject them, whilst their members at the other works were instructed to block all transfers of work from Horwich, Shildon and Temple Mills. The unions also gave a general instruction that all of their members should refuse to cooperate with BREL management in any rationalisation schemes at the other workshops.

Export orders did not provide any respite which may have given the company work to keep the workshops open. The order from Northern Ireland Railways which was under discussion at the end of the 1982 had still not materialised in March 1983. The proposal had been complicated by what BREL's directors referred as a 'very cheap French bid' for stainless steel trains. BREL responded with a cheaper alternative based upon a combination of the Mark I coach underframe and the Class 510 body, for a cost lower than the French bid and within the budget which Northern Ireland Railways had informed the company was available.

The order was received by BREL shortly thereafter with work to commence on the new trains for Northern Ireland at Wolverton workshops in October. The order consisted of three three-car diesel electric multiple units with an option for another six units if Northern Ireland Railways decided to take that up, depending upon the availability of budget in Belfast.

Despite the difficulties being experienced by the company, BREL continued to invest in apprenticeships to preserve skills for the long term in the workshops which were envisaged to still be needed in the future. The intake for 1983 reported to the board in July was 490, the lowest in ten years, but still the largest single apprenticeship scheme in Britain at the time.

The railway gave authorisation for an additional refurbishment programme which would provide some respite for the company in the short-term during August 1983. The railway decided to embark on a programme to extend the life of the Class 303 EMUs used around Glasgow. Fifty sets of three cars each were to be overhauled and refurbished for use by Provincial ScotRail at a cost of just over £16million. The completed sets

The workshops at BREL undertook contract work for the preservation movement as well as industry. London and South Western Railway M7 30053 is in the training school workshops at Derby Litchurch Lane, 2 April 1982. *Colin J. Marsden*

were to be turned out in the new bright orange and black livery introduced by the Strathclyde Passenger Transport Executive.

More good news was received by BREL in November when Córas Iompair Éireann opted to take up an option for an additional fifty-two Mark III coaches, worth just over £9.5million, which had been an option on an older order. The BRB also placed an order for a new batch of sixty Mark III coaches worth just over £11million. The coaches would provide work for Derby Litchurch Lane for the immediate short term.

The company's efforts to find alternative revenue streams had moved forward during 1983. The company had discussed the possibility of selling the Class 141 lightweight DMUs to the railways in the United States and South America with British Leyland who had agreed to allow BREL to sell the trains in the Americas as a representative of the joint construction venture. The company had thus registered the names 'BREL Inc.' and 'BRE-Leyland Inc.' within the United States. Proposals for the structure of the new American subsidiary of BREL remained under discussion by the board but were progressing toward fruition.

The new agreement relating to the Americas included the improved lightweight DMU which would become the Class 142. BREL and British Leyland had agreed to extend their joint venture during late November 1983, in order to bid for requirements from British Rail for a replacement multiple unit to meet demand on lightly used routes and to increase the availability of units above the twenty Class 141 units currently in service on the railway. BREL and British Leyland both saw a potential for the new units to form the basis of an export train which both companies could potentially benefit from commercially. The possibility of any export orders, if any were to be forthcoming, for the trains from the Americas was still a long way in the future.

The annual report and accounts for the year reflected the economic difficulties which the company had been experiencing over the last two years. The Chairman's review of the year stated that the company had experienced difficult trading conditions. The volume of new build and repairs had reduced with British Rail's requirement forecasts continuing to decline. Whilst overhead savings of around £16million had been achieved it had also been necessary to reduce staff employed by BREL by 3,600. The company had announced that as a result of reduced work coming into the workshops, Shildon and Temple Mills were to be closed completely whilst only the foundry facilities at Horwich would remain open, the rest of the site being closed. Closures of Temple Mills and Horwich were to have been completed by the end of 1983, with Shildon closing by mid-1984. The announcement had been made by letter to all the affected trade unions on 18 February.

Turnover continued to decline compared to the previous two years, the achieved turnover for 1982 standing at £470.4million down on the 1982 figure, with the turnover for 1983 declining again to £436.97million. Profits were however still being made with the profitability of the company increasing slightly from £6.62million in 1982 up to £10.82million in 1983.

The volume of work being undertaken had declined drastically with only twenty-seven new locomotives completed in both 1982 and 1983. New build coaches had declined from 140 in 1982 to just 87 in 1983, although the number of new Diesel and Electric Multiple Units had increased from 195 to 226. The most dramatic decline, and clearly this was behind the rationale that the works at Shildon should be closed, was a reduction from 832 new 'Revenue and Service wagons' in 1982 to a paltry 93 completed in 1983.

Repair work was dwindling in the same manner as new build over the two years. Locomotive repairs were down 1,013, to 937 in 1983. Coach repairs had declined from 7,870, in 1982 to 6,584, whilst wagon repairs had fallen from the 1982 completion figure of 14,544 to 10,541.

One note of optimism was sounded in the accounts for the year, with hope that the delivery of the first 'new lightweight, fuel efficient Railbus' in late 1983 would be followed by the commencement of production of railbuses for South East Asia, Europe and the United States, even though firm orders had yet to be received.

First generation DMMU stock was overhauled by various BREL sites, including Derby Litchurch Lane, Doncaster, Glasgow and Swindon. Class 101 DTCL No. M56392 is receiving a general overhaul at Litchurch Lane, 2 April 1982. *Colin J. Marsden*

Whether the optimism expressed in parts of the report would become reality, or whether the declining fortunes that the company was experiencing would continue would be revealed in the new year.

One other small reason for optimism arose as the year ended. BREL's continual lobbying of the BRB for more clarity and a more structured working relationship achieved a small improvement in visibility of workload. British Rail agreed to provide a contract relating to overhaul requirements relating to the Mark II(d) fleet of coaches over the next three years, providing a small degree of certainty against which BREL could plan.

An initial trial was to be undertaken for twelve months beginning in January 1984, with the contract to be reviewed and renewed annually in advance. All shopping was to be controlled centrally to ensure adherence by both sides to the plan, and the computerised vehicle shopping system being trialled at Wolverton should be used. The railway guaranteed to provide 186 coaches for classified repair and overhaul in 1984, 175 in 1985, and finally 165 in 1986. Further overhauls would be planned as each year progressed. The planned work was to be undertaken at either Derby Litchurch Lane, Glasgow, Wolverton or York, although any optimism felt at Glasgow would be destroyed by events that would transpire during the autumn of 1984.

BREL Wolverton Works wheel shop, 17 August 1985. *Colin J. Marsden*

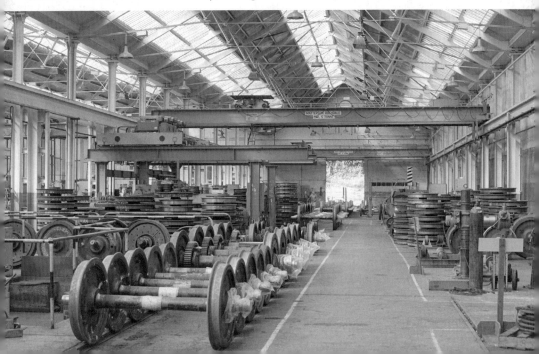

Chapter 10

CONTRACTION AND REORGANISATION

The year 1984 began with a decision to introduce short time working at York. Whilst the workshops had a reasonable amount of EMU related work, it did not provide full utilisation of the facilities at the site and short time working was chosen as an alternative to job losses.

Temple Mills and Horwich workshops had been closed, with the exception of the foundry at the latter site. A cadre of 110 staff remained at Horwich, who were engaged in clearing and securing the closed parts of the works, but who were expected to have left the company by the end of April. Further staff reductions were effectively achieved by the board's decision to not undertake any apprenticeship programmes at all in 1984.

The company also looked to rationalise the use of its office facilities in Derby during the early part of 1984. The headquarters functions located within Derwent House in the Rail Technology Centre located opposite Derby Litchurch Lane Workshop were to be relocated into an office building located in the centre of Derby. St Peter's House in Gower Street became the new centre of operations away from the London headquarters office with staff moving into the building during the early part of the year. The building still stands but has now been converted into flats.

The company continued to attempt to find new work from outside British Rail, although the board continued to lobby the BRB for the acceleration of decision making relating to new trains and were hopeful of achieving agreement on increased and more regular maintenance of the railway's fleet of locomotives and rolling stock. The BREL board was also considering the possibility of extending the railbus concept to create a range of light rail vehicles for sale to municipal authorities, both at home and abroad, who were revisiting their urban transport requirements.

The company directors still believed that an export drive was an important part of their commercial strategy going forward. The formation of a sales company in the United States to gain both a presence in the Americas and a share of what was hoped would be a lucrative export market throughout all of North and South America for British-made trains. To that end, the formation of BRE-Leyland had been progressed with the BRB finally giving authorisation for BREL to proceed with the creation of the new subsidiary companies.

The requirement for permission to be given by the railway board illustrates again how little autonomy the company had in reality, despite the intention when it was created that it should be a completely independent private company which just happened to be owned solely by the BRB. The unwillingness of the BRB to let BREL control its own commercial activities, and interference from the Department of Transport under various governments from both the main political parties, would prevent the company from achieving its full potential.

Once able to do so, BREL immediately embarked on the creation of two separate American subsidiary companies to operate throughout the Americas using the names already registered in the United States. BRE-Leyland was formed to sell and service the Class 141 and Class 142 railbuses into the North and South American countries, although all manufacturing would be undertaken in BREL workshops in Britain. BREL Inc. was created to sell and service all other products manufactured by BREL other than the BRE-Leyland Railbuses.

The export drive progressed in other directions with the development of the international coach progressing well. The demonstration coach was to be ready for operational testing by the middle of the year with a view to having a full demonstration train in place after testing had been completed. British Railways Investment Committee gave approval for the budget needed for BREL to create and operate a demonstration train to accommodate visiting dignitaries from both overseas governments and overseas railways with a view to winning orders for, what was hoped to be, large numbers of the new export vehicle. The coach was to be part of a ten coach demonstrator train, with meeting facilities, catering and meeting rooms on board to meet the needs of the sales team representing BREL in attempting to win orders for the new vehicle. The new train was to be operated on behalf of BREL by the railway and would be based at Willesden depot in North London for maintenance and when not in use. The demonstration set was to operate between London and Manchester with the first demonstrations for potential overseas customers to run from May 1986.

An International Coach at Derby Litchurch Lane after completion. *Colin J. Marsden*

The company had already sold a first batch of international coaches to the railways in the Congo and Gabon. Export orders had also been received from Northern Ireland for diesel electric multiple units, more bogies for Taiwan, and a confirmation from the Republic of Ireland for an optional further quantity of coaching stock from an existing order. The orders on hand for export to be delivered during 1984 amounted to a total of £30million, with firm orders for 1985 and 1986 on the books worth £23million and £24million respectively.

The company was engaged in negotiations relating to orders potentially worth a further £12million in 1985 and £17million in 1986. These orders included coaches for Malaysia, Kenya and the Ivory Coast, and EMUs for

Egypt. Railbus orders were under discussion with representatives of the railways in Cameroon, Indonesia, Malaysia, Mexico, Panama, Thailand and the United States. The optimism placed in the potential for large orders for the railbuses would sadly not come to fruition. The workload to be generated by the export orders on hand was insufficient to provide a reprieve for the workshops notified of closure or contraction, although they did provide work for Derby Litchurch Lane, Wolverton and York.

The export potential did not include any wagons and so the plan to close Shildon Works continued, with notice being given that the site would close in its entirety on 30 June with the loss of 2,463 jobs. The impact of these job losses would have a huge impact on the local area which had already been affected particularly badly by the lack of employment locally as other businesses had reduced their staff numbers. With unemployment already being high, the plan to close Shildon Railway Works was met with vociferous local opposition. Sedgefield Council appealed to BREL to reverse the decision and approached the Department for Trade and Industry to request their intervention to help save the works. A strong local campaign to save the works gathered momentum and a lot of media coverage, however their efforts were in vain as BREL simply had no work to allocate to Shildon other than that which had been reallocated to Doncaster to keep the wagons works there utilised.

The campaign did have one positive outcome. In order to mitigate the 'vociferous local opposition', which had also involved the Labour Party leader, Neil Kinnock, who visited the works on 28 April to join the calls for the works to be reprieved, the company looked at what it could do to help, although a reprieve was ruled out. In an attempt to help their employees in the troubled works, BREL introduced an 'Alternative Employment Policy' for the staff there. The company would, though the scheme, make finance available to provide resources to assist the staff in finding employment elsewhere. BREL, alongside Sedgefield and Shildon District Councils, set up the Shildon and Sedgefield Development Agency. BREL provided £50,000 towards the cost of the running the new development agency with another £1.6million provided from the company to fund grants and loans to support any projects which would result in the creation of alternative employment for the BREL workforce who were to lose their livelihoods when Shildon works closed.

The company also made it known that it was open to the possibility of the buildings on the redundant site being 'sensibly' used by any firm who wished to set up a facility there, or to use parts of the site for expansion. BREL also made available assistance should any company wish to take up the offer.

This was not the end of railway engineering in the area though. In the future Hitachi Rail would move into a purpose built construction facility on a nearby site at Newton Aycliffe producing the InterCity Express Programme (IEP) trains. In Darlington a group took occupation of the old Hopetown Carriage Workshops to construct the first new build mainline steam locomotive to be built in Britain since Evening Star left Swindon Works in 1960. The A1 Steam Locomotive Trust completed 'Tornado' its first locomotive and moved on to build other lost LNER designs keeping the legacy of steam locomotive building alive in the north east.

BREL approached the BRB to request permission to dispose of the freehold of the majority of the site in order to allow the redevelopment of the area with the aim of selling the site to developers who wished to create new industrial facilities on the site, which may support regeneration of the area. The company would be able to realise a surplus of £197,000 in excess of the book value of Shildon, which could be used as part of the assistance package on offer from the company.

The company aimed to keep one small part of the site. The wagon repair shop was to be split into small, self-contained industrial units. The smaller units would be more attractive to smaller engineering and manufacturing companies who might thus be drawn to the site, offering employment to the BREL staff who would be likely to have the skills the new companies needed. The last two buildings not covered by BREL's disposal plans were to be acquired by Sedgefield Council who would redevelop them as part of an ongoing job creation programme.

The company provided assistance to soften the blow to the local economies caused by the closure of the maintenance workshops at Horwich through a grant of £157,000 to Bolton Metropolitan Borough Council to partly fund the running of a similar regeneration agency in the area to be called Bolton Business Ventures.

August 1984 saw some good news for the company. The BRB placed a large order with BREL, announced in a press release dated 3 August, for fifty new two-car Class 150 DMU trains, worth around £22million to the company. The first train was due to be delivered to the railway in 1985 to begin the replacement of 200 older multiple unit vehicles. The press release also included a review of orders which had been placed with BREL that year. New construction orders of £100million had been placed, made up of sixty Mark III coaches to be constructed at Derby Litchurch Lane (worth £11million); 209 EMU vehicles at York (£48million); fifteen Class 58 locomotives at Doncaster (£15million) as well as the Class 150 order. A joint order had also been placed for 100 'lightweight DMU' vehicles to be manufactured by the joint BREL and British Leyland consortium.

The lightweight vehicles referred to in the press release were in fact Class 142 'Pacer' units. The manufacture of the vehicles was to be undertaken in a novel manner. The frames, and power units were to be constructed by BREL, with the body shells being constructed by British Leyland. The body shells were to be fully equipped with complete control desks in each driver's cab, with electrical and control systems ready to be plugged directly into the BREL built element. The interiors of the bodyshells were to be fully fitted out using standard British Leyland bus fittings. The completed body shells were to be transported to the BREL workshops by road. Upon arrival, the bodies would be lifted by crane onto the completed chassis assembly, with the body locating pins dropping into prepared mounts for fixing. At this point the remaining 'plumbing' would

After repair at Derby Litchurch Lane, LDM395673 an Overhead line maintenance train vehicle is stabled in the paint shop there, 30 September 1985. *Colin J. Marsden*

be connected to join the electrical and control systems to the power unit, braking systems and electrical supplies on the underframes.

An additional order had been placed for seventy-five vehicles, but not all was as it first seemed. The order was split between the BREL and British Leyland consortium for fifty of the vehicles, the remaining twenty-five being allocated by the BRB to Walter Alexander and Company (Coach Builders) Limited of Falkirk for bodyshell construction, with the railway underframes and equipment being constructed by Andrew Barclay and Son Limited in Kilmarnock.

The decision to split part of the order away from BREL created a strong backlash from the trade unions. Letters were exchanged between S. Hoggart, the Director of Employee Relations at the BRB, Ray Buckton the General Secretary of the ASLEF union and Jimmy Knapp, the General Secretary of the NUR. The latter two gentlemen were extremely unhappy about the allocation of work away from BREL.

The Class 142 'Pacer' units were manufactured jointly by BREL and British Leyland. The bodies were constructed in Workington and delivered complete, by road, to Derby Litchurch Lane. A body is in the yard at Derby, 30 September 1985. *Colin J. Marsden*

The complete body shells of Class 142 'Pacer' units were lowered onto a completed frame in BREL's Derby Litchurch Lane workshops. The connections between body and frame would be joined and the unit would be ready for testing. A body is being lowered onto a frame in Derby, 30 September 1985. *Colin J. Marsden*

The unrest spread to other unions, with the British Transport Officers' Guild's General Secretary James Dalgleish making direct representations about the split order to Robert Reid, the then Chairman of the BRB. Dalgleish informed Reid, in a letter dated 20 August 1984, that the union's members were 'most concerned about the prospect of work being allocated outside of BREL' during a period of time when the company had closed three works and was seeking substantial reduction in its workforce due to lack of work coming into the company.

The BRB responded to all of the trade unions who had questioned the decision to award part of the Class 142 order to an outside consortium by letter on 21 September. It was explained that the board felt that the Scottish consortium was best placed. They were able to offer a better delivery date in the tender at a better price and design than that provided by the BREL and British Leyland consortium. The board confirmed that it had viewed BREL as having come in second place on the bid despite their ability to meet delivery dates for the whole contract, which the Alexander-Barclay consortium was unable to do. BREL were more expensive than Alexander for the production of the wider bodied vehicle required.

The TSSA added to the debate with a letter to Hoggart dated 1 October 1984. The union asked the BRB to explain the rationale behind awarding part of the order for the new trains to a consortium outside of BREL when the company was having to make redundancies and close workshops. The union also questioned if the decision that had been taken was really in the best interests of British Rail and raised the question again of why the correspondence so far between the railway and the unions, had indicated that BREL was actually the second placed contractor in the bid and not the first. The dispute would continue to cause bad feeling among the unions for some time.

The new year dawned with a challenge for the company not of its own making which originated in the United States. BREL was being sued by a group of American passengers who had been on board a train which had been involved in an accident. The bogies on which the train ran had been supplied by BREL but were nothing to do with the cause of the accident. Nevertheless, BREL's name was being dragged through the courts and even though the company would ultimately be found to have nothing to answer for, its reputation was being damaged. In order to avoid any links to the legal proceedings that were ongoing in America, the BREL board opted to temporarily abandon the two companies which they had begun to set up in the United States. BRE-Leyland and BREL Inc. were left as inactive companies and to replace them, a new company, ART Inc., was registered in America. The new company was to operate under the same arrangements that had existed between BREL and British Leyland, with both companies being equal shareholders in the American operation. British Leyland had agreed to the arrangement and to take up half the shares in ART Inc.

The company was still finding it difficult to attract export orders late in the year and with the reduced work being received from British Rail still not providing the utilisation it needed in all its workshops, BREL was struggling to provide work for all of its workforce. One small additional order for 150 export bogies had been received from Taiwan worth around £2.3million but little else had been committed to by potential overseas customers.

1985 saw a further threat emerge for BREL's workshops in Glasgow. The BRB published a new strategy for its requirements in Scotland which would have huge impacts for the workshops in Glasgow. The new strategic plan was based upon the results of a study undertaken by a British Rail working party into future ScotRail requirements. The 'British Rail: Traction and rolling stock maintenance strategy for Scotland; residual workload' plan resulted from the study and would sound the death knell for the works. The new policy was formed in response to a revised future requirement defined by the Traction and Rolling Stock Maintenance and Repair Strategy for Scotland. BREL's Glasgow Works was involved in providing comprehensive vehicle and component repairs to the fleet of locomotives and rolling stock allocated to Scotland. The reduction in rolling stock which the report recommended would result in the work at Glasgow being considerably reduced, threatening the future of the works as it stood.

The new policy resulted in BREL only needing a smaller facility to meet the demands upon it from Scottish Region. A smaller maintenance facility would be created on a reduced part of the same site, to be known as 'Springburn Depot'. This would only handle 'fast turnaround repairs involving component swaps and light structural repairs to stock'. Component repairs and heavier vehicle repairs were to be handled elsewhere using BREL's other facilities. The workshops were no longer to carry out light repair work, instead these tasks would be transferred to local regional depots. No heavy or unclassified repairs were to be undertaken at the new Springburn Depot, with all overhauls of controlled spares and repairable components to be sent away to other locations.

The residual workload relating to new build projects and general overhauls of locomotives, as well as the in progress class one and class two overhauls of coaching stock would be completed but no further work was to be allocated. The overhaul of some locomotives would, however, continue to be undertaken at Springburn. Class 08 shunter overhauls on the fleet allocated to Scotland currently being undertaken elsewhere were to be transferred to the works to avoid the need for the locomotives to travel to Doncaster and Crewe. The remaining Class 20 fleet allocated to Scotland was small enough for overhauls to be handled by the works with little impact on workload. The Class 26 and 27 fleet was being run down and no repair requirements were envisaged after the closure of the existing workshops in Glasgow, while the Scottish Class 37 fleet was not envisaged to need any major overhauls for at least ten years following the current overhauls and installing of electric train heating equipment.

No decision had been made in respect to the Scottish Class 47 fleet, but it was planned that any work would most likely be undertaken at Doncaster. The rundown of the existing DMU fleet in Scotland and its replacement by the new Class 150 units removed the need to further maintenance work that had historically been carried out in Glasgow, with the new units anticipated not to need any major overhauls before the mid-1990s.

It was viewed, as a result of planned requirements, that BREL no longer had need of its workshops in the form they existed at that time, and that they should be required to close them as outlined in the traction plan. The new arrangement being imposed upon BREL foreshadowed what was to come as the company was prepared for disposal and privatisation. As a result of the lack of a viable future for the workshops in Glasgow as they existed at the turn of the year and British Rail's less than optimistic – for BREL – traction plan, the company issued notice in January that the workshops would be run down with an associated reduction in staffing from 1,550 staff to just 500–600. The site was also due to contract from the present 42 acres to around no more than 16 acres.

Returning to January 1985, the response of the trade unions to the closures and reduction in work force at BREL's works, as well as the allocation of orders away from BREL based purely on ability to deliver by a required date and not only on cost was less than supportive. The union's

Class 47 No. 47162 receives attention, including a repaint, at Doncaster, 6 April 1982.
Colin J. Marsden

criticism and dissatisfaction was aimed squarely at The BRB and not BREL, although some of BREL's decisions were questioned.

The trade unions representing the staff at Glasgow protested at the impending closure of the works due to the railway's future plans, and granting of orders for rolling stock to companies other than BREL whilst the company was having to lay off staff due to lack of work. In principle, the unions had no problem with work going outside BREL, if the workshops were busy and jobs were not put at risk by awarding contracts away from the company.

The NUR printed articles about the general rationalisation of the workshops and the reasons behind the demands being made by British Rail earlier in the year. The union also published the railway's plans to replace their aging diesel fleet with a smaller fleet of locomotives, especially freight locomotives. The *NUR News* magazine outlined that British Rail would not be reducing its fleets until the period between 1990 and 1996, when according to the article in the March 1985 edition, the railway claimed it would achieve locomotive fleet reduction through the use of push/pull and the replacement of locomotive hauled services on provincial routes with DMUs.

The author of the article claimed, however, that the reduction would be achieved through cuts in services as even the introduction of the planned new diesel and electric multiple unit trains would not even replace the existing units on a one to one basis, let alone also replacing locomotive hauled trains. The reduction in the freight locomotive fleet was also said to be planned for around 390 locomotives, although the dramatically declining freight traffic on the railways which was leaving many of the freight locomotive fleet with nothing to do was not mentioned.

The author of the *NUR News* article went on to discuss the plans being made by the BRB to '… create the maximum opportunity for open competition between potential suppliers.' According to the article, and a point which appears to be backed up by the case of the order for the Class 142 units, delivery dates were the main concern of the railway board and not cost. The railway had also, apparently, stated that they had not ruled out purchasing from foreign suppliers either. In the railway's favour was the announcement, outlined in the article, that they intended to place orders for 100–200 locomotives at a time, giving the manufacturer four to five years' continuous work, and hopefully a resulting reduction in costs per unit.

The articles in the *NUR News* are particularly interesting, in that whilst scathingly critical of the BRB, the union was very supportive of BREL, and the difficult position it would be in due not only to competition for new work from across the world, but also the likely reduction in maintenance work as a result of the new trains and locomotives needing less heavy overhauls for some time and also being designed to run longer between maintenance visits. The union outlined that the struggles that BREL was experiencing was likely to result in job losses.

The union was however mildly critical of BREL around the subject of Swindon and Glasgow. The run down of Swindon Works announced in May 1984 due to lack of workload for the site after March 1987, which management had, according to the article, stated that low utilisation and lack of forecast workload placed the workshop's future in jeopardy, with closure likely by the end of 1986. Management at Swindon were said to have since played that statement down, with assurances that many of the jobs at Swindon would be safe. This may actually be due to changes to allocations of work, with projects being assigned to Swindon instead of Eastleigh and so forth, to try to preserve the jobs at the works, although management at Swindon at the time of the discussions with the unions, would, to be fair to them, have not known about the plans being discussed at board level in BREL.

The rundown of Glasgow Works which had begun before the traction plan for Scotland had been published had been 'exposed' with the same comments being made about BREL's actions in running down

Class 33 No. 33029 is seen in the main loco bay at Eastleigh Works on 25 April 1984 while undergoing a General Overhaul. *Colin J. Marsden*

the workshops, whilst also reassuring staff that their jobs were safe. It seems that BREL was sadly stuck with British Rail's plans causing them to have to make decisions that it appears from the board minutes they did not want to have to make, but commercial reality was forcing their hand. The company and the unions were due to hold open discussions about the situation at the BREL Joint Consultative Committee meeting scheduled for 12 April.

In the meantime, the NUR were urging their members to blacklist the 'Class 143 Railbus' units being built by Walter Alexander and Andrew Barclay, the first of which was due to be delivered to the railway in May 1985 for use around Newcastle. The union urged their members to make every effort to support the National Executive Committee's decision and refuse to work on these units, especially since the decision on the allocation of an order for 240 Class 150 vehicles had not yet been made. It would seem that, in view of the strong letters being written directly to the BRB by the British Transport Officers Guild and by the Associated Society of Locomotive Engineers and Firemen (ASLEF) which represented only footplate crews, that these other unions were also likely to be supporting a black listing of vehicles not manufactured by BREL.

The announcement that the workshops at Glasgow were to contract was received with anger by the NUR, although the union did say in a letter to its members dated 11 April 1985, that discussions with BREL had indicated that the plans were only tentative and dependent upon allocation of work from British Rail but had not taken into account the outcome of the British Rail Working Party's report as it had not yet been published at the time of the letter. As outlined above, the result would not be good news. The union believed that despite this, the likelihood was that the workshops would be forced to close, and its members based both at the BREL workshops and the British Rail regional depots across Scotland had called for a day of industrial action in protest on 17 April as part of a greater campaign to save 'the last remaining Main Works in Scotland'. The National Executive agreed and called for the strike to go ahead in Scotland.

The union instructed its members in Scotland to withdraw their labour from one minute past midnight on 17 April for a period of twenty-four hours '… as a measure of our concern at the BR policy of cutbacks in [workshop] capacity'. The strike would involve all the union's members with the exception of those working for Traveller's Fare (British Railway Board's catering subsidiary). Staff in Permanent Way, Signal and Telegraph,

Clerical, Supervisory and Regional Shopmen would all strike, however apprentices were not to be called on to strike. The union also instructed its members that no train should be worked past a signal box being manned by railway management in an effort to undermine the effectiveness of the industrial action being taken. The members of the union working on buses were instructed not to join the strike but to refuse to run rail replacement bus services whilst the strike was ongoing. A meeting was also to be arranged not with BREL but the BRB to demand a change in their policies across the whole network, as the threats affecting Glasgow were believed to be part of a national problem affecting all of Britain.

The meeting with the BRB went ahead on 15 April in Euston Square, London with representatives from the BRB and the NUR present but without representatives from BREL. The union was unwilling to call off the strike and the railway board refused to change their policies but might consider further discussions if the strike was called off. The union warned the representatives from the BRB that strike action may spread further as the membership across Britain was becoming increasingly disaffected by British Rail's policy-making. It is interesting that the union seemed to be very understanding of the position that BREL was in, and also strange that no representatives from the company had been invited to attend the discussions. Consensus was not reached to delay the strike at the meeting.

The announcement by BREL of the substantial job losses at Glasgow and also at Swindon was accompanied by a similar initiative to that created for Shildon. A new development agency was formed in both Glasgow and Swindon in cooperation with local authorities in order to attempt to provide alternative employment for every member of the workforce who was to be made redundant from the railway workshops, who had not opted to take the early retirement packages on offer. The BREL board provided an initial funding of £750,000 over three years to support the initial work of the new development body, Swindon Holdings. The company began negotiations regarding working with 'Glasgow Opportunities' to find work for all the workforce who needed jobs after they had left the railway works. The company was planning to provide initial funding of around £500,000 to support the workforce in finding alternative jobs once their time with BREL came to an end.

BREL issued a communication to the BRB on 1 May 1985. The 'British Railways Management Brief' covered the planned future of the workshops which the BREL board had established based upon forecast workloads for the next few years. The paper informed the BRB that the unions representing the staff at BREL's workshops had been informed that the continuing decline in the workload coming from British Rail and further reductions forecast in the rail plans for the short term future would result in a reduction of manpower over the next three years. An additional reduction of around 1,300 staff above that already forecast for the period up to 1987 would be required in the short term.

The forecast workload reductions would result in the need for further manpower reductions between April 1985 and March 1987 of 4,800 staff. The unions had also been informed that Swindon Works would now close in its entirety by 31 March 1986. It would also be necessary to reduce the workforce at Glasgow to just 460 staff by March 1987 once the current EMU refurbishment programme was complete. The workforces at Eastleigh would need to be reduced by 400 with the number of staff at Doncaster being reduced by 350.

After withdrawal a few of the 1936-design 4SUB units visited BREL Eastleigh Works for parts recovery. Set 4719 is seen in the works yard, outside the old container shop, 13 April 1984. *Colin J. Marsden*

Space at BREL Eastleigh was always at a premium, with most of the trains overhauled being 3, 4 or 6-car formations. A part overhauled DTC from Brighton-allocated 4BIG No. 7032 is 'dumped' by the container shop, 13 April 1984. *Colin J. Marsden*

The forecast workload reductions and the resulting concerns about the future that were being caused within BREL as a result, were accompanied by outside protests to the BRB and central government relating to the closure of Shildon Works, which were, on occasion, quite supportive of BREL's own unsuccessful attempts to stave off the closure. The public protests questioned the basis upon which the decision had been made, controversial evidence being found in leaked internal memos relating to declines in rail freight traffic which was still available but had been lost to road freight during 1985. The loss of the traffic had been one of the main factors which had contributed to the closure of the works at Shildon during the previous year. In a letter to the BRB, Shildon Town Council protested that the reasons for the closure of the works in the town had been wrong. The town clerk, writing on behalf of the town council, expressed concern about the content of a 'leaked document' that had been read out to the annual conference of the NUR in Ayr on 27 June 1985. The document, an internal British Rail memo, a copy of which was attached to the letter caused great concern.

According to the original memorandum from British Rail's Freight Director, dated 11 June 1985, the railway was losing freight revenue to road transport as Railfreight was unable to provide '… a satisfactory service …' due to the lack of locomotives and wagons being available to meet the volume of business that was being offered to the railway. As a result, Railfreight's customers were diverting traffic to road in anticipation of the freight services the railway was able to offer being unable to handle their traffic. The memo outlined a small sample of the reasons that Railfreight was failing to be able to win goods traffic even though it was being offered to them.

The railway had a shortage of mineral wagons, with 40 per cent of the fleet being stopped due to failures and maintenance requirements, whilst 17 per cent of the railway's steel carrying wagons were also stopped for the same reasons. The fleet as a whole was gradually building up numbers of wagons which would shortly need maintenance, which was likely to increase the cripple rate. A general lack of available motive power was also impacting the sector's ability to fulfil freight traffic demands. The Director of Freight appealed to the BRB to consider improvements in maintenance support which would improve availability rates of freight locomotive and wagon stock in order that Railfreight could take advantage of the revenue on offer.

The Shildon Town council letter referred to the content of the memorandum as a 'kick in the teeth' for the erstwhile staff of Shildon Works who had lost their jobs exactly one year before, because the construction and repair facilities at Shildon were surplus to requirement. The council letter stated that the content of the leaked memo would cause resentment and bitterness in the area, and accordingly the council had resolved to take action. The council resolved to express their strongest resentment directly to the prime minister, Margaret Thatcher, and the Board of British Rail. They had resolved to also ask the leader of the opposition, Neil Kinnock, to demand or institute a public enquiry into the reports which had been used to justify the closure of Shildon's workshops. Lastly, the town council instituted the creation of a report to ascertain what '… an act of this nature …' could mean to a community reliant upon a single industry.

BREL's export drive yielded results in August with the company agreeing a joint venture which would provide work for Derby Litchurch Lane and additional revenue for the company as a whole. The company announced the signing of a collaboration agreement in the in-house BREL magazine *BRE International*. The agreement involved the manufacture of coaches, vehicle bogies and collaboration in repair and maintenance systems and programmes with a company in Mexico. The agreement between BREL and Constructora Nacional De Ferrocarril (CNCF) covered the construction of 500 International Coaches worth around £200million with the initial export of fully completed coaches from Derby to Mexico to be followed by sharing the work across both companies. The cooperation agreement would not only cover Mexico but other territories within South America as well potential sales to railways in the United States and Canada. The agreement also covered an agreement for BREL to potentially manufacture the products, such as the range of subway trains, that had been developed by CNCF.

Swindon Works finally closed its doors on 26 March 1986 with loss of the remaining 2,300 jobs at the site. The company did however provide assistance to the workforce in a similar way to the support that was offered to the staff at Shildon and Horwich. The BREL board authorised the creation, in a joint venture with the local council, of a regeneration company tasked with creating employment in the local area which could provide jobs for those who needed them. An early retirement package was offered to those who were within the final years of their working lives before retirement, whilst other staff were assisted by being given time to attend interviews and so forth before the works was closed. The remainder of the staff who had no jobs to go to once the works were closed were helped through a programme of retraining in Swindon Work's school which remained open for a time to run these courses. The company invested £1.4million into the Swindon Alternative Employment Programme, and reported in an internal memorandum, dated 1 February 1988, that by the time of the memo 860 jobs had been created by the programme. The company was still helping its staff as it recognised that by the beginning of 1988, 400 of Swindon's erstwhile workforce were still out of work, but that efforts were being made to continue to assist them with finding employment.

The short term future of Crewe Works had been assured by early 1985. The BRB gave approval for the construction of the Class 91 for the east coast mainline at its meeting on 14 February 1985.The tender for the Class 91 programme was provided to BREL as the construction subcontractor to either ASEA, Brush Traction, or GEC. All three companies had opted to include BREL in their bids, but General Electric's bid was viewed as being the most acceptable to the BRB due to the inclusion of BREL as a subcontractor for the mechanical parts of the locomotive with GEC supplying the electric traction equipment directly to BREL for installation in the Class 91s. The contract was awarded in February 1986 for thirty-one locomotives with an option for an additional twenty-five. BREL allocated this to Crewe Works, although GEC had enquired about the possibility of buying Crewe from BREL in view of a potential requirement for a large number of locomotives in the medium term which had been hinted at by the BRB. The enquiry for the purchase of the workshops came to nothing but at least the work supported the continued existence of the workshops at Crewe.

The company continued to recognise that a key part of its future and fundamental to the survival of the company as a viable engineering concern were exports. The BREL board suggested that a new effort to attract export sales should be undertaken in 1985 and on into 1986. The sales drive was to focus upon exports of locomotive hauled coaches, multiple units and light rail vehicles. The board also agreed that the maximum assistance should be sought from the government in achieving success in export markets. An additional offering was to be included in the future export efforts; the sale of part completed vehicles. This had already been successfully undertaken for the Republic of Ireland and was on offer to SEPTA in the United States. The future modular approach that was approved by the board at the April meeting was designed to give the most flexible offering to potential customers whilst retaining the maximum value add from BREL which would be reflected in the revenue achieved. The Class 150 DMU was also attracting a lot of interest from potential overseas customers and BREL was optimistic about its potential.

The trade unions had continued to oppose the manufacture of Class 143 units by W. Alexander Limited with ongoing instructions to blacklist the units being provided to their members, with the decision to continue the blacklisting of the new units being shared with the company at the BREL Joint Consultative Committee. The unions also told BREL that they were both concerned and disappointed that BREL had not been allowed to bid as the main contractor for the Class 91 programme.

The April board meeting saw the announcement that the chairman of BREL at the time would be resigning from his position on the board due to a conflict of interest as he also sat on the board of British Rail, which was no longer deemed as acceptable to the Department for Transport. The meeting minutes state that he was resigning reluctantly but felt that it was necessary for BREL's future success given the continuing moves by the BRB to push the company away to an arms-length relationship. The resignation was effective from 30 April, with his replacement elected as the new Chairman and Managing Director effective from 1 May.

The summer saw the company active in the United States searching for new sales. The company began a programme of Railbus demonstrations in Cleveland in May with a view to selling the trains to the American market, although the effort was complicated by lack of support from British Leyland in the United States. In June, the company received Department of Transport authorisation to complete the formation of their subsidiary company in the United States. ART Inc. thus came into existence with a share capital of $50,000, with shares rapidly being taken up. The initial directors of the company were to be Messrs P.A. Norman (Chairman), P.S. Coventry, C.R. Wood and Cortland Linder (President). British Leyland decided they no longer wished to be involved with the American company and signalled their intention to withdraw from ART Inc., which they confirmed in November. British Leyland would withdraw with effect from January 1986 and in response BREL would buy out the British Leyland shares in the company and go it alone.

June also saw the company achieve some new successes. The export drive gathered momentum with representatives of the company in China working on a contract to redesign a rail factory with a view to licencing construction of the international coach there. The month saw BREL win the first competitive repair contract from the BRB. A contract for the repair of 450 VDA covered vans was awarded to BREL with the work allocated to the wagon works at Doncaster.

The company was starting to see returns on its efforts to make itself viable and to win more export and outside engineering work; however the storm clouds were gathering as moves being made by the BRB to divest themselves of the company began to gather momentum.

Chapter 11

THE ROAD TO PRIVATISATION

In order to unravel the process which resulted in the final disposal of BREL, we must return to 1981. The beginning of the year saw the first tentative steps on a path that would result in the sale of BREL.

In April, minutes of the Department of Trade and Industry's group looking at their involvement with supporting British exports of railway equipment and rolling stock reported that the department was assisting both GEC and Hawker Siddeley with their export initiatives. The department minutes did not mention any assistance being given to BREL, which seems surprising given BREL's frequent appeals to government for support in competing with foreign companies whose governments appeared to be providing subsidies or financial arrangements to allow them to compete at an advantage.

Department minutes relating to a meeting between Sir Fred Walker MEP and H. Pryce from the Department for Transport, mentioned the receipt by the BRB of the report that had been commissioned through independent consultants to investigate the arrangements under which British Rail was managing its manufacturing and maintenance requirements, specifically with reference to BREL. The 'Manufacturing and Maintenance Review' recommended that the relationship with BREL should be severed as far as construction of new stock was concerned and that a new company, completely separate from BREL should be formed. The consultants seem to have not appreciated that the whole rationale behind the creation of BREL during the late 1960s and its founding in 1970 was to achieve exactly the same aim. The BRB, unsurprisingly, rejected the findings of the report, but the seeds had been sown which would influence the future of the company.

BREL's future as a semi-independent company was threatened further with the publication of the Serpell Report in late January 1983, with the

BRB and BREL receiving pre-publication copies of the report in late 1982. Sir David Serpell was a retired senior civil servant who chaired a committee with had been commissioned by Margaret Thatcher's government to examine the state and long term future of British Rail. Serpell had served as Undersecretary at the Treasury between 1954 and 1960 and then in the Ministry of Transport, becoming Permanent Secretary from 1968. IIe had been responsible for implementing the Beeching Cuts under the Conservative Minister of Transport, Ernest Marples and the Labour Minsters of Transport Tom Fraser and Barbara Castle. In 1974, having retired from the Civil Service, Serpell joined the BRB. Popularly seen as being the natural choice for chairmanship of the committee, *The Guardian*'s obituary in 2008 stated that the then Liberal Party leader David Steel was considered first but Serpell was selected instead.

The two parts of the report looked at the state of the railways at the time and the options for the future as defined by the committee. BREL was impacted by the recommendations for the future of Britain's railways and criticisms of the railway as it was structured in 1982. In a letter to David Serpell dated 9 September 1982, BREL criticized the initial report. The letter outlined the sections of the report which referred to BREL, extracting the '… fundamental problems' that BREL had in 1982, specifically with reference to statements made on page ten of the Serpell Report.

The report was to state, firstly, that the company had excess capacity which should be dispensed with in view of the future plans for the railway. The second concern raised in the report covered the commercial relationship between British Rail and BREL, criticising the monopoly that BREL enjoyed on the provision of new rolling stock and locomotives to the railway. Finally, the report complained that the relationship between the BRB and BREL was too close. It was believed that the railway board would be unable to achieve an 'arms-length' relationship with BREL whilst the company remained wholly owned by the BRB.

The Serpell Committee had outlined three options for the future of BREL, one of which was privatisation. The letter from BREL pointed out that whilst the committee had pointed out the negative in the relationship between BREL and the BRB, no positives had been outlined. The letter was also highly critical of the committee's report, specifically that while three potential options had been outlined, none of them had been worked through in any detail, which made them almost impossible to justify. The report was also criticised for not suggesting any way in which the potential future options would result in the proper maintenance and renewal of the railways rolling stock and locomotives fleets going forward.

The report, when published in January 1983, was extremely critical of the ownership of BREL. In a response to the report, it was pointed out by the BRB that whilst the Serpell committee did not believe, it was said, that the advantages to be gained from competitive tendering and dual sourcing could be achieved whilst BREL remained a wholly owned subsidiary of the BRB, the committee had failed to consider that competitive tendering was already underway between BREL and Metro-Cammell for the supply of the prototype DMUs. The board also stated that they favoured maintaining the 'arms-length' relationship with BREL through continued ownership of the company in order to maintain control of maintenance functions and supply of new rolling stock. The board believed whole heartedly that privatisation was not the correct way forward for BREL and that the company should continue as a wholly owned subsidiary of the railway board. It was believed that all that the Serpell report advocated could be achieved without any change in ownership of BREL.

The BRB had implemented a policy of competitive tendering in 1980, long before the Serpell report which had completely ignored British Rail's change in direction. The 'BREL Manifesto' which had been published in the April of the same year was also completely ignored by the committee. The manifesto had stated that the company should move towards being a '… fully accountable and profitable subsidiary …' of the BRB. It also laid out that BREL should fulfil the requirements of financial and performance criteria expected of any company in the private sector. As part of the manifesto, BREL was expected to have to bid for work from British Rail relating to new traction and rolling stock, all of which would be put out to tender. The existing manifesto, to some degree, made a nonsense of the assertations being made in the Serpell Report relating to BREL. The company had already been placed 'at arms-length', a fact which the committee behind the Serpell Report had totally ignored, and which made the parts of the report relating to BREL at best debatable. The report was, however, published and both the BRB and BREL had to live with it, and ultimately would have to put in place preparations for the divestment of BREL from railway ownership.

The Department of Transport had intervened in the BRB's decision making process in February 1985. The Secretary of State for Transport, Nicholas Ridley, had a meeting with Robert Reid, the Chairman of the railway board on 13 February 1985. The meeting discussed the situation regarding locomotive maintenance and supply to the railway. Reid said that British Rail's requirement for only 100 new locomotives over the next ten years could only support a single British supplier. He was concerned that, however BREL was restructured, the railway could be in the hands of a monopoly supplier. BREL was already exploring cooperative arrangements with overseas companies such as General Motors of the United States and ASEA of Sweden to supplement capability it didn't have and to provide additional capacity if needed in the future which would give the company a more compelling offer.

The Secretary of State saw a potential problem with substantial foreign involvement in supplying a highly subsidized nationalised industry and the possible perception of how public taxes were being spent that might result and blocked the move.

As a monopoly UK purchaser, Ridley felt that the railway needed to ensure that all of their potential suppliers remained in business and where possible competed in tendering for the railway's business. The railway should also only purchase from domestic suppliers wherever possible even if that meant dividing work among them in small quantities.

In April 1983, the BRB and BREL had set up a new design function within the structure of BREL in Derby. The new department was tasked with creating a new series of market led, competitive products for both the British and export markets. British Rail transferred all of the staff involved in traction and rolling stock design to BREL who were no longer required by the railway, initially affecting 250 employees with another 60 to follow once their current work had been completed. The existence of a design team wholly located within BREL would allow the company to be more independent of the BRB, but also in the longer term would allow the company to be separated entirely from the railway and sold off into private ownership.

Responsibility for all procurement related to BREL's activities was transferred wholly to the company in 1984. BREL had previously only been able to purchase items up to a minimal level of expenditure, but from 1 April the company no longer had to apply to the BRB director of supply for purchases of materials, machinery and other items required by the workshops and the company. BREL would now become completely autonomous with regard to its supply chain and purchasing policies, arguably something which should have occurred with the creation of the company in 1970.

The future of BREL as part of the BRB had begun to look bleak even before the Serpell Report had been published. A review had been commissioned by the Secretary of State for Transport and the Department of Trade and Industry regarding the possibility of privatising the company in October 1983. The Secretary of State had set Sir Robert Reid the objective of reviewing options for the future of BREL, including the possibility of privatisation. In a letter to the Secretary of State for Transport, Paul Channon, dated 24 November 1987, Reid outlined the results of the BRB's study. The railway board, with the assistance of Price Waterhouse had considered the future of BREL and had concluded that privatisation was the best option for the company. The continued ownership of BREL by the BRB was viewed by the board as being contrary to British Rail's core activities, the sale and provision of train services. Secondly, retention of BREL would inhibit development of competitive sourcing policies that were to be increasingly implemented by the railway board, and reduce the benefits to be achieved. Finally, the BRB believed that BREL's ability to diversify its range of activities would be assisted by private ownership.

The first mention of the review into the future of BREL appears in the BRB minutes files under minute number 82/85 from the railway board meeting held on 4 February. On 23 February 1982, James Urquhart, a director of BREL, reported to the BRB at the time that '... the discussion with the Secretary of State ...' mentioned in the minute had yet to be held but that members of the board might be interested in the two papers which had been prepared for the meeting with the government.

It must be borne in mind that at this time members of the board of directors of BREL also had seats on the BRB. The Chairman of the BREL board and two other directors were constant members of the railway board until later in the 1980s and those positions had sat on both boards since BREL had been formed in 1980. In fact, the Chairman had always been appointed by the BRB and the other directors of the BREL board were mostly appointed by the railway board.

The first paper intended for the meeting with the Secretary of State was an overall review and report into the current plans for capacity reduction, which involved the run down and closures of works and reductions in manpower across other sites which were covered in the previous chapter. The paper also outlined the importance of expanding export initiatives with a view to using business won through that channel to allow the workshops to remain not just viable but profitable. The second paper introduced the idea of introducing private capital into BREL in the long term, but that the first priority of the company was rationalisation of the production capacity across the entire company.

The first paper mentioned a study which was to shape the future of BREL. The publication of the Manufacturing and Maintenance Study referred to in the paper, and mentioned above, was the first time thought had been given as to how BREL's functions might be structured going forward into the late 1980s and into the 1990s. The segregation of manufacturing and maintenance raised as a possible future structure in the study produced by the BRB 'Manufacturing and Maintenance' Steering Group would be seen again when BREL was prepared for sale as its contents had been endorsed by the BRB in April 1981 according to the BREL paper.

The original report has been commissioned by the railway board through a firm of outside consultants in February 1979 but was not published until nearly a year later. The report outlined that cost cutting and

BREL carried out a reorganisation of workflow at Eastleigh to remove delays in the process, reducing the time the units spent in the works. The coaching stock work flow line involved each work station carrying out a set procedure with booked times for vehicles to be 'moved' to the next work base, 18 September 1985. *Colin J. Marsden*

efficiency improvements were needed in order to reduce manufacturing and maintenance costs and improve management effectiveness. The improvements were required in order to reduce the cost of ownership of rolling stock by British Rail. The paper stated that the report had revealed a number of organisational and managerial shortcomings which were being addressed. BREL had responded with the publication of the 'BREL Manifesto'.

The manifesto, the paper said, had outlined the four core principles by which BREL was to operate. The company was to be profitable and be able to remain the principal contractor for the BRB's rolling stock requirements, despite the railway board's plan to enter into a policy of competitive tendering for all its needs. The company was also to become a leader in design, build and sales of rolling stock for selected international markets, whilst seeking joint venture and cooperative arrangements both in the United Kingdom and abroad, thus sharing risk and investments needs. The arrangement with Constructora Nacional De Ferrocarril of Mexico and the attempts to create a new sales company in the United States were clearly driven by the thinking that the new company 'manifesto' had created.

The Manufacturing and Maintenance Steering Group undermined BREL's plans a little, however. New contracts were being created against which any prospective supplier of new rolling stock for British Rail would have to bid. At the same time, the railway was revisiting the contractual arrangement it had with BREL for maintenance of its fleets of locomotives and rolling stock. BREL would still suffer from the imposition of commercial arrangements by the BRB. Objective two of the new arrangements outlined in the paper to be presented to the Secretary of State stated that the new contracts for maintenance work would set precisely agreed 'unit cost prices against an agreed work content' which BREL had to abide by once they had been agreed by both parties. In their favour, however, objective three stated that recompense would be made for underutilisation of BREL facilities if the railway failed to meet the contracts, although the same held true if BREL were not to meet contracts with the railway.

In 1985, BREL privatisation was gathering momentum, although the rolling stock manufacturers outside of BREL were also seeking to clarify the future of the rail supply industry. An informal meeting was held between Edward Hosker at the Department of Trade and industry to discuss the future of the sector. Representatives from GEC, Hawker Siddeley (the owners of Brush since 1957) and Metro-Cammell were present but no representatives from BREL were invited.

A BRB press release dated 10 April 1985 presented two new policies which had been officially adopted by the board. Firstly, the railway board announced that it now operated a complete policy of competitive tendering for all new traction and rolling stock. Secondly, the railway board announced that it had severed all links between the BRB and the BREL board. BREL would no longer have representation on the BRB. The latter announcement had been forced on the railway by political pressure being applied by members of parliament and other railway equipment manufacturers, who claimed that there was a conflict of interest among the directors who sat on both boards, and also that BREL received an unfair commercial advantage by being aware of discussions which were held in the BRB meetings to which other companies were not privy. The press release had been issued in response to discussions held at the Department of Transport with the Chairman of the BRB between 1983 until 1990, Sir Robert Reid (not to be confused with his successor Bob Reid).

A memo resulting from the meeting, dated 2 April 1985, outlined the concerns that both Reid and the Department of Transport had about three of BREL's board members also sitting on the BRB. The concerns related to Messrs. Urquhart, Myers and Casey. The concern was mainly that their position as members of both boards gave BREL an unfair advantage in competition against other manufacturers, or at least opened the possibility of accusations of such an advantage. The memo interestingly refers to the need for the BRB to strengthen its decision-making control so as not to prejudice any options for the future of BREL.

Reid's solution to the problem was to ensure that the independent Manufacturing and Maintenance Steering Committee was made up only of members of the BRB. Myers and Casey were reported to have already left the BREL board by the time of the meeting at the Department of Transport, with Urquhart to cease to be chairman of BREL, and to resign from the BREL Board. P.A. Norman would succeed Urquhart as Chairman of the BREL Board and would report to the Manufacturing and Maintenance Committee. The committee would from that point be made up of Urquhart, Myers, Casey and Norman. The BREL Board would be restricted to decision making relating only to the daily operation and business requirements of the company. The company would defer to the Manufacturing and Maintenance Committee for all 'Strategic Matters' including tendering for British Rail construction contracts and agreement on long term maintenance requirements, three quarters of the members of which sat on the BRB.

BREL board meeting minutes show that Casey and Myers had indeed resigned from the company's board at the March 1985 meeting. The company's relationship with General Motors and ASEA was also outlined in the same meeting. The company had approached ASEA for assistance in bidding for the forthcoming construction of Class 91 locomotive. The approach to General Motors related to the plan to bid for the BRB's tender for a new freight locomotive using its Class 38/Class 48 design which would have used a General Motors engine. The Class 38 would never be built as the need for it disappeared with decreasing freight traffic on the railways, although, as has been discussed previously, Railfreight may not have agreed. The planned relationship was not just being questioned in the halls of government. A number of questions had been raised as to whether this ought to be allowed given BREL's position as British Rail's main contractor.

The early months of 1985 saw the end of the first part of BREL. The deteriorating relationship between the company and Metro-Cammell had meant that no tenders for export work had been submitted through BRE-Metro for some time. BRE-Metro had effectively become a dormant company. It was proposed at the March BREL board meeting that the remaining BREL directors of the BRE-Metro company should formally resign and be replaced by the election of a single director. The BREL representatives were accordingly all replaced by A.D. Vickers, the Chief Accountant at BREL, with Metro-Cammell making exactly the same change. The export company was then to be wound up as soon as possible.

The BREL board raised concerns about the disruption to the business that the planned decision to group the company's workshops into either New Build or Repair functions would cause. The Engineering Director raised the concern that consideration had not been given as to the facilities that would be required in order to create a standalone New Build Group and the impact upon maintenance facilities which had previously been shared where commonality of processes existed. The Chairman agreed with the concerns, and it was decided to form a sub-committee to be led by the Engineering Director and tasked with examining what needed to be done to split the company into two divisions.

Chapter 12

ENGINEERING AND MAINTENANCE: THE DIVESTMENT OF BREL 1986 TO 1988

BREL had been informed by the BRB that it needed to be able to operate as a completely free standing company by April 1987. The BRB's decision to place the contracts for thirty-one Class 91 locomotives with GEC but with BREL as the sub-contractor building and fitting out the locomotives in their own workshops using GEC traction equipment and the twenty-nine Class 87/2 locomotives with BREL but with GEC as the subcontractor placed the company in a difficult position. It was widely made known that it was important that the Class 87 project should be successful. The company had lost the bid to construct the Class 150 series of DMUs which had been awarded to Metro-Cammell.

The company continued its efforts to win overseas orders, despite the threat of privatisation. A healthy order book would be of benefit in making the company more attractive to potential purchasers. To this end, BREL embarked on a series of demonstrations and trials in Canada of both the Class 141 and 142 railbuses. The board of the company was informed at the July board meeting that the trials were progressing well and considerable interest was being shown in the trains by the Canadian railway authorities. The company sought permission from the BRB to continue the trials, with the railway board agreeing to leave them running in Canada until early 1987. The situation in Canada and the need to gain permission to continue a promising programme shows again how the company was being limited throughout its existence by its relationship to its owner, the railway board.

The workshops at Swindon having closed were to be sold off, and so the company approached the BRB for permission to begin the process.

BREL proposed to sell the site through tender, with a decision to be made on the final purchaser by mid-Septmeber 1986. The site had been independently valued with the assets believed to be capable of achieving in the region of £1.4million at public auction. The sale itself was likely to prove trickier due to the number of listed buildings on the site. Additionally, the local council had a negative view of the closure of the works and were against high-tech or retail uses of the site. The Railway Board gave permission for the sale of the site at Swindon to go ahead in late May, so BREL was able to send out the tender documents to twenty-two prospective purchasers in June. The company received bids for the site from a number of prospective owners with Trafalgar House submitting the best bid, although it was still short of BREL's expectations. After negotiation, Trafalgar House agreed to submit an improved bid to the company which was received in November. The BREL board viewed the new offer which included the costs involved in redeveloping the site and encompassed BREL's Alternative Employment Scheme for Swindon, as likely to also be acceptable to the Railway Investment Committee to whom it was submitted for final acceptance after being accepted by the BREL directors.

Meanwhile, the situation at Horwich Foundry had been deteriorating. Performance had been getting progressively worse with delays and late deliveries to the railway becoming increasingly common. The foundry was engaged mainly in making iron brake blocks in large quantities for the railway as well as other castings used both within BREL and across the railway, although the production of brake blocks remained its main workload. BREL opted to engage the services of external consultants to look at the foundry at Horwich to establish what improvements could be made.

As the year came to a close, BREL was confronted by an unexpected approach from British Leyland. The company was informed that Leyland wished to continue with the joint venture agreement for manufacture and export of railbuses beyond the expiry of the current arrangement at the end of November 1986. The change in interest was mainly due to the potential management buyout of Leyland Bus from the main company as part of the privatisation of British Leyland which was to spin off the bus manufacturing part of the company into a separate entity 'Leyland Bus' which management were looking to buy. The arrangement would be of benefit to a privatised BREL so negotiations began.

The situation with regard to the remains of the workshops at Swindon became complicated when the BRB awarded the contract of sale to White Horse Holdings Limited towards the end of 1986.

1987, the last year in which BREL existed in its current form, began with the sale of Swindon being discussed by the board. Due to various discrepancies found in the sale to White Horse Holdings, the sale was re-awarded, this time to Tarmac Properties, a subsidiary of Tarmac Plc. The former apprentice school was not to be included in the sale, but instead was to be taken over by British Railways Property Board and leased to the local authority under the same arrangements which had been in place between BREL and the local council as part of the Alternative Employment and Manpower Commission Schemes.

The year also began with a meeting of the British Rail Council at which the Manufacturing and Maintenance Policy was revisited in order to define the future of BREL. The outcomes and notes for attendees at the meeting relating to this item on the agenda were embargoed and were not circulated to trade unions members. The background to the discussion was a remit from the Secretary of State for Transport to consider options for the future of BREL, including privatisation. The meeting chose to try to get the best of both options, with a decision made to prepare BREL for privatisation through the creation of a 'New Build Group' which would comprise Crewe, both works in Derby, York as well as Horwich Foundry.

The BRB claimed that it was vitally important that the board retained control and ownership of the maintenance functions performed by BREL in the long term. To that end, a new division, British Rail Maintenance Group with Wolverton, Doncaster, Eastleigh and Glasgow works would be created, that would remain in the ownership of the railway regardless of the fate of the new build group.

BREL was approached in February about the workshops at Derby Litchurch Lane. An offer was made by Beechdale Engineering to acquire 100,000ft² of the existing workshops in order to accommodate planned expansion of the company. The discussions were still ongoing with British Railways Property Board in March.

The BRB continued on the path to the privatisation of BREL in the background. In April, the board headquarters administration minutes show an entry, Instruction 126, which had been passed by The BRB for the creation of a new company to be called 'British Rail Maintenance Limited' which was to be formed from 1 April 1987. Property was to be transferred

The main works associated with 25kV ac loco repairs was Crewe, where classified and casual attention was given. Class 86/3 No. 86322 is seen, 6 April 1982. *Colin J. Marsden*

from BREL to the new company with immediate effect on the date of incorporation of the new concern, namely the workshops at Doncaster (with exception of the Wagon Works), Eastleigh, Glasgow (Springburn) and Wolverton. All staff working there were to be transferred on the same date.

A preliminary report into the privatisation of BREL commissioned by the BRB through a firm of independent consultants, outlined some of the challenges facing BREL, and which also impacted upon the attractiveness of the company to any prospective buyer. The main concern raised in the report related to the level of competition that had entered the arena since the BRB's introduction of competitive tendering. GEC and Hawker Siddeley were competing for locomotives and power units, whilst Metro-Cammell, Leyland Bus and W. Alexander Limited were competing with BREL for passenger coaches, EMUs and DMUs. It appears, though, that the consultants involved in the project were unaware of the joint venture between Leyland Bus and BREL. The report finished by stating that competitors were making a determined effort to take work away from BREL, the evidence to support this assertion being seen as the contract for the Mark IV coach being awarded to Metro-Cammell, whilst Hawker Siddeley had won the Class 89 locomotive contract.

The Railway Board and BREL circulated the plans for the restructuring of the business in a report published on 20 May 1986, although the circulation list seems to have been restricted. At the time of the report, BREL employed 22,850 staff but this was planned to be reduced to 22,100 by March 1987, with further job losses reducing the staff employed by the business to around 16,900 by 1989. The staff were to be split between two new divisions of the company; BREL New Build Group (employing 12,700 staff), and British Rail Maintenance Group (employing up to 4,200 staff).

The workshops would be split out into the new divisions or closed. The New Build Group would comprise the workshops at Crewe, Derby Locomotive Works, Derby Litchurch Lane, Doncaster Wagon Works (now added to the group), Horwich Foundry and York. British Rail Maintenance Group would be allocated part of Doncaster Works, Eastleigh, Springburn (the remnants of Glasgow Works) and Wolverton. The remaining parts of Doncaster with the exception of the National Component Stores would be closed during 1988 or 1989. In reality, the situation would be different.

The BRB issued a press release the same day outlining the fate of BREL. The release stated that the trade unions had been informed that a workforce would be retained at the remaining eight sites in operation under BREL's auspices, although it seems they may not have been party to the detail contained in the British Rail Report, given the restriction of the notes from the British Rail Council in January. The needs of the business were to result, according to the press release, in the loss over the next three years of around 4,205 jobs. These losses were to be in addition to the 1,750 jobs losses previously communicated to the unions.

The railway announced, however, that in the same period it would need to recruit around 20,000 staff. A new senior director would be appointed to the BRB with responsibility solely to work with BREL to help those affected to find alternative employment within and outside the industry. The release also announced that Doncaster Works would continue to carry out wagon manufacture and repairs and would become part of British Rail

Maintenance Group, although in reality the wagon works at Doncaster would be sold off. Doncaster would also become the home of British Rail's new National Component Store, although the workforce was planned to reduce from 3,100 to between 1,430 and 1,690 over three years depending on the railways long term needs.

Eastleigh Works was announced to have a less certain future. In the short term it would continue to refurbish and overhaul Southern Region third rail electric stock. Its short term future was guaranteed by the difficulties involved in moving trains to and from workshops in the north, although its long term future depended upon the railways boards expectations of improved productivity and reduction of overheads being met. Nevertheless, the workforce was planned to be reduced by up to 500 jobs. The bad news being announced in the press release continued.

Glasgow was to be closed and adapted as a Regional Maintenance Depot for ScotRail on a proportion of the current site. The new depot would provide work only for 200 staff. Wolverton was also to be impacted by the rationalisation plans. Heavy repairs were to cease at the works, with it becoming purely devoted to high volume bogie exchanges on coaching

Towards the rear of Eastleigh Works were a number of two and three car length sidings which were used for vehicle storage, these were fed by traversers. A collection of different EMU vehicles await attention, 13 April 1994. *Colin J. Marsden*

and multiple unit stock. The changes were expected to result in a reduction of the workforce at Wolverton from 1,900 to between just 650 and 850 staff.

The BRB had split off the wagon workshops at Doncaster into a new company, with a view to selling them separately. Doncaster Wagon Works Limited had been formed despite the original intention to include them in the reformed BREL New Build Group. The board received an offer for the wagon works in the form of a management buyout. The interested parties had already formed a company 'RFS Industries Limited' with a view to acquiring the Doncaster Wagon Works. The promoters of the RFS Industries purchase were a mix of BREL and British Rail management staff who wished to keep the wagon works trading. The BRB announced that, subject to gaining the required financial backing, RFS Industries Limited had made a bid to purchase the entire shareholding of Doncaster Wagon Works Limited.

The railway board provided a report to the prospective buyers outlining which parts of the site at Doncaster were to be included in the sale and details of the company as it stood in railway ownership. The Doncaster Wagon Works had achieved sales of £21.67million to the end of the 1986 tax year in March 1876, £4.52million had been for new wagon construction whilst £10.3million had been achieved against wagon and wheel repairs. A map included in the report showed that the sale included all of the buildings and rail links which had previously made up BREL's wagon

CSA 'Presflow' used for Fly-Ash movement, B874035 outside Doncaster Works wagon shops after a classified overhaul, 4 February 1986. *Colin J. Marsden*

works at Doncaster located behind the BREL offices which faced the railway station. The site to be acquired included the car park, the entire wagon repair shop building, machine shops and the old apprentice school. The sales of the wagon works was concluded on 16 December 1987, with RFS Industries Limited becoming the new owners with a purchase price of £4.9million being agreed.

In November 1987, The BRB sent a communication to all the unions impacted by the planned sale of BREL to a new owner outside of British Rail. The letter was intended to clarify the final plans for the divestment of BREL since the final plan differed a little from what had previously been discussed. A letter, dated 24 November, was sent to Jimmy Knapp, the General Secretary of the NUR; C.A. Lyons, General Secretary of the TSSA; A. Ferry, General Secretary of CS&EU; N. Milligan, General Secretary of ASLEF; and finally J.M. Dalgleish, the National Secretary of the British Transport Officers' Guild. The letter gave a detailed account of the plans for the railway workshops and included copies of workload slides used in presentations given to the Rail Council earlier in the month.

The document clarified the terms under which BREL was to be sold. The company was to be acquired through purchase of the shares owned by the BRB. Staff were to be protected through contracted agreement with the new owner that all staff contracts would be honoured in full, and that conditions of service, rates of pay and bargaining procedures and other agreements made between BREL, staff and the trade unions would all remain unchanged.

As far as the workshops themselves were concerned, all the remaining workshops in the ownership of BREL would pass to the new owner with the exception of Horwich Foundry which would be retained by the BRB for separate sale as a going concern in mid-1988. The workshops allocated to the maintenance company would be transferred back into the direct ownership of the BRB and would remain owned by the railway for the performance of maintenance activities on the railway's rolling stock. Doncaster Wagon Works, having already been sold was not covered by the sale of BREL.

To meet the requirements of the BRB, BREL in its current form would be split into two groups. BREL (New Build and Repair Group) would be a fully integrated company capable of design as well as all the tasks associated with new traction and rolling stock construction and outside engineering work. The company would be expected to enter into competitive tenders for all work for the railway alongside any other companies who wished to bid. The company would be the part of BREL to be sold on to a new owner. British Railways Maintenance Limited was to be formed in order to cover the maintenance and repair needs of both the BRB and the railway operations management. The new concern would be controlled directly by the railway board and would be retained after the sale of BREL. All light repair work would no longer be undertaken in railway workshops; instead, the work would be allocated to British Rail depots.

Wolverton Works, to be retained by the railway after the sale of BREL, was to be reduced in size due to the reduction in workload and types of work to be allocated to the workshops. The consultancy company Conran Roche had been retained by the BRB to recommend uses for the site. Their report indicated a preference for a mixed use for the old BREL site which was no longer needed by the railway. It recommended that the surplus area of the site should be sold for development, but planning permission should be sought prior to sale of the site in order to increase its value and thus the likely return on the sale. The mixed-use approach recommended by the report included half an acre of 'employment' related development, and 5 acres of residential property to include 175 new houses. An area of 0.33 acres was to be reserved for 'leisure' use. 'Market and speciality shops' were to occupy just over an acre of land across the old site, with the same space reserved for a large supermarket. The railway would retain just under 2 acres of its old 12 acre site, the balance being used for open space and car parking in the new development.

Chapter 13

1988, NEW OWNERS AND THE END OF BREL

The new year dawned with progress being made in the sale of BREL to a new owner. The budget for the new year is extremely revealing. The budget report introduction makes it clear what the situation was within the company. The company anticipated that the year would be one of major change with privatisation being the major concern occupying the directors of the company. The BRB had declared its intention to sell the company by the end of the year, and to that end BREL had been divided in two at the start of 1988. The BREL budget thus only covered the four remaining works under its control, Crewe, Derby Litchurch Lane and Derby Locomotive Works, and York.

Allowance had been made for any remaining liabilities relating to workshops that had been closed over the previous two years. Horwich Foundry was subject to a separate budget due to the BRB's intention to retain the foundry for sale separately from BREL and its incorporation into a separate entity 'Horwich Foundry Limited', which was now owned by the BRB.

January also saw the publication of a report into the future of Horwich Foundry Limited. The report had been created by an independent firm of consultants whose study had been undertaken in connection with the proposed sale of the foundry separately to the sale of BREL. At the time the company consisted of a mechanised iron foundry accompanied by a small manual iron foundry, and a spring manufacturing works. The company also owned four industrial units on the site. The company employed 330 staff. The mechanised foundry brought in around three quarters of the company's revenue. The foundry workshops were mainly involved in the production of brake blocks for rolling stock with 70 per cent of the company's business coming from that source. The remainder of the company's business relied on casting chairs and baseplates for railway

York Works bogie and wheelset overhaul shop, 5 February 1986. *Colin J. Marsden*

York Works new build shop with various vehicles and parts for the Class 317, 318 and 150 builds, 5 February 1986. *Colin J. Marsden*

tracks, but also included an amount of outside work providing low value castings sold as weights for tractors, trawler nets and washing machines. The manual foundry was viewed as being uneconomic and only operating at half capacity. The spring shop was very profitable. Its main work was the provision of laminated bearing springs to BREL for rolling stock. It also supplied the BRB with all of its leaf spring requirements for locomotives and rolling stock, although the contract for the latter was due to expire in March and would be subject to a competitive tendering process. The spring shop was seen to be working at about half capacity so there was ample room for growth, however the plant and machinery in it were coming to the end of their economic working life.

The industrial units owned by the foundry company were all leased to companies outside the British Railways Group, although the leases were administered by British Railways Property Board. The income from the units was viewed as insignificant, the importance of the units being that their ownership secured rail access into the site.

BREL was also in the process of rationalising its works with the resultant reduction in jobs that would result. Crewe and York were to lose jobs as a result of reducing workloads, with Derby Litchurch Lane Works to contract in size. Job losses were announced for May 1988, with 1,020 staff to be made redundant at Crewe, 1,420 at Derby and 500 at York. The redundancy notices were withdrawn at Derby due to an increase in workload being awarded to BREL which was being allocated to the works.

The site at Crewe was also to be reduced in size over two phases. Phase one would see a reduction from 90 acres, 35 of which were covered by buildings, down to 76.75 acres, of which 30.5 acres were covered. A reduction in staff by 600 jobs would follow. Phase two would see the site shrink to 70.5 acres, 20.5 covered. The contraction would result in the loss of fifty-five further roles.

A final phase of rationalisation would see the site reduced in size to only 44 acres, with 15.33 covered. The wheel and bogie repair as well as electric traction motor repairs were to be transferred to the erecting shop. The asbestos removal plant was to be closed and replaced with a smaller unit more suited to stripping components as most asbestos had by now been removed from rolling stock and locomotives. The steel foundry at Crewe was to be closed completely.

A new canteen would have to be provided, which was to be achieved by transferring it from the current location in one of the oldest buildings remaining on the site which had been originally constructed by the London and North Western Railway in the nineteenth century. The building was now too far from the remaining activities being undertaken at Crewe, too large for the number of staff remaining employed on site, and more importantly, was frequently subject to pest infestation. BREL was to purchase West Street Junior School on the edge of the remaining site, from the local authority, and convert it to the new canteen.

A similar plan was scheduled for Derby Litchurch Lane. The blacksmith's shop was to be rationalised, and the tool room to be re-sited to a more logical location in the works. The buffer shop, now unused, was to be cleared, with the Maintenance Store being demolished and the supply activity moved into it. New office accommodation was to be provided through the construction of a new building.

Privatisation moved into its final phase when the BRB incorporated a new company which was to be sold. On 25 March 'BREL (1988) Limited' was incorporated. The new company was to acquire by transfer everything held by BREL which had not already been transferred to British Railways

47468 and 56049 stand outside BREL Crewe Works, ex-works, awaiting test, 4 July 1987. *Colin J. Marsden*

Maintenance Group. The company was prohibited from using any of the terms British Rail Engineering, British Rail, or British Railways in any way, a restriction which would apply to the future owners of the company.

The opening share capital was set at £100 in £1 shares, later raised to £1million. The shares were to be allocated to the BRB with the exception of one single share which was allocated to Brittravel Nominees Limited. With the railway board owning the new company, it could sell it as it saw fit. The reason for forming the new company was to enable the railway to write off existing debts. The creation of BREL (1988) Limited saw BREL cease to exist as an operational company.

BREL (1988) Limited started life with some troubles of its own though. The BRB refused to provide guarantees and a performance bond against a new order that BREL had received from Thailand for the supply of twenty DMU vehicles. The board wrote to the Secretary of State for Transport stating that they would only be prepared to provide the bonds and guarantees whilst BREL remained in its ownership and were not prepared to extend them to BREL (1988) Limited.

The BRB commissioned an independent report into the potential restructuring that might be undertaken in order to prepare BREL to be divested from the ownership of the railway board. The 'British Rail Engineering Limited: Draft Report on Restructuring' was delivered on 31 March 1988 by the consulting firm Peat Marwick McLintock. The report outlined the company as it existed at that time with proposals on what options might be undertaken in order to prepare BREL for sale. The report also outlined the costs involved in pursuing those options should the railway decide to do so.

A proposal was received by the BRB from York Area Economic Development Unit regarding the future of Holgate Works in the City. The Economic Development Unit had commissioned a report from consultancy firm Steer, Davies and Gleave (dated July 1987). The report concluded that the future of the workshops in the city was best served by the works being sold off as a completely independent entity from the rest of the BREL estate. York City Council agreed, however the BRB was not interested in splitting York Works out separately.

The final decision to sell the new company was made in August. The BRB appointed Lazard Brothers of London as their financial advisors in the sale with the Memorandum of Sale being provided to interested parties shortly afterwards. All expressions of interest in acquiring the shares in BREL

York was separated into two main areas. New build, concentrated on multiple units, and repairs. This view shows the coaching stock repair shop with various MK1 and Mk2 coaches receiving attention. *Colin J. Marsden*

(1988) Limited were to be sent to the offices of Lazard Brothers in London by 7 October 1988.

The reason for sale was stated as having been due to the BRB's intention to dispose of BREL as part of its strategy to concentrate its financial and management resources purely on running the railway. The reasons for sale also outlined that the sale of BREL was 'one of a series of sales of businesses' which the board believed would also assist in the policy of competitive tendering being undertaken by the railway. It also believed that BREL would benefit from not being under railway ownership with the constraints that entailed. The company, according to the memorandum of sale, had been unable to diversify due to statutory restrictions in place whilst it was owned by the BRB. The company was said to have 'already targeted areas' outside of its traditional business. The diversification areas that the company had been exploring included modular buildings for construction, and work, including repair and new build for the defence industry. The previous work carried out by BREL for the Ministry of Defence which, among other jobs, related to both the Spartan Armoured Personnel Carrier and the Samson Armoured Recovery Vehicle in the army's CVR(t) family of light tracked armoured vehicles seems to have been overlooked.

The workshops which were to be included in the sale were to be those at Crewe, both the works in Derby and the works at York. The headquarters facilities in Derby were also to be included. One of the selling points that the board promoted was the skilled and experienced workforce, as well as the modern equipment located in large industrial premises which the new owner would receive. Despite the workforce being viewed as one of the selling points that the company offered, the memorandum of sale went on to outline the plans for headcount reduction already in place. The company was said to employ 8,568 staff across the five sites included in the sale. A rationalisation programme was said to be underway with a view to reducing the number of employees to between 7,900 and 8,100 by the end of March 1989, although the changes were to be dependent upon workload.

Interestingly, the memorandum of sale of BREL included both the business groups created in BREL. The New Construction Group and the Manufacture and Repair Group were now both included in the sale, although the BRB had transferred some of the assets and workload related to maintenance activities into British Rail Maintenance Limited. Assets which would pass to the new owner included British and international patents on a number of items of advanced technology that were held by BREL.

The memorandum of sale outlined the financial performance of the company. In hindsight, it must be asked how this was relevant to BREL (1988) given the reorganisation of BREL prior to sale, and the removal of Horwich Foundry and Doncaster Wagon Works for separate sale which had removed part of the revenues from what the new owner was purchasing. Nevertheless, the company was presented as having made a loss for the last two years of its existence prior to the creation of BREL (1988) Ltd. The company was, however, shown to have been profitable up until the end of the 1986 tax year with profits made in 1983 (£10.82million on a turnover of £443.3million), 1985 (£23.48million on £538.37million turnover) and 1986 (£4.36million on £471.3million). Losses were shown for 1987 (£5.32million against £452.256million) and 1988 (£6.77million against £305.4million). Why the financial figures for 1984 were not included in the sale proposal is unknown.

The conditions of sale were laid down in the memorandum of sale, specifically in regard to staff employed by BREL (1988) Limited. Pensions had been provided through the British Rail Pension Scheme in which the majority of members of staff were enrolled. The provision was to cease with the sale of BREL to a new owner, however the BRB required the new owner to undertake to provide a new pension scheme to which all the staff would be transferred. The benefits of the new pension scheme provided by the future owner of BREL should be 'no less favourable than those of the relevant BR scheme'. Membership of the new scheme was to be aggregated with the existing time each employee had been enrolled in the British Rail scheme to give 'continuous service' as far as pension benefits were concerned, with all accrued benefits being protected after transfer to the new company's ownership.

The employees of the company were also entitled to concessionary travel, on both British Rail and London Underground services as well as some overseas railways services and shipping lines. These benefits remained in force after redundancy and retirement, and also applied to their immediate dependents. The concessionary travel arrangements also remained in force for the dependents of a BREL employee after their death. The BRB required that the purchaser of BREL would make arrangements to provide the same benefit to all its staff going forward from the date of sale. The railway board would provide facilities to the new company up to a value of £300 per year, linked to increases in travel fares. With regard to existing arrangements with overseas railways and shipping lines, it was required that the new company purchase tickets on behalf of its staff under the same arrangements currently in force.

The new company was expected to honour the railway's current redundancy arrangements, whereby employees facing redundancy were entitled by their current terms of employment to settlements greater than the current statutory amount. It was a policy of BREL, which was expected to be continued by the new owner, that a further supplemental redundancy payment would be made equivalent to the notice period if the employees leave on a date specified by management, regardless of whether that date were within the notice period or afterwards.

The financial results included in the memorandum showed the interest payable on loans, all of which were due to the BRB against loans provided by the railway. Loans amounting to £64million were outstanding. Section 12 of the Memorandum stated that the BRB would 'release the Company from any further liability in respect of BREL loan stock' after the completion of the sale. As a nationalised company, the BRB had to request permission from the European Commission to write off the £64million loan that had been made to BREL. Permission was finally received, by fax, on 5 April 1989, which would allow the sale, by then agreed in principle with the final owners, but awaiting authority from Brussels to go ahead.

By the time of the permission being received from the European Commission for the financial adjustment which would allow the sale to go ahead, the BRB had chosen their preferred bidder for the company.

An open bidding process had been undertaken for the sale of BREL (1988) Ltd to a new owner. A number of bidders had expressed an interest. The bid documents had been sent out to Alsthom, ABB (on their own), BN, Bombardier, Finmeccanica, FKI, GEC, General Electric, General Motors (who withdrew early), Hawker Siddeley, a BREL Management Buyout team, Metro-Cammell, Trafalgar House (on their own) and Vickers Shipbuilding and Engineering Limited. The Management Buyout Team, Trafalgar House and ABB soon arranged to form a consortium to buy out the company together.

Meanwhile the BRB was looking to dispose of Horwich Foundry as a going concern through a separate sale to that of BREL. The intention to sell the foundry was originally announced on 24 November 1987, with the new company, Horwich Foundry Limited incorporated on 27 January 1988. The process was delayed due to the foundry being a supplier to the Ministry of Defence. Certification was received from the ministry and the sale of the foundry was advertised in the *Financial Times* on 15 March 1988. After an open bid tendering process, the foundry was sold to the Parkfield Group in July.

Most of those who had expressed an interest and received the bid documents had withdrawn by the end of 1988. Queries had been made about various elements of BREL and the impact they might have upon any offers made to purchase the company. One of the most common queries raised was related to the status of subsidiary parts of the company. In a letter dated 7 December 1988 to GEC from the BRB the position was made clear. BRE-Metro had not yet been wound up and was still part (50 per cent) owned by BREL, although the company had not traded since May 1984. ART Inc. in the United States was wholly owned by BREL but had not traded in the 1987/88 tax year. BRE Inc. in the United States had also not traded in the year, having operated as a sales office based in Arlington until December 1987.

The bidders had been reduced to just two who had expressed an interest and were willing to continue with the bidding process by the end of 1988. The bidders were GEC, who had bid just £3.7million and a Consortium made up of BREL Management, Trafalgar House and ASEA Brown Boveri (ABB) who had made a conditional bid which changed dependent upon the availability of final accounts from BREL (£13.6million without, £23.6million with).

The trade unions were invited to meet with the prospective new owners. The CS&EU, NUR, and TSSA met with the bidders and expressed their views to the BREL Sale Committee. The TSSA supported the Consortium bid as it offered better prospects and security for BREL staff. The NUR and CS&EU responded by saying that they supported none of the bidders and were totally opposed to the privatisation of the company.

The new year began with the BRB informing the preferred purchaser that they had been successful. The potential new owners were the consortium of BREL Management, Trafalgar House and ASEA Brown Boveri (ABB). The agreed purchase price was £14million. The President and Chief Executive of ABB, Percy Barnevik, wrote to Sir Robert Reid to say how delighted he was that the consortium had been chosen as the preferred bidder. He also stated that the consortium was committed to taking BREL forwards, building on what had been achieved already to create a leading engineering company upon which British Rail could depend. The letter promised that transfer of ABB technology and management experience to BREL would be used to achieve the development of the company. Sir Robert Reid replied, his letter including the statement that the BRB would be 'very reliant on the consortium as one of our principal suppliers'.

The negotiations undertaken between the consortium and the railway board had resulted in agreement being reached on what the future BREL would look like. A major restructuring programme was to be undertaken after the sale aimed at reducing capacity to a level deemed more suited to the potential work that the company could expect to bring in over the short term, with operations being streamlined to achieve economies that would allow the company to be competitive in the open market for railway and general engineering business. The restructuring of the company was estimated to cost in the region of £75million. As a result of the agreement to write off the loans made to BREL to allow the new company to begin its existence in a better financial position, the European Commission required that the BRB and the board of the new BREL must submit annual reports to Brussels via the British government on the progress of the restructuring plan starting in March 1990.

Whilst the sale of BREL (1988) was in progress and negotiations were proceeding between the BRB and the interested parties, the railway continued to place work with the company. In March, contracts were placed with BREL (1988) for the construction of three batches of vehicles for the Class 321 and a number of Class 319 EMUs to be built at the Holgate Road Works in York. At the same time, contracts were placed with the company for the Class 165 Networker, and Class 158 Sprinter DMUs to be built at York and Derby Litchurch Lane respectively. The job losses planned for Derby were halted with the award of the Class 158 contract to the company as the workforce would now be required in order for the new company to be able to fulfil the order.

The contracts were covered by a letter of intent, sent to BREL (1988) Limited long before the sale and purchase contract relating to the final disposal of BREL (1988) Limited to the BREL consortium was signed. The letter of intent was aimed at preventing any accusations of a link between the disposal of BREL (1988) Limited and the placing of the orders on the new company. The letter of intent, dated 16 March 1989, stated that the contract for seventy-seven Class 158 vehicles was to be placed with BREL (1988) Limited within the next fourteen days for a total value of £43.646million. Additionally, further contracts were intended to be placed with the company for Class 158 (56 vehicles), Class 321 (152 vehicles) and Class 319 (24 vehicles) which required final endorsement by the BREL Consortium after purchase of the company had been completed.

At the same time as the final negotiations for the purchase of the BREL (1988) Limited were beginning, the consortium was given some good news by the BRB. In an effort to assist the new company and to support the new owners, the board announced that it would be prepared to enter in negotiations with the new BREL for construction of 200 new Networker vehicles for Network South East. The railway viewed the new family of diesel and electric Networker classes as the most important new build programme they had currently planned, although at the time of the communication with the BREL consortium the programme was subject to final sign off by the Department of Transport. In the same letter, dated 5 April, the railway board made it clear that it had every intention of allowing the new BREL every opportunity to participate in future new build programmes and substantial repair work contracts intended to be offered to the private sector.

The sale was concluded on 18 April 1989. The BRB issued a press release to confirm the news to the media on the same day. BREL was no longer part of the railway and would now forge its own future. Reducing workload from the railway and the reduction in size of its locomotive fleet saw the Locomotive Works in Derby close in 1991. The company would continue to use the BREL name until 1992, when Asea Brown Boveri bought out the other shareholders. The company was then merged into ABB Transportation and BREL ceased to exist, bringing to an end the brief but eventful existence of a company that promised much when it was created and may have achieved so much more than it was able to if it had been allowed more autonomy. It was sadly not to be.

BIBLIOGRAPHY

Brandon, David and Upham, Martin, *Ernest Marples: The Shadow behind Beeching* (Pen & Sword Books, Barnsley, 2002).

Marsden, Colin, *BREL* (Haynes Publishing, Yeovil, 1990).

Myler, Chris, *The Life and Times of York Carriage Works: 1884-1995* (ABB Rail Vehicles Limited, 1995).

National Archives Kew, various papers in: AN18; AN109; AN111; AN112; AN129; AN171; AN174; AN180; AN181; AN184; AN192; AN199; MT124; PV13; T539.

Rail Magazine, 'Class 91's…Promise unfulfilled' (27 July 2019).

Sansick, John, 'The Jewel in British Rail's Crown: An Account of the Closure of at Shildon Wagon Works' (PhD Thesis, Durham University, 1990).

Smith, M.D., *Horwich Locomotive Works Re-visited* (Amadeus Press, Cleckheaton, 2021).

Vaughn, John, *BREL Locomotive Works* (Oxford Publishing Company, Oxford, 1981).

Walker David, 'Sir David Serpell: High Ranking Civil Servant known for his '"Hatchet Job" report into Britain's Railways' (*The Guardian*, 11 August 2008).

INDEX